Just Development

Just Development

Beyond Adjustment with a Human Face

Edited by

Tariq Banuri
Shahrukh Rafi Khan
Moazam Mahmood

Karachi
Oxford University Press
Oxford New York Delhi
1997

Oxford University Press, Walton Street, Oxford OX2 6DP
Oxford New York
Athens Auckland Bangkok Bombay
Calcutta Cape Town Dar es Salaam Delhi
Florence Hong Kong Istanbul Karachi
Kuala Lumpur Madras Madrid Melbourne
Mexico City Nairobi Paris Singapore
Taipei Tokyo Toronto
and associated companies in
Berlin Ibadan

Oxford is a trade mark of Oxford University Press

ISBN 0 19 577830 8

Printed in Pakistan at
Continental Offset Printers, Karachi.
Published by
Ameena Saiyid, Oxford University Press
5-Bangalore Town, Sharae Faisal
P.O. Box 13033, Karachi-75350, Pakistan.

Justice is the Strife

Heraclitus

Contents

Appendix

NGOs IN PAKISTAN: AN OVERVIEW

Khawar Mumtaz

Tables

Chapter 1

Chapter 2

Chapter 3

Chapter 4

Chapter 5

Chapter 6

Contributors

Tariq Banuri	Sustainable Development Policy Institute, Islamabad, Pakistan
Giovanni Andrea Cornia	World Institute for Development Economic Research, Finland
A. R. Kemal	Planning Division, Government of Pakistan
Shahrukh Rafi Khan	Sustainable Development Policy Institute, Islamabad, Pakistan
Moazam Mahmood	Pakistan Institute for Development Economics, Islamabad, Pakistan
Khawar Mumtaz	Shirkatgah, Lahore, Pakistan

Acknowledgements

The writers of this volume received help from a number of sources, all of which are gratefully acknowledged. The initial impetus for the study was furnished by Arshad Zaman, then Chief Economist, Government of Pakistan. Subsequently, Akhtar Hassan Khan, Secretary, Planning and Development Division, and Pervez Tahir, Chief, Policy Planning Section, Planning and Development Division, gave both criticism and advice. Kunio Waki and Steven Allen of UNICEF, Islamabad, provided comments as well as guidance throughout the work. Gamani Abeysekera designed the terms of reference and made a very useful contribution in the initial stages of the work. Nigar Ahmed provided invaluable assistance in the design phase of the study. Helpful comments and criticism were also provided by the participants at the annual conference of the Pakistan Society of Development Economists, January 1992.

The personnel of UNICEF, Islamabad, provided help in a number of ways. The assistance of Jason Weisfeld, Fernando Mujica, and Sarfraz Khawaja has been especially valuable.

The research and support staff of IUCN-Pakistan, SDPI, PIDE, and Shirkatgah provided invaluable support in typing and formatting of the text. The person who should be singled out for gratitude is Mohammad Shehzad. Finally, many thanks are due to Nauman Naqvi for a very careful reading of the first proofs.

The research has been conducted by consultants and staff of UNICEF, and the judgements contained here do not necessarily reflect the views of UNICEF or of the parent institutions of individual researchers.

Editors' Note

It is virtually impossible for a book such as this to be current when it eventually reaches the reader. For example, while going through the third proofs, we found that the macro environment had changed, due to the introduction of the New National Finance Commission Award and the New Economic Measures of the re-elected Nawaz Sharif government (1997-). While we have integrated the salient features of these specific measures in the text, there will inevitably be other changes that will not have been incorporated by the time the book gets to the reader. It is, therefore, important to highlight here that, while we draw on policies and data to convey our message, the critical aspect of the book is the message of just development, and how it is possible to go beyond adjustment with a human face. We expect this message will continue to be relevant until it is seriously addressed.

PART ONE

INTRODUCTION

1

Just adjustment and just development

Tariq Banuri

INTRODUCTION

This study is a follow up in the Pakistani context of the issues raised in UNICEF's classic contribution to the political economy of development, *Adjustment With a Human Face* (Cornia, *et al.* 1987, henceforth *AWHF*). It examines why, despite four decades of development, there has not been a significant move towards meeting the basic needs of the population. This imbalance is evident in Table 1.1 which shows Pakistan to have poor human resource development despite a respectable growth performance.

Due to a number of reasons, concerns over this imbalance have acquired greater force in recent years. First, the very magnitude of the dissonance between economic and social indicators is a major source of concern. Second, the emergence of large budgetary and payments deficits since the 1970s, shifted government policy increasingly towards the pursuit of short-run targets, to the neglect of social infrastructure and ultimately, from the basis of sustainable and just development. The Social Action Plan, evaluated in later chapters, represents an attempt to redress the imbalance between economic and social indicators. Third, this development has been further compounded by a shift in intellectual fashion towards privatization and liberalization, which is increasingly becoming an excuse for the abdication of basic social responsibility by governments in Southern countries. Fortunately, there is a growing recognition that human resource development is an essential prerequisite even for other 'hard-nosed' objectives, such as economic growth or industrialization.

All this is well known, though unfortunately not yet universally conceded. The recognition has led to a number of prescriptions for policy reform, among which UNICEF's *AWHF* is significant. These reforms centre around the enhancement of financial allocation to social sectors by governments, either by a transfer from other sectors, such as the military, or by additional resource mobilization. At the macroeconomic level, the *AWHF* approach focuses on a less deflationary path and on active mesoeconomic policies in the foreign exchange and credit markets, and in support of the informal sector and public works. The prescriptions also advocate the explicit setting of targets of human resource development in government plans and pronouncements. Much less is said, however, in the field of governance and on the political economy of the overall approach.

In Pakistan particularly, and elsewhere generally, the problem is much deeper—it cannot be rectified by a simple transfer of resources. The Government today appears to neither be able to raise additional resources, nor to reduce expenditure in other areas. Moreover, in some cases, the issue is not simply the provision of more financial resources, but also a fundamental reform in the way particular services are delivered or even thought about. In other words, even if resources were available and were provided to the social sector, they would not necessarily produce the desired results. In investigating this issue, it is important to learn not only from past successes, here or elsewhere, but also and perhaps more importantly, to learn from failures: Why have governments been unable to raise or divert resources? Why have governments focussed mainly on the inputs into the social sector and not as much on the outputs that these inputs are supposed to produce? Why has it been so difficult to incorporate concerns about the quality of outputs into decisions and plans?

In this volume, we start with the conventional set of concerns and corresponding policy prescriptions as applied to Pakistan in the 1990s. But from there we go on to discuss the underlying political economy of the failures of development. For this purpose, it is very useful in methodological terms to shift the existing fount of values, the forum for choices and priorities, the beneficiary of developmental programmes, and the cradle of monitoring institutions.

The question then is not why a government does not wish to increase spending on particular items, but why a society is incapable of organizing collective public action to pursue its valued goals. Thus, a central element of the analysis is governance, namely the ability of a society to make and implement collective decisions. The state then is viewed not as an autonomous and monolithic entity, but as one possible institution for collective decision making, albeit the most significant one. (Amadeo and Banuri 1991). Similarly, underdevelopment and associated problems are seen not purely as a lack of resources or technology, but rather as a form of 'social helplessness'; namely as a condition in which a society, whether in the North or South, is unable to deal with problems created by social change. (Zaman and Zaman 1991). As a result, the issue of redefining the social role of the state is added to the set of issues identified in earlier studies on adjustment. In particular, we take up issues of participatory development, the involvement of local populations and the potential role of NGOs in future developmental activities.

This focus leads to another argument for the pursuit of human resource development, even under the pressure created by adjustment programmes. The argument is that the pursuit of human development and the protection of vulnerable groups is essential for the establishment of a just society, which is a prerequisite of governance and the maintenance of social harmony, and therefore of economic growth—indeed of any valued societal objective. In other words, political objectives such as the improvement of the human rights record, the social and legal status of women and the administration of justice are essential for long-run development; indeed development will not be sustainable unless it is also just. Hence the title, *Just Development*.

Structural adjustment, namely, changes in a country's production and consumption structure, becomes necessary when expenditures begin to exceed incomes systematically. However, orthodox adjustment programmes have often been criticized because they have tended to retard growth in poor countries and to shift the burden onto vulnerable groups. In the tradition of this literature, we do not argue against the necessity of structural adjustment, but against the adverse effects of such adjustment and for people centred development.

Furthermore, much of the criticism of orthodox adjustment programmes derives from an absence of justice in these programmes, and indeed from an absence of justice in any aggregate concept of welfare or development. This provided another reason to demand that development as well as adjustment, should be based on a society's norms of justice and fair play; in other words, that there should be 'just' adjustment and just development.

Our argument is that reliance on the cultural norms of justice and humanity—particularly with regard to vulnerable groups—as the basis of choosing priorities and designing policies is a means, and not an obstacle, to sustainable growth and structural adjustment. In other words, the goal is not only just adjustment, which is a short-run objective, but also just development, a long-run strategy that is not based upon the sacrifice of weak and vulnerable groups in society.

However, all this does not mean that government policies are viewed as unimportant or given less importance. On the contrary, government policies are seen by us not only as a means of pursuing the direct objectives of human development, but also of pursuing the indirect objectives of promoting institutional changes which are necessary for the achievement of the direct objective. As a result, this study provides guidance for the selection of wise government policies as in *AWHF* and related analyses. However, these policies are society-centred rather than state-centred, hence the subtitle: *beyond adjustment with a human face*.

1. OVERVIEW OF THE STUDY

The broad dimensions of the Pakistani political economy are detailed in Part II, chapters 2 to 5. In chapter 2, we describe the salient features of economic development in Pakistan since independence in 1947; in chapter 3, we look at the human development record in the same period; in chapter 4, we describe the nature of, and trends, in poverty and income distribution; and in chapter 5, we look at the policy framework in operation, particularly after 1970. Thus, in these four chapters we detail the initial conditions, the changes, the policy framework and the economic and social problems confronted by Pakistan. In chapter 5, we also focus on structural adjustment and the likely impact of the macroeconomic policies this entails on the economy and socially vulnerable groups. This represents the mainstream approach to resolving Pakistan's economic and social problems. In Part III chapters 6 and 7, we suggest an alternative and complementary agenda for socio-economic policy reform. In chapter 6, we portray successful experiences in Pakistan and elsewhere to argue that ambitious human development targets are possible. In chapter 7, we review past failures and suggest an agenda for institutional reform. These last two chapters represent analyses and proposals for 'just adjustment' and 'just development'.

In chapters 2 and 3, we bring out the main features of socio-economic development in Pakistan, as well as the reasons for recurrent concern. A decent rate of economic growth has not been matched by improvement in the quality of life or living standards. The impact of social action on human development is low, even though the share of public expenditure allocated to social sectors has increased steadily (as in the rest of the South, though to a comparatively lower level), and the per capita income has doubled over the past 25 years. Social indicators for Pakistan reflect a dismal picture as evident from Table 1.1 below.

Table 1.1 shows that Pakistan's growth in per capita GNP between 1985-94 was respectable in a cross-country perspective. However, it was behind in achievements in the social sectors. This is particularly the case for literacy and primary education where performance is even below than that of low income economies. It is encouraging to see that life expectancy at birth now exceeds the average of low income economies and that female life expectancy now exceeds that of males. However, the gap is much smaller than one might biologically expect. Once again, while its infant mortality rate matches the average of low income economies, the numbers for the more prosperous economy groups show what a long way Pakistan has to go. Progress will not be easy since Pakistan has a very high fertility rate and so social services have to catch up with a large and growing population. The large budget deficit, high external debt, low revenues, low reserves, and high military expenditure will compound this difficulty.

Table 1.1 : Comparative statistics on social and economic development

		Pakistan	LIE@	LMIE	UMIE	HIE
GNP/capita, 1994 ($)		430	360	1,590	4,640	23,420
Growth rate of GNP per capita, 1985-94 (% per year)		1.3	−1.1	−1.2	1.4	1.9
Adult illiteracy, 1995	Male	50	37	na	12	na
	Female	76	55	na	14	na
Primary enrolment, 1993 (% of age group)						
	Male	80	82	105	104	104
	Female	49	67	101	104	104
Infant mortality rate, 1994 (per thousand)		101.8	86	36	36	7
Life expectancy at birth, 1993	Male	61	54	64	66	74
	Female	63	57	70	72	80
Total fertility rate, 1994		5.4	5.1	2.7	2.8	1.7
Current account balance, 1994 ($ million)		−2020	na	na	na	na
Reserves, 1993 (in months of imports)		1.4	4.2	na	4.7	2.7
Government revenue, 1993 (% of GNP)		18.4	na	na	na	na
Budget deficit 1994 (% of GNP)		5.8	na	na	na	na
Expenditure, 1993 as % of government expenditure:						
	Education	1.1	na	na	na	na
	Health	.04	na	na	na	na
	Defence	26.9	na	na	na	na

Source: *World Development Report 1995* and *1996*.

Notes: na = Not availablle

@ = Excluding China and India.

LIE = Low income economies. LM, UM, and H represent lower middle, upper middle and high respectively.

Besides the poor mobilization of resources, we show in chapter 2 that resource allocation is also poor, and there is inadequate diversification of the industrial base, low employment elasticity in the formal sector, low investment and saving ratios, and inefficiencies in the production structure. Water-logging and salinity plague Pakistan's agriculture, in which productivity is also low by international standards.

In chapter 3, we show that apart from the shortcomings depicted in Table 1.1, Pakistan's social and economic conditions include poor housing, unpredictable availability of physical infrastructural services, inadequate nutrition, lack of improvement in the role and status of women, and the inability of the society to protect its children. Pakistan has also had an inconsistent record of human rights, an accelerating process of environmental degradation, and a worsening of the overall security and protection available to citizens. At the same time, there are concerns about the breakdown of the civil order, as manifested in growing civic intolerance and political violence, corruption and irresponsibility in public services, cynicism towards public institutions and public morality, and a virtual collapse of the system of higher education.

In chapter 4, we look specifically at the poor and vulnerable groups in society. Historical data reveal that the incidence of poverty—as defined by access to a nutrition level of 2,550 calories per capita per day—has declined steadily since 1970 (although income distribution worsened for much of this period) but still includes about a fifth of the urban and rural population. The poor have deficient access to social services, including health and education, and are extremely vulnerable to abrupt changes in policy or economic conditions. The chapter also shows that government fiscal policies have not made a dent in the problem of poverty.

In chapter 5, we provide a broader look at the policy framework in Pakistan. We show that there have been two major shifts in the policy stance. In the early 1970s, a Keynesian-Populist (KP) regime launched a significant but short-lived effort in the area of social development. The second shift, occurring at the end of the 1970s, reduced the resource allocation for the social sectors rapidly. This was done partly to adjust the chronic imbalance between incomes and expenditures introduced by mismanagement during the KP period. There are signs that, at least as far as social sectors are concerned, a third shift is taking place. However, this is being inhibited by the severe resource constraint that has become worse despite more than a decade of structural adjustment programmes. The chapter also shows that a major reason for the resource constraint is the very institutional basis for policy making. Finally, we also investigate the evidence with regards to the likely impact of structural adjustment policies on vulnerable groups.

In Part III, we carry the discussion forward to provide prescriptions for human resource development as well as resource mobilization and institutional change. In chapter 6, we draw upon the experience of successful implementation of human resource development programmes in Pakistan and elsewhere, to argue for a massive increase in resource allocation to the social sector. We also provide guidelines for resource mobilization. In chapter 7, we explore the failure of earlier policies to argue for institutional reform in the form of decentralization, popular participation, and NGO involvement in programme implementation.

2. GOVERNANCE AND COLLECTIVE DECISION-MAKING

To start with the ideal of learning from failure, one has to ask why the state has been unable to pursue valued societal goals. In an article on the developmental crisis in Latin America, Fishlow (1987, p. 27) comments upon this situation:

> The correct solution to deal with the continuing problem of economic recovery in Latin America is not the uniform application of orthodox remedies. . . . The right question is how to reconstruct a Latin American developmental state that can consistently implement the right policies, not just register the right prices.

Fishlow's advice is equally relevant to other Southern countries which are increasingly finding themselves unable to pursue their social as well as economic objectives effectively.

The most significant obstacle to the pursuit of social objectives is what may be described as the crisis of governance. Governance is a nuanced concept, including in particular the government's capacity to make and implement policies, especially policies which require attention to detail, such as targeting, selection or judgement. The crisis of governance includes an excessive degree of centralization; overburdening and rigidity of the government machinery; the absence of local participation which can provide the requisite attention to detail; deterioration in the professionalism, competence, and integrity of public functionaries; and the weakening of judicial and quasi-judicial institutions.

All these characteristics can be observed in Pakistan. The government has become excessively centralized over the years, participatory institutions have eroded and are virtually non-existent today and there are repeated expressions of concern about the quality of bureaucratic and political elites. In this situation, while the government would still be able to pursue a few aggregate goals, anything which involves qualitative concerns will not be addressed.

This implies that if the government and civil society take the task of governance seriously, some attention will have to be given to supportive institutions. Broadly speaking, this means the following:

the strengthening, restoring, and nurturing of participatory institutions; the improvement in work conditions of the bureaucracy; and the strengthening of judicial institutions partly as a check on the bureaucratic and political elites, and partly as a means of ensuring coordination and accountability in democratic and participatory institutions.

Governments in Southern countries have become ineffective because of a number of reasons. The proximate reasons are easily established. Breakdown in professional standards, overburdening and overcentralization, lax supervision, arbitrary procedures encouraged by venal politicians and bureaucrats, and consequently, a minimization of the attention to detail that makes for good training of public functionaries. Some obstacles to governance are purely economic in character, even though their removal would involve a broad understanding of social processes. Foremost amongst these is the fiscal crisis of the state.

Another economic obstacle is the balance of payments which in Pakistan's case has almost always been in deficit (see chapter 2). This creates an obstacle in the pursuit of social objectives, since payment difficulties have a tendency to make government policies hostage. Erratic changes in export and import flows, trade policies, terms of trade and workers remittances have also led to sharp variations in the balance of payments. Except for a few years, the overall balance has been consistently negative. While workers' remittances grew sharply over the period from 1974-5 to 1982-3 and financed a large part of the deficit, the fall in workers' remittances since then has led to a sharp deterioration in the balance of payments. (*Economic Survey* 1995-6, 160).

Other obstacles have emerged in the monitoring and information systems. All systems which provide a means of supervision, monitoring, and regulation have eroded over time.[1] Because of legal restrictions, the system of property registration has become erratic and real estate as well as automobiles are often registered in fictitious names. On the one hand, the absence of effective, impartial, and trustworthy institutions for gathering information renders social data meaningless, and on the other hand, it imbues public information with power and thus results in information hoarding as well as corruption.

The obstacles to governance may have less to do with economic than social causes. The most important obstacle, again, is the violation of the social norms of justice by public functionaries, and hence a gradual erosion in their legitimacy and motivation. The loss of legitimacy has also been accompanied by a decline in their real incomes which has therefore induced a shift towards illegal earnings. An important consequence has been the loss of a spirit of service, which results in the decline in the quality of service. This then impinges upon the ability of the state to raise revenues through formal mechanisms and hence in its ability to provide adequate work conditions for its functionaries.

Two reforms are essential for breaking this vicious circle and restoring collective institutions. First, the establishment of a strong and independent judiciary. The object is to make public functionaries act in the public interest, no matter what policy they pursue. Second, society must fashion institutions which bring the individual incentives faced by all public functionaries—e.g. politicians, bureaucrats, teachers, journalists, doctors, or researchers—into harmony with the public interest.

The upshot is that what needs to be studied is not development, but underdevelopment—not in the sense of a lack of financial or technical resources, but in the sense of the failure of collective mechanisms and of the inability of managing collective goals. The failure of collective action is linked directly to the inability of civil society to influence its educational and cultural life. A start can be made by transferring the control of primary schools to community organizations (see chapter 7). It would be essential to involve women directly in such activities. This would not only restore the role of women as the guarantors of cultural continuity, but also humanize the functioning of the educational system.

The point is that collective action is impossible without direct participatory institutions. Given that these institutions have eroded over centuries, their renewal and restoration will not be an easy task. It will require support and protection from the government as well as other powerful groups in society.

3. THE ROLE OF THE STATE

The discussion of governance raises another set of issues, namely the role of the state in society. The literature on development in general and human development in particular, is focussed almost exclusively on what the state *should* do without seeking to address the more fundamental issue of the role of the state in society, i.e what the state *can* or *cannot* do. Indeed, the 'human' objectives are presented not as if they were the values held by a living community, but rather as the values of 'outsiders', be they policy makers or international advisors. In this sense, the prevailing discussions of human development continue the quasi-colonial tradition of conditionality, whereby all good things are to be pursued only as a compact between government policy makers and financing agencies.[2]

This is partly because the discussion has been dominated by economists, who tend to recognize only the individual and the state as decision makers. A perception of the society as composed of various collectives—community based organizations (CBOs), village organizations (*tanzeems*), villages, urban communities, unions, co-operatives, professional and business associations, ethnic groups, school and college students—would give a different slant to the issue. To the extent that these collectives are autonomous and active, they can help identify issues, articulate and pursue social values, create institutions, supervise public functionaries, and maintain the social and economic health of the society.

In this alternative perspective, the persistence of such problems as underdevelopment, poor quality of life, social violence, crime, corruption, or industrial pollution appear not as failures of the state (which can be corrected through coercive or other means) but as 'social helplessness', namely as the failure of social homeostatic mechanisms through which healthy societies normally cope with problems. (Zaman and Zaman 1991). The reasons for this helplessness include the societal conflicts and growing polarization that militates against the emergence of a collective synthesis. This means that policy attention must be given to remedying these conditions, not as human rights objectives alone, but also as economic objectives.

This also helps to underscore the fundamental issue of quality of services. While the state measures its performance and actions by the 'inputs' that go into the process of, say, education (e.g. number of schools, or teachers, or school enrolments), society is interested only in the 'output' of such a process, in this case the inculcation of 'initiative', the ability to work with others and the ability to understand and influence society'[3]. An important aspect of this dissonance is the tendency of the Pakistani state to finance investment but not recurring costs of establishments, thus enhancing the quantitative bias. Investment is but an input; the output is produced by the continuous operation of institutions. (Burney 1991).

This perspective is also useful in identifying alternative solutions to a problems. Different groups, depending on their capacity, can reach the same goals through methods which differ in terms of technology, scale, nature of knowledge, nature of the organizational input required and the financial package needed. This can also distinguish between spheres where state action can be effective, and those where it cannot operate. Given the tremendous variation in cultural systems and social structures, no two societies would have an identical distribution of legitimate and illegitimate areas of state action.[4]

Finally, this alternative perspective also enables a discussion of the efficacy of the state, including the professionalism of its functionaries, the degree of co-ordination between them, and the division of functions of federal, provincial, and local governments, and non governmental bodies.

4. LEARNED HELPLESSNESS

The analysis of failure can help understand why some societies are incapable of achieving certain goals. Zaman and Zaman (1991) have argued that conventional concepts of development and underdevelopment are inappropriate for understanding or reforming societies in the Third World. Besides the fact that conventional development approaches 'suggest implicitly that the levels of consumption accumulation achieved by Europeanate societies is available to all mankind', they are looking at the wrong things:

> We believe that development . . . is an epiphenomenon, like the speedometer of a car which registers speed, but neither causes nor explains it. The primary phenomenon which needs to be studied is human behaviour, in its widest sense, which is not in some sense 'pro development' (as in Europeanate society) but instead sustains poverty, disease, illiteracy, etc.

The point is that many Southern societies find themselves incapable of pursuing even collectively valued objectives. While a considerable amount of research needs to be conducted into the causes of such disabilities, a few points can be made.

First, although it has become a cliche by now, there are strong reasons to believe that an important cause of such helplessness is the traumatic encounter between colonized and colonizing people in the previous centuries. (See Nandy 1988.) The impact of this encounter is sustained by the nature of South-North interaction in the post-colonial period.

Second, the hostility of state policies and state action in the post-colonial period towards participatory institutions has led to the gradual erosion of the self-confidence, the skills, and the institutions needed for organizing collective action.

Third, the exacerbation of social dualism and conflicts over identity, partly as a reaction to misguided state action in the early days of independence, has made it difficult to agree upon national values and national institutions.

Fourth, an educational system which has sought explicitly to produce technicians rather than citizens, militates against the creation of new syntheses and new compacts that must underpin any initiative for collective action.

Fifth, the belief of many experts that all desirable social values are to be imported from outside has made both agreement and creativity impossible. For instance, as long as there is the belief that Pakistani society, left to itself, will violate the rights of women, minorities, or other vulnerable groups—or that the protection of these groups is valued only by outsiders—it would be impossible to introduce reforms that are both democratic and legitimate.

5. JUSTICE, ADJUSTMENT, AND DEVELOPMENT

Adjustment with a human face provides an economic argument for what had before been seen only as a moral agenda. We argue that it is not that citizens have inalienable human and civic rights, important as they are, but also that, first, long-run development is impossible, without the protection of these rights and the participation of the entire population, both men and women, in development activities; without the maintenance, and improvement of the health and educational level of the people; and without the conservation of the natural environment. Second, that development programmes and adjustment policies of governments have often failed to protect these rights, and thus have not only violated the inalienable human rights of their populations, but have also harmed their long-term prospects. Third, that this need not have been so: there are policies and programmes that could have enabled these countries to pursue simultaneously the goals of economic growth, structural adjustment, and human resource development.

This reveals that the implicit target of all critics of development is the absence of justice in development programmes. This has emerged in a number of ways: the focus on inequality and income distribution; the introduction of the concept of basic human needs as an alternative to aggregative income based measures of development; the invocation of the rights of women, children, minorities, and other vulnerable groups; and more recently, the concern with the natural environment.

Before proceeding, it may be useful to distinguish between two concepts of justice: 'justice as equality', and 'justice as quality'. The former refers to the idea that everybody is equal in some ontological sense and ought to be treated equally. The latter is, in a sense, a contrasting view, i.e. that every individual has to be treated differently because every one is a unique individual and not a cipher. The idea of justice as quality emerges from concern over the bureaucratization of the world and the tyranny of aggregates.

Southern countries are confronted with both kinds of injustice. On the one hand, people are not treated equally—before the law, before a tribunal, or in society in general. On the other hand, people do not receive the personal attention and trust that they need to develop their potential and to contribute effectively to society. In other words, the object is not only to provide education to everybody, but good education to everybody, education that contains the personal attention and devotion of the teacher; the idea is not to provide a doctor for every community, but to provide a doctor who will exert himself/herself for the community.

The establishment of justice requires first the protection and strengthening of judicial or quasi-judicial institutions—not only judges, but also teachers, doctors, bureaucrats, politicians, election commissioners, service commissioners, and cricket umpires!

Second, it is also necessary that the services of these quasi-judicial functionaries be recognized and rewarded. It cannot be over-emphasized that the provision of justice is a wealth creating activity. A just society can resolve its problems more readily, and can enable people to pursue their ordinary business of living, effectively and productively. Just as financial institutions, entrepreneurs or traders are rewarded not because they produce wealth, but because they are essential to the production of wealth in a society, so also the personnel of judicial and quasi-judicial institutions must be rewarded as if they were the producers of wealth.

Finally, the greatest obstacle to the establishment of a just society is the uncertainty and unpredictability created by centralized structures. Unpredictability militates against people making long-run agreements with each other and abiding by those agreements, i.e. against people treating each other fairly and justly. In today's world, a government which takes arbitrary actions, which changes the rules of the game frequently, which bases its legitimacy on patronage, and which is corrupt and unprincipled, creates an environment of uncertainty in which it is in no one's interest to follow the dictates of justice.

The undermining of justice is perhaps the most serious charge that can be levelled against orthodox adjustment policies and orthodox development strategies. By violating the societal norms of justice, these policies and programmes undermine their own long-run potential. The resulting climate of injustice is not conducive to the creation of wealth. More importantly, the perception of injustice creates a reaction down the road and weakens the social fabric that is crucial to ordinary economic decision making

In other words, the issue is not whether a government follows populist or orthodox economic policies. The issue is whether it obeys the norms of justice in its own society while following its selected policy. A weak, disorganized, and corrupt government will not be able to attend to all the details that the provision of justice necessitates.

NOTES

1. To give a simple example, taxi meters are a means of regulating the relationship between taxi drivers and their customers; they provide an easy method for the inspector to check on this relationship. In Pakistan, however, because of the arbitrarily fixed fare rates, and because of corruption, these meters do not have any meaning any more. The result is that the customer and driver have to waste their time haggling.
2. This attitude may derive from the perception, expressed for example in the World Bank's Social Action Plan documents, that there is a 'lack of a strong constituency for public expenditures in basic social services'. See World Bank (1991, p. 1).
3. Raven (1989, p. 460). Presumably, the state too would be interested in outputs but it simply does not have the ability to measure or monitor them.
4. For instance, many Western people would consider it quite legitimate for a Western state to take away a woman's child on the grounds that she is not a good mother. In Asian countries, like Pakistan, while people may be coerced into accepting such an action, it will simply not be viewed as legitimate.

PART TWO

THE PAKISTAN EXPERIENCE

2

Economics Trends

Tariq Banuri and A. R. Kemal

INTRODUCTION

The following four chapters describe the developments in Pakistan's political economy since its independence. However, the focus of attention is on the post-1970 period, after Bangladesh attained independence. We have relied as much as possible on domestic data sources. An alternative was to use the World Bank and IMF data sources which are conveniently available on diskette. However, on occasion, we found large discrepancies between the two sources and opted for the domestic source, since the Bank and Fund often do not generate their own data.[1]

We have also focused on Pakistan's performance as a whole, and compared it with that of low income economies and South Asian economies, which represent Pakistan's reference group of countries.[2] The main result is the dissonance between changes in aggregate economic measures and stagnation, and even reversal, in the quality of life of citizens. The problems identified in this chapter provide the backdrop for the discussion of mainstream structural adjustment policies in chapter 5, and the alternative just development prescriptions of chapters 7 and 8. Some of the chapter sections are brief because of our focus on covering new ground.

1. INITIAL CONDITIONS[3]

Pakistan inherited an agrarian economy with poor physical and social infrastructure and virtually no industry. As a result, growth was slow and exhibited sharp fluctuations. The per capita income at independence was only Rs 316 ($115). Agriculture accounted for 60 per cent of GDP and manufacturing no more than five per cent (and that too in what is now called the informal sector). There were only three large-scale manufacturing units in the areas which constituted Pakistan.

While Pakistan inherited a good railway system with 8,554 route kilometres, the road transportation system was totally inadequate. For a population of 35 million and an area of about 884,000 square kilometres, there were only 22,238 km of roads (out of which only 8,130 km were of 'high type'), 25,000 motor vehicles, 11,575 buses and trucks, and 1,125 taxis. There was only one port and that too was undeveloped. Merchant shipping comprised of three obsolescent cargo ships with a total dead-weight of 18,500 tons. Telecommunication facilities were equally inadequate, with two radio stations (with a combined power of 15 megawatts), 45,426 radio sets, 3,036 post offices, 7 telegraph offices, and 12,436 telephones. There were 81 bank branches and one head office, and the latter shifted to Pakistan at the time of independence.

Social infrastructure was even poorer. The literacy rate was 13.2 per cent of the total adult population, and 8.6 per cent of the adult female population.[4] The new country inherited only 8,413 primary schools, 2,190 middle schools, 408 high schools, two universities, and no professional colleges. The health situation was even bleaker with only 13,769 hospital beds, and less than 1,500 registered doctors.

1.1. Local Institutions

The prolonged period of colonial rule had effectively destroyed local institutions for self-governance.[5] At the advent of colonial rule in the 18th and early 19th centuries, autonomous villages governed their day-to-day activities. The *Imperial Gazetteer of India* gives the following description of a 'typical' Indian village: 'The inhabitants of (a typical Indian village) pass their life in the midst of these simple surroundings, welded together in a little community with its own organization and government, which differ in character in the various types of villages, its body of detailed customary rules, and its little staff of functionaries, artisans and traders.'[6]

A number of actions of the colonial government led to the gradual decay of these institutions. First, under the centralized colonial administration, the traditional village headman and accountant became paid government servants. Land revenue collection, vested in village councils, was allowed to lapse in favour of direct dealing with tenants. Local leaders were thenceforth recognized only as individuals—either as low-paid government servants, or as parasites of the state—and not as representatives of the integrity of the local community.[7]

Second, the colonial system of judicial administration refused to enforce the local panchayat court's decisions. Even though the newly established regular courts took local customs and practices into account in rendering their decisions, these usages became mummified and rigid.

Once written in 'the village red book', the customary usages regulating the conduct and rights of the members of the community became static and often oppressive, instead of the earlier situation when they were constantly, though unconsciously, modified to suit the changing conditions.[8]

Over the next sixty-five years of British rule, a variety of local bodies were established or reformed—municipal corporations, municipal committees, notified area committees, cantonment boards, district boards, taluka boards, and finally, in the 1920s, village panchayats.[9] Yet, report after report recognized the failure in introducing local autonomy.[10] For example, the 1907 *Royal Commission on Decentralization* (1909, p. 236), one of the many unsuccessful attempts by the British government to reform local government, admitted that Indian villages 'formerly possessed a large degree of autonomy', but

> This autonomy has now disappeared, owing to the establishment of local civil and criminal courts, the present revenue and police organization, the increase of communication, the growth of individualism, and the operation of the individual *raiyat-wari* system . . . Nevertheless, the village functionaries, the headman, the accountant and the village watchman, are largely utilized and paid for by government, and there is still a certain amount of common village feeling and interest.

The Report went on to recommend what can be called an administrative form of decentralization, namely one in which the panchayats would be under the administrative control of the district authorities, headed by the (appointed) village headman and comprised of an elected or appointed council. It could then undertake such local functions as adjudication of petty cases, village sanitation and minor civil works, construction and maintenance of school buildings and some local control of school management, management of small fuel and fodder reserves, and management of village cattle pond and local markets. In the spirit of its recommendation, the report suggested that the revenue of the panchayat should come mainly from grants by district authorities or from assignment of a portion of the land cess. Purely local, though minor, revenue sources were receipts from cattle ponds, markets and fees on civil suits filed before the panchayat.[11] Some of these recommendations were implemented through the Village Panchayat Act 1920, but the consensus appears to be that this initiative did not succeed in producing the desired result.

Even after independence, matters did not change much. The attitude of bemoaning the passing of the local systems of self-governance, while hastening their demise through policies and actions, is common in post-colonial societies, and Pakistan has been no exception. A major reason is an unconscious belief, shared by development experts as well as local intellectuals, that the destiny of the country cannot be left in the hands of illiterate or ignorant villagers. Only the recognition of the failure of the development project in recent years has led to some rethinking on the issue.

Five decades of independence have seen a consistent attachment to centralized administration of the economy and the polity, even though, as we shall see later, it has not been conducive to the achievement of societal objectives. The centralization of powers and functions inherited from the colonial period was maintained during the subsequent period as well. While a number of initiatives were introduced to improve the functioning of local institutions, the commitment to local self-management was never clear and consistent enough to permit significant progress. As a result, local institutions are still far from being autonomous or effective. They depend upon the provincial governments for the bulk of their finances, they are subject to supervision by provincial departments of local government, and their powers of making and implementing laws are virtually non-existent.[12]

2. TRENDS IN GROWTH AND COMPOSITION OF GDP

In the forty years between 1949-1950 and 1989-1990, the gross domestic product (GDP) grew at an annual average rate of 5.2 per cent as shown in Table 2.1.

Some observations and conjectures based on Table 2.1 are notable. The 1960s represented a boom decade, particularly for manufacturing which grew at over ten per cent per year—although it should be kept in mind that the growth was built on a small base, and that sustaining it becomes progressively more difficult. After 1970, the civil war and subsequent division of the country, the oil price hike, devaluation, the nationalization of industry and adverse weather conditions all affected the growth rates adversely. The revival in the late seventies could be accounted for partly by an increase in remittances and favourable weather conditions. Growth rates of manufacturing are likely to have picked up again in the early eighties on account of liberalization and the increased inflow of foreign capital. The subsequent decline in growth rates in the late eighties coincides with a decline in remittances, which peaked as a percentage of GDP in 1982-3 (see Table 2.14), and the increase in debt repayments. This decline in the growth rates in the 1990s structural adjustment period should be of concern to the policy makers.

The growth of GDP has been accompanied by a radical change in the structure of production as shown in Table 2.2. The share of agriculture declined by more than one half, from 53.2 per cent in 1949-1950 to 24.7 per cent in 1994-5. In this period, the share of transportation and communication doubled, manufacturing and construction tripled, and finance and banking quadrupled (from a small base). There has been little change in other services, public administration, defence, and the ownership of dwellings.

Though Pakistan's GDP has grown at a respectable rate, it is still classified amongst the least developed countries on the basis of both per capita income and human resource development. While the continued growth of population at an annual rate of 3.1 per cent has constrained the growth of per capita income, human resource development has been hindered by the low priority accorded to the social sector. Moreover, inadequate physical and social infrastructures, growing fiscal deficits, low rates of savings and investments, rising unemployment and under-employment, sluggish growth and instability of export earning and rising balance of payments deficits are threatening even the prospects of high growth rates in Pakistan.

Table 2.1 : GNP, GDP, and sectoral growth rates

	GNP	GDP	Agriculture	Manufacturing
1949-50 to 1989-90	5.5	5.2	3.4	7.6
1949-50 to 1959-60	3.1	3.1	1.6	7.7
1959-60 to 1969-70	6.8	6.8	5.0	9.9
1959-60 to 1964-65	6.8	6.8	3.8	11.7
1964-65 to 1969-70	6.8	6.7	6.3	8.1
1969-70 to 1979-90	5.4	4.8	2.3	5.4
1969-70 to 1974-75	4.4	4.3	0.8	4.6
1974-75 to 1979-80	6.4	5.3	3.9	6.2
1979-80 to 1989-90	5.5	6.1	4.0	8.2
1979-80 to 1984-85	6.4	6.7	3.7	9.5
1984-85 to 1989-90	4.6	5.7	4.3	6.9
1989-90 to 1994-95	4.4	4.8	3.9	5.6

Source: Based on data from *Economic Survey 1995-96*, Statistical Appendix (1996, p. 31).
Note: National income accounts methodology changed in 1989.

2.1. Agriculture

Except for the second half of the 1960s when, spurred by the Green Revolution grew the agricultural sector, at a rate of 6.3 per cent, its growth rate has been a more modest 3.4 per cent over the 1949-50 to 1989-90 period (Table 2.1). During the eighties, the growth rate did not exceed four per cent. Agricultural output falls significantly short of its potential due to various problems relating to pricing policy of agricultural outputs and inputs, lack of diversification in agricultural output, improper use of fertilizers, credit constraints, rigid water management practices, uncertain availability of improved seeds, unsustainable pest management, and weak agricultural extension programmes.

Table 2.2 : Composition of GDP (percentage shares)

	1949-1950	1959-1960	1969-1970	1979-1980	1989-1990	1994-1995^R
Agriculture	53.2	45.8	38.9	24.8	26.0	24.7
Mining	0.2	0.4	0.5	0.5	0.5	0.5
Manufacturing	7.8	12.0	16.0	17.0	17.8	18.2
Construction	1.4	2.5	1.2	5.1	4.1	4.0
Energy	0.2	0.5	2.0	3.0	3.1	3.8
Communication	5.0	5.7	6.2	6.8	9.6	10.0
Trade	11.9	12.5	13.8	14.3	16.6	16.2
Finance	0.4	1.0	1.8	2.5	2.1	2.4
Housing	5.1	5.0	3.4	3.0	5.4	5.5
Public Admin.	7.0	6.2	6.4	10.1	7.2	6.5
Other Services	7.7	8.3	6.7	7.2	7.5	8.2

Source: *Economic Survey 1991-92 and 1995-96,* Statistical Appendix, (1991, p. 26-7; 1996, p. 30).
Note: R = Revised estimate.

The government of Pakistan uses support prices to guarantee a minimum return to the producer, thus providing an incentive for a sustained growth of agricultural output. However, these support prices diverged greatly from international market prices. Although, this difference narrowed during the eighties, domestic prices continue to be significantly lower than their world market prices.[13] A pricing structure geared towards comparative advantage of the country, agricultural research, technical know-how and extension services would help both in the diversification process as well as in the acceleration of output growth.

To encourage agricultural production, agricultural inputs such as fertilizers, pesticides, and the sinking of tube wells, were subsidized throughout the sixties, seventies, and the first half of the eighties. While the subsidy on the consumption of nitrogenous fertilizers has been phased out, the use of phosphatic and blended fertilizers, irrigation water and credit continue to be subsidized. The remaining subsidies were expected to be eliminated as part of the conditionalities imposed under the Structural Adjustment Program of the World Bank. However, because the subsidies on non-nitrogenous fertilizers are being provided to improve the soil phosphate to nitrogen ratio, its withdrawal might involve efficiency losses.

Pakistan has relied on mechanization rather on than the development of biological technology for enhancing productivity in agriculture, even though the former is labour saving and the latter is capital and land saving technology. Also, while a large proportion of Pakistan's total geographical area is water-logged (about 10 per cent in 1990) and saline (about 2.5 per cent in 1990), very little progress seems to have been made towards the resolution of these problems.[14]

2.2 Industry

The manufacturing sector grew at a rate of 7.6 per cent between 1949-50 and 1989-90 (Table 2.1). Although this is a respectable growth rate, it has neither been able to generate sufficient employment (in a labour surplus economy), nor ensure sufficiently high and stable foreign exchange earnings to overcome balance of payments problems. However, there has been diversification of output in the manufacturing sector; textiles and food processing industries accounted for almost a half of manufacturing output in 1969-70 and only about a third by 1987-8.[15]

Table 2.3: Investment in industry

Year	(As per cent of GDP) Private	Public	Total	Share of Private Investment in Total
1980-81	1.7	3.8	5.5	31.3
1981-82	1.8	3.4	5.2	34.1
1982-83	2.0	4.1	6.1	33.3
1983-84	2.1	3.5	5.6	37.1
1984-85	2.2	3.3	5.5	40.8
1985-86	2.5	3.4	5.9	42.1
1986-87	2.5	3.7	6.2	40.3
1987-88	2.5	3.3	5.8	43.5
1988-89	3.2	4.2	7.4	42.9
1989-90	3.7	3.7	7.4	50.5
1990-91	3.8	3.2	7.0	54.3
1991-92	5.0	3.4	8.4	59.2
1992-93	5.0	3.2	8.2	61.4
1993-94	4.8	3.1	7.9	61.7
1994-95[R]	4.4	3.4	7.8	57.4

Source: Based on GOP, *Economic Survey 1990-1991*, Statistical Appendix, (1996, pp. 34-8), *Economic Survey 1994-95*, Statistical Appendix, (1994, p.29).

Note: R = Revised Estimate.

The most important problem facing this sector is gross inefficiency in resource allocation as well as in operation. In order to improve the efficiency level and stimulate private investment, the government introduced deregulation and privatization policies in the early eighties. While some concerns have been expressed regarding the social costs of these policies, they may have contributed to doubling the share of private investment in total investment and tripling it as a per cent of GDP between the early 1980s and the early 1990s (Table 2.3).

It is also interesting to note that private investment in industry increased from 31.3 per cent in 1980-1 to 57.4 per cent in 1994-5. Nonetheless, in absolute terms, such investment at 4.4 per cent of GDP in 1994-5 is still low, compared to the high performing East Asian economies (section 3). The failure of investment-GDP ratio to rise further may have been due to various constraints, including a distorted incentives structure, industrial regulations, inadequate credit availability, lack of infrastructure, and the absence of a clear-cut policy on closure.

2.3. Employment

The rapid growth of population has constrained the growth of per capita income on the one hand, and has led to unemployment and under-employment on the other. While the gross national product increased at the rate of 5.5 per cent, per capita income growth was less than about 3 per cent as shown in Table 2.4.

Table 2.4: Average annual growth of population, per capita GNP, and labour force

	Per Capita GNP Growth	Population Growth	Labour Force Growth
1960-80	2.8	na	na
1970-80	na	3.1	2.7
1965-90	2.5	na	na
1980-93	3.1	3.1	2.8
1990-4	1.3@	2.9	3.3

Source: *World Development Report*, (1982, p.112; 1992, p.218; 1995, p.162, p.210).
Notes : @ represents data for 1985-94.

Due to the high population growth rate, the labour force has also grown at a rapid rate of 3.3 per cent over the 1990-4 period. This exceeded growth in the labour force of all low income economies by 0.7

per cent (*WDR* 1996, p.194). A faster growth of labour force than that of population reflects a decline in the labour force participation rate, from 43.16 per cent in 1990-91 to 42.0 per cent in 1993-4 (*LFS* 1993, p.xv; 1995, p.16). This suggests that labour market adjustments in Pakistan take place via adjustments in the labour force participation rates rather than in open unemployment rates. The latter has been reported to be around three per cent for a long period. However, using new definitions, the 1993-94 *Labour Force Survey*, found that the unemployment rate of 3.6 per cent increased to 6.3 per cent (*LFS* 1993, p. x, xiv).

Another aspect of employment is the distribution of the unemployed by gender and age. According to the *Labour Force Survey* 1993-4 (1995, p.16), the refined participation rate for women was 13.3 per cent, less than one-fifth that of men. While this statistic grossly understates the actual participation rate for definitional reasons, it nevertheless also reflects genuine obstacles to women's participation in the labour force. This is particularly true for urban and educated women. Similarly, official figures indicate that 12.3 per cent of the children between the ages of 10 and 14, and 33 per cent between the ages of 15 and 19 are in the labour force (ibid., p.17). These statistics represent a large incidence of child labour.

The occupational structure of those in the labour force has also been changing, though in a less marked manner than the changes in the structure of GDP, as shown below in Table 2.5.

Table 2.5 : Sectoral distribution of employed labour force (percentage shares)

Period	Agri.	Mfg.	Const.	Elec/Gas	Tpt.	Trade@	Other
1969-70	57.03	15.57	3.93	0.41	4.73	9.89	8.44
1974-5	54.80	13.78	4.20	0.49	4.87	11.09	10.77
1978-9	52.65	14.66	4.92	0.74	4.73	11.08	11.22
1984-5	50.56	13.84	5.60	0.69	5.20	11.54	12.57
1990-1	47.45	12.38	6.62	0.83	5.24	13.24	15.22
1994-5	50.04	10.12	6.50	na	4.95	12.78	15.56

Source: *Economic Survey 1995-96* (1996, p. 12). The information has been drawn from *Labour Force Surveys* for the respective years.

Notes: @ = Wholesale and retail trade
Mfg. = Manufacturing and mining
Const. = Construction
Tpt. = Transportation

Not unexpectedly, the share of agriculture in total employment has declined by about seven per cent. However, the share of the manufacturing and mining sector in employment, quite surprisingly, has fallen continuously since the late 1960s. The remaining categories represent employment in services and all these show increases.

The changes in the employment distribution are mainly due to differences in employment elasticities with respect to output (i.e., how employment growth responds to output growth), which are reported in Table 2.6.

Table 2.6 : Employment elasticities

Period	Agri.	Mfg.	Const.	Elec/Gas	Tpt.	Trade@	Other
1963-4 to 1969-1970	0.07	0.40	3.99	0.05	1.14	0.83	0.18
1969-1970 to 1979-1980	0.99	0.37	0.72	1.33	0.48	0.84	0.60
1979-1980 to 1989-1990	0.49	0.12	1.05	na	0.16	0.31	0.30

Source : Kemal (1991)
Notes: @ = Wholesale and retail trade
na = Not available

The elasticities of employment in the formal sector vary quite significantly not only across economic activities, but also over time. Almost all the sectors experienced a decline in employment elasticities over time. Manufacturing had the lowest employment elasticity in the eighties. A major reason could be capital cheapening tax holidays, tax credits, accelerated depreciation allowances, and low rates of interest. Another reason is the high labour costs produced by various types of interventions in the labour market (Kemal 1986, 1989). The relatively higher elasticities in the services sector probably represent less government intervention in these sectors.

An elasticity of 0.12 means that ten per cent growth in the formal or large-scale manufacturing sector would generate about one per cent increase in manufacturing employment. Thus an employment strategy concentrating on the manufacturing sector would make little sense. Pro-employment alternatives focus on the informal sector and on the creation of off-farm employment opportunities in rural areas since employment elasticities in these activities are believed to be much higher due to their greater labour intensity. However, such alternatives suffer from inadequate domestic demand for goods and limited export prospects. Export prospects could be improved with feedback between importers, exporters, and small producers, and by ensuring quality control. Both these activities could be undertaken by the Export Promotion Bureau.

Another obstacle in generating more employment in the informal sector is the absence of detailed knowledge on the internal functioning of the sector, especially with regard to its mode of governance, i.e., its methods of resolving disputes, of co-ordinating activity, and of its system of providing credit.

3. SAVING AND INVESTMENT

Pakistan has more than doubled its investment and saving ratios from a low base in 1959-60 of 9.7 and 6.5 per cent respectively as shown below in Table 2.7.

Table 2.7 : Trends in growth of GDP, investment, and savings

Year	GDP	I/GDP	GNS/GDP	GDS/GDP	I-S
1959-60	na	9.7	6.5	na	3.2
1964-5	na	17.3	10.5	na	6.8
1969-70	na	14.3	13.1	13.1	1.2
1979-80	na	15.3	6.2	13.4	1.9
1982-3	6.8	15.5	12.6	na	2.9
1985-6	6.4	15.3	11.9	5.2	3.4
1986-7	8.8	16.1	14.1	9.7	4.0
1987-8	6.4	17.6	13.3	10.7	4.3
1988-9	4.8	17.2	12.4	na	4.8
1989-90	4.6	18.0	13.4	na	4.6
1990-1	5.6	18.3	13.6	na	4.7
1991-2	7.7	19.9	14.5	na	5.4
1992-3^{R}	2.3	20.4	13.4	na	7.0
1993-4^{R}	4.5	19.9	14.6	na	5.3
1994-5	4.4	18.6	14.6	na	4.0

Source: GDP growth rates have been drawn from the 1992-3 and 1995-6 *Economic Surveys*, Statistical Appendices (1993, p.34; 1996, p.31). Investment and saving data are revised estimates drawn from the first chapters of the *Economic Surveys* for the corresponding years, p. 6 of the *Economic Survey* 1986-7 and pp.20-1 of *Economic Survey* 1982-83, Statistical Annexure.

Notes:
GDP = GDP (factor cost) growth rate
I/GDP = Investment GDP ratio
GNS/GDP = Gross national saving GDP ratio
GDS/GDP = Gross domestic saving GDP ratio
R = Revised estimate
I-S = Column 3 - column 4
na = Not available

Despite the increase in Pakistan's investment ratio over a period of time, it is still below the average investment ratios of 30 per cent and 26 per cent for low (including India and China) and middle income economies, respectively in 1993 (*WDR* 1996, p.212). Also, Pakistan's investment ratio is far below the investment ratio of leading performing Asian economies in the 1960-85 period, which averaged over 35 per cent (*WB* 1993, p.41). It is puzzling how Pakistan has been able to generate fairly high growth rates with relatively low investment ratios.

Again, while the national saving ratio has also grown steadily, the domestic saving ratio (for the few years for which data are available) is much below the averages for countries in a similar economic situation.[16] The difference between national and domestic saving represents the inflow of remittances. Nonetheless, even with high remittances, the gap between investment and national saving is very high (column labelled I-NS) and continued to grow over time. This gap had to be bridged by the inflow of foreign funds, which over a period of time has imposed a considerable burden on the economy in the form of high debt service requirements.

The government is partly responsible for the resource gap due to its inability to generate enough revenue to meet its expenditure (see Table 2.8). Consequently, it has to draw on the pool of national saving, which results in the gap between investment and national saving. In order to finance its excess spending, the government, besides using external resources, has squeezed a substantial portion of the non-government savings through borrowing.[17] It is often argued that the diversion of non-government savings to the government sector may promote growth in income and result in additional savings. This seems improbable in the case of Pakistan, because even though there exists much excess production capacity, it cannot be mobilized due to a number of constraints (e.g. inadequate power, poor communications infrastructure and shortage of skilled manpower).[18]

4. BUDGET DEFICITS AND THE PUBLIC DEBT

A major obstacle to the establishment of effective support mechanisms is the fiscal crisis of the state. In 1994-5, Pakistan spent roughly 9 per cent of GDP on debt servicing and about 5.4 per cent on the military, which left under 4 per cent of the 17 per cent of GDP collected as tax and non-tax revenues to fund everything else, including general administration, law and order, and social services (*Economic Survey* 1995-6, p.138-42). Since the debt burden is increasing over time, an increase in state support for the social sector would occur only if one of the following three things happen: a fiscal reform helps restore the solvency of the state; additional external resources are tapped to free the social sector from governmental patronage; or alternative and innovative funding mechanisms are devised. What follows is a picture of the fiscal crisis with a few suggestions.

4.1. Public Debt

Both external and domestic debt ballooned over the last two decades. Table 2.8 shows the size of both domestic and external debt as a percentage of the GDP.

Table 2.8 : Domestic and external debt as a percentage of the GDP

Year	Domestic debt as % of GDP	External debt as % of GNP
1970-1	25.5	26.2
1974-5	19.1	34.1
1979-80	24.2	30.2
1984-5	30.5	29.7
1988-9	43.0	33.0
1994-5RE	42.0	56.6

Source: For external debt 1993-4, *World Development Report 1996* (1996, p. 220); For domestic debt, *Economic Survey 1995-6*, (1996, p. 143).

Note: RE = Revised estimate.

The two debts reached parity in 1970-1 and then again in 1984-5. Since then, the domestic debt has grown at a much more rapid rate, and in 1988-9 had reached 36 per cent of GDP when the external debt was one-third of GDP. This trend has again been reversed and the external debt in 1994-5 was more than half of GDP. The rapidly rising domestic interest payments account for the rapid rise in internal debt.

4.2 Fiscal Deficits

The budget deficit started growing rapidly in the 1970s, when public sector activities increased sharply. Table 2.9 shows how the budget deficit has increased over time and the factors responsible for this increase.

Table 2.9 : Budget deficit, the military, subsidies, debt service, and public investment as a percentage of the GDP (mp)

Year	Deficit	Subsidies	Debt service				Military	PI
			RF	IF	ID	T		
1959-60	0.8	na	na	na	na	1.3	6.5	6.0
1969-70	3.6	2.1	na	na	na	2.1	6.3	7.0
1979-80	6.3	1.6	2.4	1.0	1.1	na	5.4	9.3
1980-1	5.3	1.8	1.3	0.8	1.1	na	5.1	9.5
1981-2	5.3	1.3	1.8	0.9	1.4	na	5.3	8.1
1982-3	7.1	1.3	2.4	1.2	1.7	na	5.8	8.6
1983-4	6.0	1.5	2.1	1.2	2.0	na	5.8	8.3
1984-5	7.7	1.4	1.9	1.2	2.1	na	6.2	8.0
1985-6	7.6	1.5	2.0	1.2	2.3	na	6.4	9.2
1986-7	8.2	1.2	2.1	1.3	2.8	4.2	6.8	9.7
1987-8	8.5	1.5	2.0	1.2	3.3	4.8	6.8	8.8
1988-9	7.4	2.0	2.4	1.2	4.3	5.1	6.4	9.0
1989-90	6.5	1.2	2.2	1.3	4.2	5.7	6.6	8.4
1990-1	8.7	1.1	2.1	1.4	3.5	4.9	6.2	8.5
1991-2	7.4	1.0	2.4	1.2	4.9	8.0	6.2	8.8
1992-3	8.0	0.6	2.2	1.2	4.7	8.3	6.5	9.0
1993-4	5.9	0.4	2.8	1.2	4.9	9.2	5.8	8.3
1994-5[RE]	5.5	0.3	2.8	1.1	4.4	8.4	5.4	8.3

Source: For data going back to 1986-7 we used *Economic Survey, Statistical Supplement 1993-4* (1994, pp. 44-5 for GDP, p.172 for the deficit, p.174 for defence, p.175 for subsidies, p.176 for debt, and p. 60 for public investment); for data going back to 1979-80 we used *Economic Survey, Statistical Supplement 1987-88* (1988, p.21 for GDP, p.105 for the deficit, p.107 for defence, p. 108 for subsidies, p. 109 for debt, p.26 for public investment); for 1959-60 and 1969-70 we used data in *Pakistan Economic Survey 1974-75*, Statistical Annexure (1975, p. 8 for GDP and pp.142-3 for the other information).

Notes:
RE = Revised estimate
RF = Repayments of principal on foreign debt
ID = Repayment of interest on domestic debt
T = Total debt servicing. We have reported the totals when only the totals were available.
mp = market prices
IF = Repayment of interest on foreign debt
PI = Public investment
na = Not available

As a per cent of the GDP, the deficit grew from less than one per cent in 1959-60 to 3.6 per cent a decade later. There are two reasons for this increase. First, the government started subsidizing wheat, edible oils, and other basic consumption goods for the poor. Subsidies, which were virtually non-existent in 1959-60, increased to 2.1 per cent of GDP in 1969-70, and then remained between one and two per cent for the next two decades, falling below one per cent only after 1991-2.

Second, the debt service burden, which was quite modest in 1959-60 at 1.3 per cent of GDP, had already almost doubled a decade later to 2.1 by 1969-70, and doubled again in the next decade to 5.4 per cent of GDP by 1979-80. Between 1979-80 and 1994-5, the combined principal repayment and interest repayment on foreign debt has been fairly steady between 3 and 4 per cent of GDP. However, given this burden of servicing the foreign debt, the government started relying on internal sources, which shows up in the steadily ballooning domestic interest payments. By 1994-5, interest payments on domestic debt alone were 4.4 per cent of GDP, and this constitutes a major factor in explaining the fiscal deficit.

Third, after the nationalization of several major industries in 1972, public investment increased from 7.0 per cent of GDP in 1969-70 to 9.3 per cent in 1979-80. Later, the privatization policy helped contain public investment especially in the manufacturing sector, but it still remained quite high at above 8 per cent until 1994-95.

Military expenditures have been high but have remained fairly constant. Since the mid-1980s, they have varied between 6 to 7 per cent of GDP.

Fiscal deficits may be financed through external borrowing, domestic non-bank borrowing, or bank borrowing. Almost half the deficit was being financed by external sources in 1979-80 and 1980-1 as shown below in Table 2.10.

By 1982-3, external financing of the deficit dropped to about a fifth of the total. Since then, it has covered from one-fifth to one-third of the deficit. However, until recently, Pakistan was able to avoid the inflationary effects that usually accompany such large and persistent fiscal deficits. This was done by relying much more on non-bank borrowing than on bank financing. Indeed, in 1988-9, bank borrowing covered only 1.4 per cent of the deficit. This changed in 1990-91 when bank borrowing jumped to cover almost half the deficit and about four-fifths and three-fifths in the following two years. The increase in the consumer price index of 27 between 1992-3 to 1993-4 is undoubtedly partly explained by this altered form of deficit financing (*Economic Survey* 1994-5, p.140). Since 1993-4, bank financing has again been contained.

Table 2.10 : Deficit financing by source (percentages)

Year	External	Domestic	
		Non-bank	Bank
1979-80	47.4	9.6	43.0
1980-1	47.7	36.2	16.1
1982-3	20.1	56.0	23.9
1983-4	19.9	48.8	31.2
1984-5	14.0	35.0	50.9
1985-6	20.6	64.7	14.6
1986-7	18.0	58.6	23.4
1987-8	22.0	53.7	24.2
1988-9	32.0	66.6	1.4
1989-90	40.9	52.8	6.3
1990-1	24.8	26.6	48.6
1991-2	20.0	0.5	80.5
1992-3	22.6	18.6	58.8
1993-4	26.7	59.7	13.6
1994-5	30.2	46.1	17.9

Source: *Economic Survey 1995-6*, Statistical Appendix (1996, p.138); *Economic Survey, Statistical Supplement 1986-7*, (1987, p.109). The rows sometimes do not add up to one hundred due to rounding off errors. The data for 1981-2 has not been reported due to a large unaccounted-for inconsistency.

4.3. Need for Tax Reform

Given the perilous state of the government's finances, as represented by the deficit in Table 2.9, the need for reform is imperative. It is widely acknowledged that tax collection is inefficient. Indeed, a former finance minister was quoted as saying that as much as one-half of the state's resources were being wasted because of leakages. Table 2.11 below shows how Pakistan's Federal Government tax effort compares with a selected group of countries.

Pakistan needs to raise more revenues and also raise the share of direct taxes, which are more progressive (see chapter 4).

As indicated in Table 2.9, the budget deficit has increased due to rising subsidies, public investment following nationalization, interest payments, and to this list we add inadequate resource mobilization. An important reason for the latter has been tax exemptions granted to various sections of the society (political pressure groups). Numerous exemptions from income tax have been granted to individuals and corporations by name.[19]

Table 2.11 : Pakistan's central government tax performance in a comparative perspective (1993)

Countries	Direct taxes as % of total current revenue	Total revenue as % GDP
Low income		
Pakistan	13.9	18.4
Sri Lanka	13.9	19.7
India	18.7	14.4
Middle income		
Turkey	35.6	18.7
Malaysia	34.5	28.7
Korea	31.4	18.9
High income		
Singapore	30.0	26.6
USA56.6	19.7	

Source: *World Development Report 1995* (1995, pp. 182-3)

There is a complete lack of will on the part of government to impose taxes in a judicious way. This is shown by the low per cent of direct taxes in total central government revenues. The 1990 National Finance Commission award did away with the practice of the Federal Government meeting the entire deficit of the provincial governments. This is a major step in providing the right incentives to provincial governments to mobilize their own resources. Provincial governments had virtually let the expenditures rise uninhibitedly because it was the federal government which had to worry about financing the expenditures. Table 2.12 below shows the discrepancy between provincial government expenditures and tax revenues as a percentage of the total.

It is clear from Table 2.12 below that provincial government expenditures far exceed their resource mobilization. In fact, there has been a decrease in provincial resource mobilization in the 1990s compared to the 1980s. This situation is not efficient. The provincial tax base should be made to match expenditures consistent with robust and sustainable provincial development, and provincial expenditures should be expected to be consistent with this resource mobilization capacity. The issue of inter-provincial development balance would then become a more prominent part of the federation's concerns.

The growth of public revenues has suffered, both from the lack of vision in policy formulation, as well as from poor tax administration. For example, granting immunity under the Self-Assessment Scheme to all those who had declared 20 per cent higher income than the incomes in the last year, and the amnesty to black money holders, and that too without any tax, led to meagre resource mobilization.

Table 2.12 : Provincial government expenditures and tax revenues as a percentage of the total.

Year	Expenditures	Tax revenues
1986-7	26.6	4.7
1987-8	24.5	4.8
1988-9	22.2	4.4
1989-90	29.5	4.5
1990-1	22.9	4.5
1991-2	na	4.5
1992-3	na	3.8
1993-4	23.3	4.2
1994-5RE	25.7	3.7

Source: Based on *Economic Survey 1994-95* (1995, p.130).
Notes : na = Not available
RE = Revised estimate

Not only have public revenues increased slowly, but increasing current expenditures have left few resources for developmental needs and for financing other expenditures. In addition, such expenditures have often not attained the desired objective or have been wasteful. Food subsidies, operated to help the poor, benefited only the rich flour mill owners and the big landlords with substantial marketable surpluses.[20] Similarly, bureaucratic inefficiency in conceiving and implementing commercial ventures are likely to have been covered up by budget subsidies.

While development expenditures fell in real terms due to privatization, budget deficits increased in part due to unconstrained growth of non-development expenditures. Current expenditure increased from 62 per cent in 1977-8 to four-fifths of the total expenditure in 1994-5.[21] The budget deficit feeds on itself as the public debt continues to increase at a rapid rate because of heavy borrowing to finance the deficit at high interest rates (see Table 2.9).

A major reason for tax evasion and low resource mobilization is the poor quality of services people receive in return for the payment of taxes and other charges. An important step for the improvement of revenue collection is the improvement of services. Yet, here the government is locked in a vicious circle: the improvement of services costs money, and more money would be available only if better services were being offered.

To break this vicious circle, the government could try to start offering better services through better paid and better motivated individuals and charge a higher fee for their services. This principle could be applied to 'higher income services', such as university education, piped water, and residential hospital care. However, even this reform will have to be accompanied by a welfare transfer programme to keep the proposal distributionally neutral.

Basic services must remain free of cost (although nominal fees may be charged). In order to make such services more efficient and beneficiary oriented, the costs and the benefits could be linked through decentralization and community participation. In this way, the local communities could take responsibility for the delivery of the service and the government could then restrict its role to providing financial support for the vulnerable or deprived communities.

Consider the following example. As things stand, local communities have no say in determining the quality or relevance of teaching in schools. Thus they have little incentive to pay more for education provided by the state for children from these communities. Decentralization to the local level (rather than district or union level) can help link the beneficiaries directly with the service, and thus improve the efficiency of the service by ensuring community supervision. This will also result in more motivated communities, willing to pay more for services they have a stake in. We take up these issues in detail in chapter 7.

An alternative to the proposals proffered above is the reliance on foreign resources. However, this is at best an interim solution, which, as shown by rising debt repayments in Table 2.9, is not sustainable.

4.4. Financial institutions

We make a few observations here pertaining to financial institutions and house building loans. For broader aspects of financial sector reform see Haque and Kardar (1994). The major financial institutions have catered mainly to government and quasi-government bodies, or to an oligopolistic business sector. The need for broader financial intermediation has been met by a succession of poorly regulated and irresponsible financial institutions which emerged in the 1980s and crashed after siphoning off a large volume of savings of small depositors. It appears that the main beneficiaries of these rackets are also the big business houses of the country.

Thus, financial markets do not perform a number of functions that they can easily do. For instance, a customary function of financial institutions is to provide credit for residential construction and purchase. In Pakistan, not only are the available funds too meagre, they are also not accessible to the vast majority of the population.

Besides legal and managerial constraints, there are two major obstacles against the effective involvement of financial institutions in house building. First, the centralized nature of the banking system means that it would be impossible for the institution to supervise credit in far-flung areas, the concentration of credit institutions in a few areas means the concentration of credit provision to the same few areas. One possibility, along the lines of the US system, would be to prohibit interstate banking, and thus promote small local banks whose main task will be to provide credit for residential construction or small local businesses.

Second, the management of information systems in the country represents a constraint. Because of legal obstacles, a large portion of real estate is owned by people other than those in whose name the property is registered. The result is that the establishment of ownership has become confused and cannot readily support interaction with the formal financial system. Title and ownership need to be clearly identified in the records, so that records acquire meaning and salience and can become the basis of financial loans.

5. BALANCE OF PAYMENTS

Pakistan's balance of payments has almost always been in the deficit. While workers' remittances grew sharply over the period 1974-5 to 1984-5 and financed a large part of the trade deficit, the decline since 1984-5 has led to a sharp deterioration in the balance of payments. This creates an obstacle to the pursuit of social objectives since payment difficulties have a tendency to hold government policies hostage.

Table 2.13 : Exports, imports, and the trade balance
(period averages, constant prices, $ million)

Year	Exports	Imports	Trade Balance
1947/48-1949/50	200.3	311.3	−111.0
1950/51-1954/55	309.8	380.4	−70.6
1955/56-1959/60	135.4	288.8	−153.4
1960/61-1964/65	171.2	553.2	−382.0
1965/66-1968/69	254.0	554.8	−300.8
1969/70-1974/75	466.0	677.4	−201.4
1975/76-1978/79	635.6	1291.4	−655.8
1979/80-1984/85	806.8	1681.8	−875.0
1985/86-1988/89	1051.2	1589.0	−537.0
1990/91-1991/92	1444.0	1867.5	−423.5

Source: *Economic Survey 1994-95, Statistical Appendix* (1995, p.153); *Economic Survey, Statistical Supplement 1986-7* (1987, p.130). The base year is 1959-60. Data beyond 1990-1 were not available.

The trade balance has been positive only three times (1947-8, 1950-1, 1972-3) since the formation of the country. As Table 2.13 indicates, while the trade balance has fluctuated, there has been a steady increase in the deficit. It remains to be seen if the decline in the deficit of the early nineties can be sustained.

The deterioration in terms of trade is likely to be a major cause of the increase in the trade deficit. Using 1987 as the base year, the commodity terms of trade declined from 124 in 1971 to 80 in 1991.[22] Had the terms of trade stayed constant, Pakistan's exports would have exceeded imports by 7.5 per cent in 1992. Because of the deterioration in terms of trade, exports are sufficient for financing only three-quarters of imports.

There is another way of looking at the trade balance as shown in Table 2.14. As a percentage of GDP, imports have held steady over the last decade while exports as a percentage of GDP show an upward trend after 1981-2. Consequently, as a percentage of the GDP, the deficit has declined from a high of 10.96 per cent in 1984-5 to the an 3.73 per cent in 1994-5.

Table 2.14 : Major balance of payment indicators as a percentage of GDP.

Year	Exports	Imports	Trade deficit	Remittances	Current account deficit
1980-1	10.53	19.25	8.72	7.53	3.69
1981-2	8.02	18.30	10.28	7.24	4.90
1982-3	9.93	18.60	9.20	10.06	1.80
1983-4	8.89	18.26	9.37	8.79	3.20
1984-5	7.99	18.95	10.96	7.85	5.39
1985-6	9.63	17.67	8.04	8.14	3.88
1986-7	11.06	16.14	5.08	6.84	2.16
1987-8	11.61	16.65	5.04	5.24	4.38
1988-9	11.64	17.56	5.92	4.74	4.83
1989-90	12.41	17.38	4.96	4.87	4.74
1990-1	13.47	16.74	3.27	4.06	4.77
1991-2	14.16	18.97	4.82	3.01	2.76
1992-3	13.18	19.23	6.05	3.02	7.13
1993-4	13.05	16.42	3.78	2.77	3.77
1994-5	13.46	17.19	3.73	3.09	3.97

Source: This is a reproduction of Table 11.3 of *Economic Survey 1995-6, Statistical Appendix* (1996, p.160)

Since 1974-5, a large part of the balance of payments deficit has been financed through workers' remittances. In fact, in 1982-3 and again in 1985-6, remittances more than covered the trade deficit. However, since 1982-3 they have been declining as a percentage of the GDP. While remittances still finance at least half of the trade deficit, this decline and the rise of debt repayments account for the current account deficits being larger than the trade deficit since 1991-2.

5.1. Trade and payments reform

Trade reforms are needed to reduce the vulnerability of the economy to external shocks. Empirical studies suggest that countries with open trade regimes and closed financial regimes have fared much better in coping with external shocks than others (Burney and Schor 1993). However, the ability to maintain closed regimes depends partly on the managerial and technical capacity of the state, and partly on the existence of co-ordination agreements between states. In other words, an effective response to the threat posed by external vulnerability requires the improvement of managerial systems in the area of financial regulation and a move towards international agreements on the monitoring of trade and financial flows.

6. SUMMARY AND CONCLUSIONS

Inadequate mobilization and poor allocation of resources, inefficiencies in the production structure and low priority accorded to the development of human resources have been the major constraints on the development process in Pakistan. This is essentially a reflection of the lack of political commitment to development objectives and is manifested in the lack of direction in public policy. This lack of commitment and direction, together with poor institutional arrangements, has led to ad hoc decisions on the one hand, and poor implementation of the decisions on the other.

But not everything has been negative. The growth rate between 1949-50 to the early 1990s has been a robust 5.5 per cent. Pakistan experienced a structural change in the move from an agrarian to a manufacturing or mixed economy, much as would be expected from a steadily developing economy (Chenery and Syrquin 1975). Exports as per cent of GDP increased several percentage points from the early 1980s to the early 1990s. Industry diversified and textiles and food went down from about fifty per cent of total manufacturing to about one-third. The private manufacturing investment–GDP ratio almost tripled from 1980-1 to 1993-4.

Despite these strengths, many fundamental weaknesses in Pakistan's economy remain. Water-logging and salinity continue to plague Pakistan's agriculture and productivity continues to be low by international standards. While there has been some industrial diversification, much more is needed to safeguard the country from external shocks. A decline in the terms of trade index of 44 points in twenty years (1971-1991) is an important cause of Pakistan's continued current account deficit despite the rise in export growth. In addition to the current account deficit, Pakistan's economy is also plagued by a large and growing fiscal deficit.

Compared to the high performing East Asian economies, investment and saving ratios are small. Domestic savings have been unable to meet even the relatively low investment ratio, and the shortfall has been met with remittances and foreign saving. Since the latter two sources cannot be relied on into the indefinite future, this remains a fundamental economic weakness of Pakistan's economy. An important reason for this dissonance between investment and saving is that the government has been spending more than the resources it mobilizes.

While successive governments in Pakistan have had the avowed objective of self-reliance, they have hardly made any effort to mobilize domestic resources. Also, they did not formulate any long-run strategy to raise foreign resources to augment domestic resources. Consequently, aid has been accepted at a high cost to the economy.

The saving rate in Pakistan has ranged between 13 and 14 per cent. While private savings can still be increased further, the low overall savings rate is essentially due to negative public savings, which reflect the huge overall budgetary deficit. The budget deficit has increased due to rising subsidies, rising public investment following nationalization, inadequate resource mobilization, large military expenditures, interest payments and the unconstrained growth of non-development expenditures. Until 1990-1, the bulk of the deficit was financed by non-bank borrowing which contained inflation. This practice changed after 1990-1 and the bulk of the deficit started being financed by bank borrowing. This is likely to have fed into the high inflation rate since 1994-5.

Both the tax collection and expenditure side of the budget have exhibited inefficiencies and waste. Immunities, amnesties, and individualized exemptions have hurt resource mobilization. At the same time, subsidies have been subverted or misdirected. Provincial government expenditures far exceed the tax revenues they generate. The 1990 National Finance Commission's decision to impose fiscal restraint on the provinces by expecting their expenditures to match their resource mobilization, must be accompanied by allowing provinces access to a reasonable tax base. This principle of decentralization also applies in a broader sense to resource mobilization. If communities have a say in expenditures, and this subsequently improves the quality of services delivered, it will also improve resource mobilization.

Without creative tax reform, the country faces the prospect of large and growing budgetary deficits which in turn limit other much needed meaningful social and economic reforms. Any attempt to cope with poverty and inequality must start with a successful employment strategy. Given the low and falling employment elasticities in the formal sector, the government must turn to the informal sector for labour absorption. Credit, technical advice, and improving feedback mechanisms between consumers, exporters, and producers are pivotal to such a strategy.

On balance, while Pakistan's economy has demonstrated the ability to produce robust growth rates and shown other strengths, it continues to suffer from several fundamental weaknesses and problems. Perhaps, one of its most major failings, which may have serious repercussions on its future performance, is the neglect of the social sectors. We turn to this issue in the next chapter.

NOTES

1. These discrepancies are sometimes pointed out in the text. Prominent examples include data on saving and investment, and school enrolment rates.
2. Pakistan is included in the low income economies by the World Bank, based on its per capita GNP.
3. Except where indicated, the statistics cited in this sub-section are from *25 Years of Pakistan in Statistics* (Government of Pakistan 1972).
4. The literacy rate refers to the 1972 definition, i.e., ability to read and write with understanding. According to the 1951 definition (i.e., the ability to read clear print in any language) the literacy rate was 18.2 per cent. *Provincial and District Population Census Reports* contain the latter definition.
5. It is often suggested that Pakistan had inherited a well-trained army and efficient bureaucracy. However, the army's effectiveness was considerably reduced by the lack of ammunition and armaments on the one hand, and by initially being under the command of British officers on the other. Similarly, the effectiveness of the bureaucracy was adversely affected by a number of factors that became significant after independence. These included the lack of requisite stationery and supplies in the initial stages; an anachronistic training system confined to administering law and order and carrying out executive orders; and, most important, an inherited contempt for the vernacular among the higher echelons of the bureaucracy.
6. Vol. vi, p. 279, as cited in Zamora (1990, p.18).
7. Ibid., p. 20.
8. Ibid., p. 21.
9. Ibid., p. 20.
10. For the many other attempts to revive local government by the British administrators in India, see Matthais (1915, pp.162-98).
11. Ibid., p. 241-2.
12. The District Social Action Boards of the last PPP administration did not represent local government even though they were introduced as such. The Punjab government's proposal on elected village councils represented potentially interesting local government reform. However, in 1996, the Punjab government was engaged in a tussle with the Supreme Court in an effort to disband local bodies.
13. This is true for cotton, maize, potatoes, and lentils, but not any more for rice (in which case the Pakistani price for basmati exceeds the most expensive equivalent from Thailand in the US market) and wheat (for which the procurement price was virtually identical to hard winter No. 2 in the US market). Both international and procurement prices are drawn from *Agricultural Statistics of Pakistan* (Government of Pakistan 1994, p.256 and pp.223-5).
14. Ibid., pp. 128-9. This source shows no progress has been made in containing water-logging from the mid to late 1980s.
15. At the time of writing, the latest Census of Manufacturing Industry, for which data were available, was for the year 1987-8. *Economic Survey* Statistical Appendix 1990-1, p.74 and *Economic Survey* 1993-94, p.60.

16. The average domestic saving ratio for low income countries (including India and China) was 27 in 1993 (*World Development Report 1995* (1995, pp. 178-79)). The eight high performing East Asian economies had an average domestic saving ratio of 37 per cent between 1960 and 1985 which exceeded even their own high investment ratio (ibid.).

17. Government bank borrowing for budgetary support generally stayed below 2 per cent of GDP (3.9 in 1984-5) but jumped to 6 per cent in 1991-2 and 4.6 per cent in 1992-93. *Economic Survey*, Statistical Appendix, (1989, p.117; 1994, p.116). Also see Table 2.10.

18. The last PPP administration (1993-1996) attempted to address the power constraint by drawing foreign investment.

19. Income Tax Act, Second Schedule. The 1997 tax reforms of the Nawaz Sharif government abolished many much exemptions referred to as SROs (special revenue orders). Its too soon to assess the overall impact of the tax reforms directed mostly at reducing tax rates and increasing the tax base.

20. Cornilesse and Naqvi, 1987.

21. *Economic Survey 1995-6*, Statistical Appendix, (1996, p.140) and *Economic Survey 1986-7*, Statistical Supplement, (1987, p.111).

22. Information taken from the data diskette of the *World Tables 1993*. (World Bank).

3

Human Resource Development

Tariq Banuri, A. R. Kemal ,and *Khawar Mumtaz*

INTRODUCTION

Human resource development has been the most neglected factor in the process of economic development in Pakistan. Social sector expenditure in 1981-2 increased from 2.0 per cent to 3.0 per cent in 1985-6, and has stayed roughly constant since then (*Economic Survey*, 1995-6, p.6). The social sector also figures low in the priorities of households; thus only 1.53 per cent of household consumption expenditure was allocated to education in 1990-1.[1]

In the past, a lack of commitment, inadequate resources, and poor utilization of the limited resource-base were responsible for the failure of the population welfare programmes and the inadequate development of human resources. Whenever there has been a shortfall in resources, the social sector has suffered the most. There are signs of change. While only 71 per cent of the overall financial allocation to education was utilized during the Sixth Plan, utilization exceeded allocations by nine per cent overall during the Seventh Plan.[2] Similarly, in the Annual Development Plan expenditures, which represent the implementation of the Five Year Plan priorities, education and health ranked ninth and tenth among fourteen sectors in 1975-6 and this ranking went to seventh and ninth in the revised estimates of the 1993-4 Plan (*Economic Survey 1995-6*, p.44-6).

The Sixth, Seventh, and Eighth Five Year Plans emphasized the development of human resources, and in the Eighth Plan the government also formulated a Social Action Plan especially to attain this goal. However, changed priorities are barely visible in the numbers as reported in chapter 2.

A number of factors are responsible for the neglect of human resource development in Pakistan. Prominent amongst them is the inadequacy of public resources. In other words, social sector expenditures are highly correlated with aggregate public expenditures. The correlation coefficient between the two series is 0.63. More precisely, an increase in public revenues of one per cent of GDP will be expected to raise the share of social sector in total public expenditures by 0.77 per cent, and in GDP by 0.29 per cent.[3] Therefore, unless major efforts are made to increase public revenues, the social sectors may still be neglected in the future.

However, as argued in chapter 4, resource mobilization must avoid placing the burden on the poor, both for equity reasons and in order not to negate the human resource development efforts.

1. EDUCATION

Pakistan started with a handicap in the education sector; as pointed out in chapter 2, the literacy rate at the time of independence was only 13.2 per cent. Due to the low priority accorded by respective governments to education, and especially to primary education, the literacy rate rose only to 26.2 per cent by 1981. While no firm data on literacy rates in Pakistan are available for more recent years, the Government of Pakistan estimates it to be 37.9 per cent in 1995-6, while UNDP, drawing on UNESCO estimates, reports it to be 36.4 per cent in 1993.[4]

While the literacy rate has increased at a relatively sharper rate during the 1980s, it still falls considerably short of the average literacy rate of 61 per cent and 79 per cent for the low and the medium human development countries, respectively (*HDR 1996*, p.145-6]). To improve the literacy rate, Pakistan initiated a number of programmes including: The Adult Literacy Programme, Iqra Pilot Project, and Nai Roshni Schools. However, they have failed to raise the literacy rate in any significant way. These programmes were not cost-effective, as the cost of education per person exceeded the cost of educating a child in a regular primary school. Moreover, there have been problems in the implementation of these programmes since they were subject to abuse.[5] A sensible change on the part of planners is apparent on this subject, evident in the Seventh Five Year Plan (nd, p.252), which aims to concentrate the government's resources on universal primary education as the most effective long-run method of countering illiteracy. NGOs are to be given incentives to launch community-based literacy programmes.

The main reason for low literacy in Pakistan is the low crude participation rate at the primary level as indicated in Table 3.1.[6] The data show a steady increase in participation rates at all levels of schooling. However, the total participation rate still falls considerably short of the crude participation rates for similar developing countries at all levels. For example, the participation rate at the primary level in 1992 for low income economies was 102 per cent and for India it was 98 per cent.[7]

Table 3.1 : Participation rates by level

Year	Primary	Middle	High
1982-3	52.8	20.0	16.0
1987-8	63.5	30.0	17.0
1994-5	73.0	46.0	32.0

Source: *Seventh Five Year Plan 1988-93* (nd, pp. 414-15); *Economic Survey 1989-90* (nd, p. 108), *Economic Survey 1995-96*, (1996, p. 111).

Notes: All numbers are estimates since population cohorts have been estimated based on the 1981 Population Census.

There appears to have been a rapid increase in the absolute growth of enrolments relative to the increase in population growth as shown in Table 3.2.[8]

Table 3.2 : Absolute growth in enrolments and population

Years	Enrolment growth Primary	Enrolment growth Middle	Enrolment growth High	Years	Population growth
1949/50-1960/61	224	180	147	1951-61	127
1960/61-1971/72	214	225	229	1961-72	152
1971/72-1980/81	136	144	131	1972-81	128
1980/81-1990/91	210	205	209	1981-91	135
1990/91-1993/94	135	133	127	1991-94	109

Source: Based on *Economic Survey 1993-94*, *Statistical Supplement*, (1994, p.16) for population data and p. 282 for enrolment data and *Economic Survey 1987-88*, *Statistical Supplement* (nd, p.178) for enrolment data prior to 1959-60

Except in the 1970s, the cumulative growth in enrolments exceeded the cumulative population growth in the corresponding period by a wide margin. However, considering that the participation rate at the time of independence was very low, the increase in enrolment has been insufficient to make a significant impact on the literacy rate in Pakistan. Even though the growth in enrolments appears to be high, compared to other low income countries and even India, the enrolment rate at the primary and secondary levels is low as mentioned above.

There is a great deal of similarity across region (urban/rural) and gender in 'the first reason cited' concerning why children and young adults between 5 and 24 were not in school.[9] In all cases, the main reason cited was that parents did not want schooling for their children.

This was the case for 19 and 26 per cent of rural and urban males respectively, and 30 and 37 per cent of rural and urban females respectively. It is surprising that this negative attitude to schooling is higher in the urban areas. Other important reasons for children not being in school is the attitude of the children, school being too expensive or too far away, and the need for children to help in the home or in work. Public policy efforts to change attitudes are still needed as are incentives for families to keep children in school.

As important as sending children to school is the educational system's ability to retain them until they complete at least primary and middle levels of education. While seventy-seven per cent of boys and girls who ever attended school complete class five, less than half complete the eighth class, and less than a third matriculate.[10] Not surprisingly, the reasons cited for leaving school are very similar to why they did not go to school in the first place. An additional reason that assumes importance is a child's poor academic progress.[11]

A large number of families mentioned school being too far away as a reason for the children not being enrolled or for having dropped out. Thus, the supply constraint continues to be important. This is particularly the case for rural females. This finding provides support for the finding from a smaller data set reported by Alderman *et al.* (1995), suggesting that a major cause for the gender gap in schooling in rural Pakistan is the supply constraint confronted by rural girls.[12] Hopefully, the government's attempts to address this shortcoming via the Social Action Plan will be successful.

By any measure, Pakistan's investment in human resources in the past has been grossly inadequate. This is evident from the comparative data for 1960 and 1990 on public expenditure on education and health for the larger South Asian countries, including Pakistan, as well as all developing countries reported in Table 6.7. Also, despite the Social Action Plan, educational expenditure at 2.4 per cent of GNP for 1995-96 is well below the 4 per cent of GNP recommended by UNESCO (*Economic Survey 1995-6,* p.6).

In rural areas, as well as in inner cities, the quality of education is poor. Most of the teachers are overburdened, poorly motivated, badly educated, ill paid, and inadequately trained or supervised. In rural areas, a single teacher is often required to teach five classes simultaneously! Many view teaching as a last-resort profession. Their salary levels, social status, and self-respect are scarcely adequate to equip them for even routine tasks, let alone the difficult, demanding, frustrating, and risky business of trying to find better ways of meeting each student's needs. Supervisory arrangements in the education system are sufficiently weak to enable some rural teachers to stay away from their duties much of the time (Kizilbash 1993).

More ominous than any of these developments is the gradual decay of the entire system of public higher education because of growing violence, corruption, cheating, and the consequent outflow of faculty members. The alienation and cynicism of students is likely to have been encouraged by three factors. First, in the last two decades, colleges and universities have remained closed up to half the time. Second, because of an excess of students as well as the growth of campus violence, the level of teacher involvement in the progress of students has consistently declined. Third, courses of teaching have become progressively removed from explicit societal concerns.

The perceived decay of public education has led parents to abandon public education on a large scale.[13] Almost one-fourth of all students in urban areas and 5 per cent in rural areas were enrolled in private schools in the early 1990s.[14] Similarly, the trend towards private higher education in the professions is by now well established, and of late, the private sector is responding to a demand for liberal arts education. It is not difficult to foresee that public sector education will go from bad to worse. Private sector education has been drawing, and will continue to draw, better teachers and students away from the public sector. In doing so, it also claims the attention of the more involved and educated parents who in many ways are the watchdogs and enforcers of standards.

What are the social consequences? Once again, it is not difficult to foresee the consolidation and entrenchment of 'the great divide'. Good schools will produce the Anglicized ruling elite, and the ghettoized public schools will provide the other functionaries if they can retain children long enough. Although it is no longer fashionable to worry about a highly class-structured society, there is reason to worry about educational dualism. It is simply not efficient. Allocations of positions in society are and will increasingly be determined by class background rather than talent. For the most part, deteriorating public schools will crush rather than nurture the talent of the majority.

The state has a moral responsibility to 'even the odds as much as possible'. The first positive step it can take is to recognize the danger educational dualism poses to public education and society. Second, it should welcome private education not as a substitute but as a challenge. The challenge is to develop institutions in the public sector that can compete with private sector results. 'Cambridge' schooling should be provided selectively in rural and urban public schools for the more talented students. To succeed, the state needs to marshall all its resources and should therefore carefully examine its policy of matching grants to private sector schools. If such grants and tax exemptions are provided to the private sector, the state should require reciprocity. One option would be to require that private sector schools adopt a number of urban and rural state schools in order to provide teacher training. In addition, they should be required to give scholarships to outstanding students from the adopted schools. This would be a small step towards bridging the divide, but it would be a start.

The state must also take on the challenge of private sector education at the higher level. Further empowering the University Grants Commission, which is suggested in the *Eighth Five Year Plan* (1994, p. 318), is not the solution. On the contrary, the solution is likely to be complete self-governance by the university faculty. But with this must come accountability. Currently, university faculty get job security on a platter soon after they join (compared to Western academic institutions) and do little subsequently to earn this privilege. Promotion is based on cultivating those in authority (to put it mildly) rather than on merit. Democratic governance and performance incentives are more likely to promote quality than further centralization.

Competing with the private sector will require better students and better faculty. Instead of matching grants to the private sector, it may make more sense to provide opportunities for upgrading faculty qualifications abroad. But those who are unable to secure admission in institutions of good standing abroad or to succeed in their studies would need to find other professions and pay back the cost incurred. Those who do succeed should be given the right incentives to return. None of this is easy, and these proposals are not intended as short-run quick fixes. Elected representatives and planners need to be confronted with a defeat to which they seem oblivious and should be goaded into taking on the private sector challenge.

2. HEALTH

The coverage of curative health facilities in Pakistan compares favourably with that in other countries classified in the low human development category in urban but not in rural areas. In the decade 1985-1995, 35 per cent of the rural population and 99 per cent of the urban population are cited as having access to health, compared to 66 per cent and 95 per cent health access available in rural and urban areas in the low human developed country group (*HDR* 1996, p.153). Health facilities measured by population per hospital, doctor, and nurse have also shown significant improvements over time as shown in Table 3.3.

Improvements in population per doctor and nurse between 1990 and 1994 dramatically slowed down, compared to earlier improvements. The population per doctor for 1990 is about half the average of countries classified in the medium human development category. However, the population per nurse was about double that of countries in the medium human development category. Pakistan was spending half the average spent by its reference group on health in 1960 (0.3 % of GDP), and by

1990 its expenditure on health at 0.7 per cent of GDP remained less than half the average of 1.6 per cent of its reference group. (*HDR* 1996, p.61).

Surprisingly, despite the low expenditure, indicators of health and longevity show that life expectancy at birth at 61.8 years in 1993 was higher than the average of 56.8 years for the low human development countries, although it was still 5 and 12 years behind the average for medium and high human development groups (*HDR* 1996, p.135-6)[15]. Similarly, at 89 per thousand in 1993, infant mortality in Pakistan was below the average of the low human development group (92), but much higher than the medium human developed group (48). Also, in all the other health indicators, including prenatal care, anaemia, low-birth-weight babies, maternal mortality rate, immunization, ORS access, and underweight children, Pakistan's performance was considerably better than the average for its reference group in the early 1990s (*HDR* 1994, p.150-1). Finally, with regard to certain diseases, Pakistan's performance matches the average of the middle human development group. For example, reported cases of tuberculosis and malaria in 1990 were 150 and 60 per 100,000, which compares favourably with the average of 155 and 190 for the middle human development group of countries (*HDR* 1994, p.152-3).

Table 3.3 : Distribution of medical facilities

Year	Population Per Hospital Bed	Doctor	Nurse
1950	2,431	na	na
1955	2,077	na	na
1960	2,038	75,470@	na
1970	2,061	15,256	na
1975	1,852	11,628	35,253
1980	1,716	7,549	15,247
1985	1,695	3,153	8,997
1990	1,512	2,127	6,511
1994	1,510	1,880	5,810
LHD 1988-91	na	7,642	5,869
MHD 1988-91	na	3,454	2,679

Source: *Economic Survey 1990-91*, Statistical Appendix (nd, p.234), *Economic Survey 1995-96*, Statistical Appendix (1996, p.238-9), *Human Development Report 1996*, (1996, pp.160-76)

Notes: na = not available
@ = number for 1961
LHD = Low human development country category.
MHD = Medium human development country category.

Notwithstanding these signs of progress, it is far too soon to become complacent. We end this sub-section with some recommendations for greater improvements in the health sector. First, there is still a bias in government priorities towards (poor quality) curative facilities over preventive facilities; this needs to be rectified; second, there is a need for an effective regulatory arrangement to cover food and drugs; third, the problem of the growing air and water pollution must be addressed on an urgent basis; fourth, there is a need for greater involvement of communities in the monitoring and provision of health services; fifth, targeted subsidies should be provided to make medicines accessible to the poor; and sixth, improved training facilities and incentives are needed for medical technicians and paramedics.

2.1. Water and Sanitation

Most diseases in Pakistan are water-borne. It is estimated that 60 per cent of infant deaths are due to infectious and parasitic diseases, most of them water-borne.[16] Therefore, the provision of safe drinking water and sewerage facilities would have a major favourable effect on the health services in the country. Between 1990-5, 96 per cent of the urban population and 71 per cent of the rural population had access to safe drinking water. This compares favourably with the low human development country group performance in urban areas (78%) and rural areas (64%) (*HDR* 1996, p.153). The statistics with regard to sanitation are similar. Three-fifths (62 per cent) of the urban population and 19 per cent of the rural population had access to sanitation facilities between 1990 and 1995. These numbers are virtually identical for the low human development country group. However, the general impression is that much of the sewage in Pakistan is discharged untreated into water courses, or burned or dumped.

2.2. Community involvement

In the past, policy discussions on health and hygiene were curiously silent on the role of the community itself. The view taken was that of 'health' as a commodity which could only be supplied by experts, namely doctors and nurses, in specific places, i.e. hospitals. However, health and hygiene are a form of knowledge—knowledge which is no longer controlled by the community. The result is that there is no popular outrage over unhygienic surroundings; the ubiquitous contamination of air, water, and food; the gradual loss of popular knowledge of nutrition and its relation to health; and about a myriad other factors that affect peoples lives. Once again, policy discussions ignored how this knowledge can and should be restored to the populace.

There was also a failure in the past to link the pollution of air and water to discussions of health and life expectancy. Most discussions began and ended with providing more doctors and hospitals, with no attention to the macro-environment which creates the need for the doctors and nurses in the first place. It was conveniently forgotten that improvements in health standards in industrialized countries came about not because of advances in curative health systems, but because of social reformers who led the campaign for hygienic improvements: clean water, clean air, and clean food. There is no such campaign in Pakistan.

The discussion of community involvement in the maintenance of health cannot be complete without mention of alternative medical practices. In Pakistan, people rely not only on 'modern' doctors but also on a variety of healers: homoeopaths, *hakims*, and spiritual healers. Most people dismiss this as superstition (which derives from the arrogance of elite knowledge systems). But this dismissal refuses to take seriously the perceptions and knowledge-base of the people. An attempt should be made first, to reach people through their own ways of thinking, and second, to streamline and regulate the functioning of the practitioners of alternative systems.

At least on a policy level, the *Eighth Five-Year Plan 1993-98* (1994, pp.351-70) did take up the issues of community involvement and traditional medicine. This is an important beginning and we hope that policy rhetoric will be realized in practice.

2.3. Housing.

Shelter and housing are important elements in the maintenance and promotion of environmental health. In Pakistan, even the total quantity of shelter has not been able to keep pace with the population's needs. In two decades between 1961 and 1981, the population growth rate, recorded at 3.4 per cent, outstripped that of the housing stock (2.4 per cent). The imbalance between the growth rates for rural population and housing stock was even sharper at 3.02 per cent and 1.95 per cent respectively (GOP 1988a, p.173).

In the same period, the number of persons per house rose from 5.7 in 1960 to 6.7 in 1980. The number in Balochistan was the highest at 7.6 per unit in 1980, and that in Punjab the lowest at 6.5. If measured by the average number of persons per room, the pressure of population on housing increased from 3.2 persons in 1960 to 3.5 persons in 1980 (GOP 1988a, p. 176). This population pressure on housing continues to be unrelenting and a 1990-1 survey shows that the mean number of persons per room increased to 4.6 in urban areas and 4.8 persons in rural areas (NIPS 1992, p.28).

The above figures do not take into account the quality of housing units. Adequate water supply, cooking facilities, sanitation, sewerage, waste disposal, and electricity do not necessarily form part of the housing facilities available to all the population.[17]

3. POPULATION, MIGRATION, AND URBANIZATION

Since the early seventies, Pakistan's compound population growth rate has been above 3 per cent.[18] This high population growth rate results from a slow decline in the fertility rate in the face of a rapidly declining mortality rate.[19] Consequently, the national growth rate leapt from 1.8 per cent in 1941-51 to 3.0 per cent in 1972-81. The rapidly growing population has resulted in a rise in dependency ratios.[20]

The fertility rate is determined by a number of factors, including the incidence of marriage, the age at marriage, the practice of breast-feeding, the use of contraceptives and a host of socio-economic variables, including the status of women, female labour force participation, education in general and of females in particular, infant mortality rate, and local systems of participation and decision-making. The slight reduction in crude birth rate from 45.0 to 43.3 per thousand during 1951-81 is attributed to reduced age at marriage, postpartum amenorrhoea, sexual abstinence, and lactational infecundability.[21]

While crude death rates have declined rapidly and life expectancy has risen by 20 per cent since 1951 (*Economic Survey* 1995-6, p.15), infant and child mortality rates have been slower to decline. Thus, while crude death rates were almost halved between 1970 and 1992, the infant mortality rate declined by a third. The decline in crude death rates between 1970 to 1993 was much more rapid (19 to 9 per 1,000 population) than the decline in the reference group of low income countries, while the decline in infant mortality rate from 1971 to 1993 (142 to 88 per 1,000 live births) matched the reference group decline. However, this decline was much less rapid than that of Sri Lanka (from 58 to 17) or China (from 69 to 30) which already had much smaller bases. Thus a substantial proportion of total deaths in Pakistan continue to be of infants and children (*WDR* 1995, p.212, 214).

The slow decline in infant mortality rates is mainly due to acute respiratory and gastrointestinal illnesses (NIPS 1992, p.120). The total fertility rate in Pakistan in 1993 was 6.1 children per woman. Although this represents a notable decline from 7 per woman in 1970, it is considerably higher than the rate of 3.3 for the reference group of low income countries (*WDR* 1995, p.212). The contraceptive usage rate amongst married women between 1988-93 was 14 per cent despite 25 years of an official Population Planning Programme. This is again in stark contrast with female contraceptive usage rates of 43 per cent in India and 40 per cent in Bangladesh.

One might expect that in urban Pakistan the fertility rate, like the mortality rate, would be lower than in rural areas, as exposure to urban facilities and a 'modern' outlook would lead to the desire for smaller families and greater contraceptive use. This, however, has not been the case; the urban marital fertility was in fact found to be slightly higher than rural marital fertility in the 1970s and 1980s by various national surveys (Government of Pakistan 1988a, p.58). However, total rural fertility rates were slightly higher than urban fertility rates and this continued to be the case in the late 1980s and early 1990s (ibid. and NIPS 1992, p.413). Probably the most important fertility differentials are found in the form of progressively lower fertility amongst women with more education.[22]

3.1. Women's status and fertility

High fertility and morbidity hinges upon very complex socio-economic and cultural factors. Poverty, illiteracy, and women's low status in society are causal factors for the high levels of population growth.[23] Absolute poverty has declined over time (see chapter 4 for details), and about one-fifth of the total population was considerably below the mean of 52 per cent for the low human development group of countries between 1980 and 1990 (*HDR* 1994, p.165). Nonetheless, almost one-fifth of the population represents a very large absolute number for Pakistan. Comparative performances in literacy and formal education are documented in detail in section 2 above.

Women's position in society has not changed in any significant manner. The majority remains illiterate (76 per cent) (*WDR* 1996, p.200). Female enrolment at the primary level in 1993 was just 49 per cent, and even out of this, 55 per cent drop out by the time they reach grade 4 (*WDR* 1996, p.200). At the secondary level, female enrolment is a bare 13 per cent. Pakistan's low female enrolment contrasts poorly with Nepal's, where female primary level enrolment has risen dramatically from 8 per cent in 1970 to 81 per cent in 1992, and with India's, where it increased from 56 per cent in 1970 to 90 per cent in 1992 (*WDR* 1995, p. 216).

Women are married early (20 years), have a shorter life (attributed to high maternal mortality and many children), and suffer from anaemia and ill health. Women's opportunities for training are few and their options for gainful employment minimal. Women's share of the total labour force in 1994 at 28 per cent was much below the average (42) for low income countries (*WDR* 1996, p.194). In short, women's dependent/secondary status precludes any significant decision-making, a necessary prerequisite if they are to control their fertility.

Thus, where poverty accounts for high infant mortality and low life expectancy (63 years), women's low status reinforces the strong son preference norm (*HDR* 1996, p.155). Sons are viewed as a means of attaining status within the family and society. The result is the desire for a large number of children, the hope being that a minimum number will reach adulthood, and that at least a few of these will be males. The desire for more than four children on average has not changed over the last 20 years. Boys are seen as assets: additional income earners who will also provide security to parents in old age. Girls, on the other hand, are perceived as liabilities: assets only to the families they are married into (as wives and mothers), rather than those they are born into. These factors colour priorities. Not surprisingly, when resources are limited the choice is almost automatically for educating or training only the male offspring. For young women, the pressure is for early marriage which has far-reaching implications for various aspects of life, especially fertility.

So far, women's needs are in fact not addressed at all when any measures for population control are introduced. Family planning services are not accessible to women; health advisers or service personnel are not available at distances where women can reach easily; and the advantages of birth spacing are not explained. The half-hearted programmes, when launched, focus on women without taking into account their subordinate position in society, or their lack of control over crucial matters affecting their lives.

It has been established that women's education, health, and income earning capacities not only have a direct impact upon their children's education and health, but also upon fertility. Unless this is understood and acknowledged, it is unlikely that the population issue will be resolved in Pakistan.

3.2. Population Planning

Population control programmes were initiated in Pakistan as far back as the late 1950s. However, because of their primary focus on the supply of contraceptives, with almost complete disregard of demand factors, the impact on fertility has been negligible. A multi-sector population programme consisting of three major components was formulated in the early 1980s which also formed the basis of the Seventh Five Year population programme. The three components of the programme are:

a) Establishment of Family Welfare Centres to provide family planning services jointly with mother-child health care, motivation/education, and community development activities.

b) Provision of gynaecological and obstetric services and contraceptive surgery through reproductive health service centres established in government and private sector hospitals.
c) Implementation of a major Information, Education and Communication Programme, through mass media, personal and group communication, to promote breast feeding, maternal and child care practices, nutrition of the growing child, responsible upbringing of the child, late marriages, and improved status of women.

The Seventh Plan allocated Rs 3,535 million for the population welfare programme to reduce the population growth rate to 2.9 per cent. However, the proposed expansion could not be undertaken in the first two years of the Plan because of subsequent financial constraints and budget cuts (see GOP 1991b). While financial allocations for the third year were increased, even a full utilization of the enhanced budgetary provision was not sufficient to overcome the history of problems. Also, the mass adult contraception campaigns have been sharply curtailed by the conservative cultural environment. Therefore, as suggested in a World Bank Report (1991), a more appropriate strategy needs to be worked out for dissemination of knowledge through community health education efforts.

Contraceptive use continues to remain low in the country, and has not contributed significantly towards a reduction in fertility. Despite some increase in the 1980s, only 9.1 per cent of currently married women reported the use of contraceptives in 1984.[24] Moreover, as has been argued by Sathar (1979), the majority of women using contraceptives in the urban areas use them only after achieving a fairly large family size.

In retrospect, a major obstacle to the effective implementation of population policies in virtually all southern countries has been the refusal of experts to take the values and concerns of the population seriously. From the beginning, population programmes assumed that experts had access to privileged knowledge of the functioning of the society, a knowledge which the population could not be expected to comment upon, except through servile acceptance. Not surprisingly, the result was a rejection of the government's attempt to promote contraception. Even today, the attempt is not to involve communities in a dialogue, but rather to sell a message.

Moreover, although research on population and demography has consistently revealed the association of fertility behaviour with socio-cultural factors, population programmes continue to be targeted narrowly on contraception rather than the achievement of broader socio-cultural goals. As shown in chapter 2 and earlier in this chapter, the social sectors that impact directly on fertility, rapid population growth, and people's development are still low on the resource allocation priorities of governments in Pakistan.

Finally, as for the other sectors, data sources insufficiently capture the reality on the ground. In the case of housing, for instance, the *Housing, Economic and Demographic Survey (HED)* is based on the national population census. NIPS advises the use of these with caution as 'usually data on households and families in population and housing censuses are subject to some important errors'. (NIPS 1988, p.170). Thus according to NIPS, the Pakistan Housing Census of 1960 and surveys of 1973 and 1980 suffer from errors and biases resulting from different concepts and definitions and untrained enumerators, and therefore, 'any major analysis drawn from the analysis of the data are to be interpreted with caution'.

3.3. Urbanization and fertility

The rapid growth of population in Pakistan is accompanied by rapid urbanization. A high rate of natural growth in population and marked urbanization coupled with limited availability of resources, have led to a sharp deterioration in the quality of life—measured by any indicator—even in the urban areas which received most of the resources allocated for the development of both the physical and social infrastructure.

The urban population of Pakistan increased at the rates of 5.6, 4.1, and 4.4 per cent over the periods 1951-61, 1961-72, and 1972-81, respectively.[25] As a result, the share of urban areas in total population has increased from 18 per cent in 1951 to 30 per cent in 1981. Rapid urbanization has also been due to the higher fertility rates in the urban areas, resulting from relatively better health facilities, the positive income effect on the demand for children, the annexation of populated territories with the existing urban centres, and, most importantly, rural-urban migration. The rate of net immigration to the urban areas, though lower than the 19.8 per cent observed in the 1961-72 period, was still quite high at 18.0 per cent during the 1972-81 period.

Low agricultural incomes, negligible manufacturing activities, and very few off-farm employment opportunities force rural workers to migrate to urban areas. As pointed out earlier, about one-fifth of the rural population lives below the poverty line. The growth of population has lowered the per capita cropped area from 0.46 hectares in 1951 to 0.31 hectares in 1981. The low rate of investment in agriculture,[26] fragmentation of land ownership, and inequalities in the distribution of land and labour-saving technical change have also resulted in a higher incidence of rural-urban migration.[27]

Since large-scale capital-intensive agricultural mechanization tends to displace rural labour, farm mechanization policies (like the yellow tractor scheme) need to be reviewed carefully. Moreover, encouraging livestock, forestry, fisheries, and poultry sectors, allocating more investible resources to rural areas, a fairer distribution of farm holdings, and better water management practices would help rural areas in retaining their population.

4. FINANCING THE SOCIAL SECTORS

This issue was discussed in detail in Chapter 2, section 4.3, and so we only emphasize the main points here. While inadequate resources have been the major constraint on the development of human resources, inconsistency in the division of resources and the functional responsibilities of provincial and federal governments have also obstructed the development of human resources. Under the 1973 constitution, provincial governments are responsible for most human resource development activities, including health and education. The National Finance Commission, which is supposed to meet after every five years, has met only three times since 1973. This forum decides the distribution of financial resources between the provincial and the federal governments. However, the Commission provides the provincial governments with sufficient finances to meet current expenditures only. Development expenditures are financed through grants made by the federal government. Moreover, local governments, which can play an important role in social sector activities, have virtually no power to collect taxes; provincial governments may delegate some of their powers to local governments.

Such a division of functional responsibilities and the power to raise finances has serious implications for the development of social sectors. No doubt, project preparation is done in the respective departments at the provincial level, but its clearance and inclusion in the development programme is authorized by the federal government. Therefore, the Annual Development Programme (ADP) proposed by the federal government may be inadequate and it may not reflect the priorities of provincial governments. Moreover, every developmental activity has implications for current expenditures. It is no wonder then that when the federal government tried to raise funds for education and health projects in the mid-1980s, provincial governments obstructed it until they were provided with grants to meet current expenditures as well.[28]

5. SUMMARY AND CONCLUSIONS

Pakistan is finally making some progress with regard to policy emphasis on the social sectors and in terms of the output indicators. Expenditure on the social sectors has more than doubled in the last decade, in part due to the Social Action Plan. Priorities also seem to have become sensible, such as the focus on primary education and rural health.

While participation rates have been rising steadily, progress in female and rural education appears to be at snail's pace compared to neighbouring countries. Similarly, Pakistan's literacy rate is still low compared even with Pakistan's reference group of low human development countries. Negative attitudes of parents, the direct and indirect costs of schooling, and inadequate school supply are the main reasons for low enrolments and high dropouts. Public policy will need to focus on changing attitudes, providing incentives, and enhancing access to schooling.

The low educational attainment of women represents one of the main reasons for the low status of women in society and Pakistan's inability to contain its high population growth rate. Nepal's ability to raise female primary schooling from 8 per cent in 1970 to 81 per cent in 1992, while Pakistan's female enrolment in the same period progressed from 22 to 31 per cent, is extremely telling. The other reason for the failure of population programmes is the government's inability to take the attitudes and values of the population seriously.

Health statistics for the early 1990s are more promising. While there is no ground to be complacent, Pakistan is doing better on all health indicators than the average of the low human development countries. The pressure of population on housing is unrelenting, as indicated by the increase over time in the number of persons per room over the last thirty years. Successful long term financing of the social sectors will require a change in the terms of reference of the National Finance Commission, to ensure that provincial governments are provided with finances to meet both current and development needs.

NOTES

1. Government of Pakistan, *Household Integrated Economic Survey 1990-91* (1993, p.109). Also see Chapter 4.
2. GOP, *Seventh Five Year Plan 1988-93*, (nd, p.417) and *Eighth Five Year Plan 1993-98*, (1994, p.519).
3. The following two equations were estimated:

$$(ES/TE) = -4.23 + \underset{(3.36)}{.773}\ (TR/GDP); \quad R^2 = 0.77, \text{ and}$$

$$(ES/GDP) = -2.67 + \underset{(2.50)}{0.291}\ (TR/GDP); \quad R^2 = 0.41.$$

Where ES is the expenditure on social sector; TE is total public expenditure; TR is total government revenues; GDP the gross domestic product. T-statistics are in parenthesis.
4. *Economic Survey 1995-96* (1996, p.11); *Human Development Report 1996* (1996, p.145).
5. Government of Pakistan, *Seventh Five Year Plan 1988-93* (nd, p.252).
6. Crude participation rates can exceed 100 per cent since the denominator includes the population of an ideal age cohort for a given level of education (5-9 for primary Pakistan) while the numerator includes the actual age group (about 5-12 for primary in Pakistan) from which students are drawn into a given level of education.
7. *World Development Report 1995* (1995, p.216). Note that this source cites Pakistan's total primary enrolment rate for 1992 to be 46 per cent. The secondary enrolment for low income countries in this source is 41 per cent which is almost double the rate cited for Pakistan (21 per cent).
8. To fine-tune the comparison of population and enrolment growth, it would be preferable to use population data for the age cohorts relevant for the primary, middle, and high schooling. However, since these are not readily available for the earlier periods, overall inter-census population growth rate estimates are presented as being suggestive of how school enrolments have kept pace with population growth.
9. *Pakistan Integrated Household Survey, Final Results 1993* (1993, pp.67-8).
10. Ibid., p.72.
11. Ibid., pp.69-70.
12. Also see Mahmood (1994).
13. The next four paragraphs are drawn from Khan *et al.* (1995).
14. *Pakistan Household Integrated Survey, Final Results, 1993* (1993a , p.71).
15. *Human Development Report 1996*, (p.161). The health expenditure number for Pakistan is drawn from *Economic Survey 1995-96*, Statistical Appendix (1996, p. 6).
16. IUCN, *The Pakistan National Conservation Strategy*, (nd, p.79).
17. See section 3.1 above for access to water and sanitation.
18. *Economic Survey 1995-96*, Statistical Appendix (1996, p.9). The population growth rate is estimated to have declined to 2.82 per cent by 1996.

19. The crude birth rate declined from 45.0 per thousand in 1941 to 43.3 in 1981 and an estimated 37.4 in 1996, while the crude death rate fell from 31.2 to 11.8 and an estimated 9.45 over the same periods (ibid.).
20. For example, the age dependency ratio increased from 92.2 in 1972 to 95.3 in 1981, *1981 Census Report of Pakistan* (Government of Pakistan 1984, p.21).
21. NIPS (1992, p. 85) and Perveen (1994, p.14).
22. NIPS (1992, p. 41). The total fertility rate declines from 5.7 for those with no education to 3.6 for those with more than secondary education.
23. The impact of poverty on fertility is discussed in more detail in chapter 4.
24. Women living in large cities reported the highest levels of contraceptive use, i.e. 30 per cent compared to 11 per cent in smaller urban towns, and only 5 per cent in rural areas.
25. Information for this sub-section has been drawn from the 1970 and 1981 population censuses.
26. Public sector expenditure in agriculture peaked during the Sixth Five Year Plan (1983-88), when it ranked 6th. Its priority has since steadily dropped and it ranked 9th in the Eighth Five Year Plan (1993-98). *Economic Survey 1995-96*, Statistical Appendix (1996, p.243).
27. The Gini coefficient has been calculated by M. H. Khan (Table 9) to have increased with a high .53 in 1980 to .57 in 1990.
28. This issue is discussed again in more detail, particularly in section 1 of chapter 5.

4

Poverty and Policy in Pakistan

A. R. Kemal and *Moazam Mahmood*

INTRODUCTION

This chapter reviews the existing data on poverty and income distribution in Pakistan and then presents head counts of the poor, identifying them in terms of their social characteristics. The first exercise involves a historical literature survey and the construction of a 'poverty map' based on data from the most recent (1992-3) *Household Income and Expenditure Survey (HIES)*. The historical literature on poverty in Pakistan is limited, in that it ignores attributes and behaviour patterns of the poor. We have tried to remedy this failing in the data analysis in section 2, but the results are only partially comparable with the earlier literature, since they have been based on a poverty line constructed from income rather than nutritional categories.

HIES is the main source of data for the measurement of poverty and income inequality in Pakistan. However, such surveys are believed to grossly understate the incomes of the highest income group and to exclude the poorest from their purview. Moreover, in urban areas, the share of the highest income group in GNP has probably risen due to the significant growth in the concentration of industrial and financial assets. Consequently, a decrease (increase) in income inequalities is overstated (understated).[1]

There are different approaches to the study of poverty. Conventional analyses have focused on what might be called a long-run definition of causal and structural mechanisms that produce and perpetuate poverty. These include, for example, various forms of discrimination, distribution of political and economic power, distribution of income earned from industrial, financial, and human capital, possible policy biases in market returns, and contribution of government policy towards the aggravation or amelioration of such biases. By calling into question the underlying socio-economic structure, this perspective helps identify policies and actions to decrease poverty.

An alternative approach is to look at the vulnerability of the poor to changes in policies or economic conditions within a given economic and social structure. Such an approach identifies ways in which the poor can be protected against unanticipated changes in policies, or in economic and political conditions. It can show, for example, whether increases in prices of food, energy, or schooling need to be avoided (or combined with compensatory actions) because they have a significant impact on consumption bundles of the poor; or whether increases in unemployment will lead male employment to encroach upon the income of female-headed households.

1. HISTORICAL TRENDS IN POVERTY ANDDISTRIBUTION

In Pakistan, as in other places, the literature has concentrated on the first approach. One tendency is to define the poor *a priori* according to class, gender, or region—and then focus on mechanisms that contribute to the poverty of the select group. For example, the debate on the creation of regional poverty in East Pakistan, now Bangladesh, focused on the causal exchange rate mechanisms (Nations, 1975). Similarly, many studies explain rural poverty as the result of government policies that create adverse terms of trade (Lewis, 1970), or of the Green Revolution that produced retarded growth. Urban poverty has similarly been explained as the consequence of state support for unbridled capitalist development during the sixties (Amjad, 1982). Women's socio-economic status was seen as the result of mechanisms that have kept them out of the formal labour market, thus constraining their incomes and upward mobility (Bilquees and Mahmood, 1990).

1.1. Trends in Poverty Level

Yet another approach to the study of poverty is estimating poverty lines, computing the headcount below them, and investigating the trends over time. The poverty line is drawn arbitrarily or on the basis of nutritional requirements or other basic needs.[2] Normally, these indicators are constructed on the basis of anthropometric surveys of caloric intake. However, such surveys are very limited in Pakistan, and certainly not stratified to permit generalization. Therefore, the alternative adopted here is to designate as the poverty line the estimated rupee value of a food basket which will deliver the Recommended Daily Allowance (RDA) for an adult equivalent in Pakistan (2,550 calories). Poverty is then defined as the proportion of the population that falls below this poverty line.

A number of studies have estimated various headcounts of poverty for Pakistan. These results have been summarized in Akhtar (1988), Malik (1991), and Malik *et al*. (1995), and are presented in tabular form in Table 4.1.

Table 4.1 : Survey of poverty estimates

Poverty Line	1963-4	1969-70	1971-2	1978-9	1984-5	1987-8	1990-1
				% Households			
Naseem (1977) (1959/60 Rs/Capita)							
Rural	250[a]	43	26	19			
	300	61	60	58			
Urban	300	55	25	25			
	375	70	59	63			
Allauddin (1975) (1959/60 Rs/Capita)							
Rural	250	57	36	42			
	300	67	61	65			
Urban	300	50	30	42			
	375	71	60	62			
Naseem (1977) % of 2100 cal RDA							
	95[b]	72	68	74			
	92	54	46	55			
	90	45	36	43			
Mujahid (1978) % of 2100 cals. RDA							
Rural	250	27	35				
	300	40	48				
Urban	300	36	29				
	375	52	46				
Irfan and Amjad (1984) (1979/80 Rs/Capita)							
Rural	109	41	55		41		
	95	32	43		29		
Krujik and Leeuwen (1985) (1978/80 Rs/HH)							
Rural	700		73		51		
Urban	700		50		30		
Malik (1988) (1984/85 Rs/Capita)							
Rural	159	37	44		29	24	
	172	43	51		35	29	
Urban	185	40	34		24	19	
	207	49	43		31	26	
Ahmad and Allison (1990) (1979 Rs/Capita)							
Rural	100				25	20	
Urban	110				20	16	
Malik *et al*. (1995) 2550 cals RDA							
Rural						20	21
Urban						9	10

Source: Compiled from Akhtar (1988), Mahmood (1989), Malik (1991) and Malik *et al*. (1995).

Notes: a = poverty lines defined on a per capita basis. See Table 4.4 for further clarification.

b = poverty estimates based on attaining different percentages of the RDA.

The Table shows that while research findings differ about the trend in poverty during the 1960s, there is a consensus that poverty has declined since then. The early studies of Naseem (1973) and Allauddin (1975) show a decreasing headcount in both rural and urban areas. But virtually all subsequent studies covering this period show a decline only in urban areas, and an increased incidence of poverty in rural areas.[3] Irfan and Amjad (1983) argue that the introduction of new technology in the agricultural sector, via eviction of tenants, had led to this observed increase in rural poverty. Subsequent declines in rural poverty have been attributed to remittances from migrant workers. In the urban areas, a rise in the wage rate due to emigration, growth of services and construction and receipts of remittances are argued to have played a major role in reducing poverty.

In the 1970s and much of the 1980s, there is unanimity in research findings that both urban and rural poverty decreased.[4] This is also supported by Table 4.2, which presents Ercelawn's (1989) estimates for the two later decades using a consistent methodology.[5]

Malik *et al.* (1995) found, as reported in Table 4.1, in a consistent comparison of poverty between 1987/88 and 1990/91, that rural poverty increased from 20 to 21 per cent and urban poverty increased from 9 to 10 per cent. While the slight increase in poverty is disturbing because it represents a trend reversal, the data also show the lowest absolute level of urban poverty that has yet been attained (more on this later). We will argue in later chapters that the increase in poverty (or at least the abatement in the declining trend) at the turn of the last decade, is associated with the structural adjustment polices followed over this period.

Aggregate trends are reported in Table 4.1. Disaggregated estimates were made by Malik (1991) and Akhtar (1988). Malik (1991) estimated the incidence of poverty in the 1980s disaggregated by province and by rural agro-climatic zone on the basis of the following three indices: simple headcount measure; the poverty gap measure; and the Foster-Gear-Thorbeck measure. The results show that over a four-year period in the 1980s both the headcount and the poverty gap index dropped for all regions except urban rain-fed Punjab. The proportion of households below the poverty line dropped from 18 per cent in 1984-5 to 13 per cent by 1987-8. Regionally, poverty was found to be more widespread in rural areas at 16 per cent compared to 7 per cent in the urban areas.[6] Also, more than half the poor are located in the rural Punjab, but the maximum incidence of poverty is in rural Sindh.

1.2. Income Distribution

The important exception to counting heads is Akhtar (1988), who uses the *HIES* data for 1987-8 to divide the poor into observable categories.

Akhtar's results, while interesting, are not comparable with those of other studies. The reason is that instead of an absolute poverty line, she uses a relative poverty line demarcating the bottom 10-30 per cent of the expenditure distribution. Since the bottom 10-30 per cent need not necessarily coincide with those that consume less than 2,550 calories, this method can both underestimate and overestimate the poor. Nevertheless, the study of relative poverty produces some interesting paradoxes, including the fact that income distribution improved even during the 1960s when poverty was on the rise, and worsened in the 1970s when poverty was falling. This is evident from Table 4.3.

Table 4.2 : Estimates of poverty

	Poor as Proportion of Population		
		Urban	
	Rural	Lower	Upper
1969-70	46	51	67
1979	36	34	57
1984-5	28	30	44
1987-8: Low Inflation	16	21	40
1987-8: High Inflation	23	29	48

Source: Ercelawn (1989).
Note: Lower and upper represent lower and upper bound estimates of poverty.

Conventional wisdom in the 1950s and 1960s was that the process of economic development will exacerbate income inequality in the initial stage and alleviate it later.[7] While this hypothesis was never uncontroversial, it does not in any event fit Pakistani data. An alternative interpretation is possible by looking at Pakistani data. Table 4.3 shows that the income distribution in Pakistan improved over the 1960s—the Gini coefficient fell from 0.36 to 0.34 between 1963-4 to 1971-2—when the growth rate of output and particularly that of the manufacturing sector was the highest (see Table 2.2 for period growth rates).[8] Inequality increased in the 1970s—the Gini rising to 0.37 by 1979—when not only were the growth rates on the decline, but public policy was explicitly oriented towards distributional concerns. During most of the 1980s, the data suggest that income distribution improved marginally, with the Gini falling to 0.348 in 1987-8, when growth rates increased sharply. Finally, the last two years of the decade and the early 1990s again display arrested growth and a worsening of income distribution. Between 1987-88 and 1990-1, the Gini rose again from 0.348 to 0.407, declining slightly by 1992-3 to 0.39, but still showing an increasing trend after 1987-8. The most disturbing point to note in

Table 4.3 is that the rural and urban Ginis for the 1990s including the most recent estimate for 1992-93, are higher than they have ever been for the last three decades—the distribution of income has never been worse.

Table 4.3 : Income distribution in Pakistan

Year	*Gini Coefficient*			*HH Income Share*	
	Total	Rural	Urban	Lowest 20%	Highest 20%
1963/64	0.355	0.348	0.368	6.4	45.3
1966/67	0.351	0.314	0.388	7.6	43.4
1968/69	0.328	0.293	0.370	8.2	42.0
1969/70	0.330	0.295	0.361	8.0	41.8
1970/71	0.326	0.273	0.359	8.4	41.5
1971/72	0.344	0.309	0.381	7.9	43.0
1979	0.375	0.319	0.380	7.4	45.0
1984/85	0.428	0.345	0.379	7.3	45.0
1985/86	0.355	0.330	0.354	7.6	44.0
1986/87	0.346	0.312	0.357	7.9	43.6
1987/88	0.348	0.307	0.366	8.0	43.7
1990/91	0.407	0.410	0.390	7.3	44.5
1992/93	0.390	0.367	0.384	–	–

Source: *Household Income and Expenditure Surveys*, various years.

Our alternative hypothesis, which seems to fit the data better, is that income distribution is correlated to the rate of growth of output. The decade of the 1960s had high output growth while the Gini dropped, the 1970s and early 1980s had low output growth while the Gini increased, the mid-1980s had high growth while the Gini dropped again, and finally there has again been a hiatus in growth at the turn of the last decade when the Gini has increased again. A comparison of the shares in income of the lowest 20 per cent and the highest 20 per cent households show similar though weaker results as evident from Table 4.3.[9]

Urban and rural differentials in income distribution are fairly consistent over the three decades shown in Table 4.3. The urban Ginis are higher than the rural Ginis, showing more skewness in the urban distribution of income.

2. IDENTIFYING THE POOR

The studies we have reviewed report the percentage of individuals or households that fall below an identified poverty line. It is also possible to identify more directly, using grouped data, what percentage of the total population or households could be categorized as poor and what their share of total income is. We have undertaken such an exercise using grouped data from the 1992-3 *Household Income and Expenditure Survey* and this complements the findings reported in the section above.

Using grouped data can be problematic because poverty is influenced not only by household income, but also by variations in household size. Some individuals in a low income class may have access to an appropriate nutritional bundle, while others in a higher income class might be nutritionally deficient. To minimize this problem, we estimated the mean nutritional status of different income groups and based the poverty line on these mean nutritional values.

We begin this exercise by basing our poverty line on the two most recent studies, Ercelawn (1989), who has estimated poverty using the 1987-8 *HIES* data set, and Malik *et al.* (1995), who have estimated poverty using the 1990-1 *HIES*. Table 4.4 gives these poverty lines in terms of monthly expenditure per capita needed to maintain a nutritional norm of 2,550 calories daily plus some required expenditure on energy, rent, health, education and apparel. This package could be purchased in 1992-3 in the rural areas for Rs 344 and in urban areas for Rs 373 given the inflation rates, prevalent between 1987-8 and 1992-3 as seen in Table 4.4.

Table 4.4 : Poverty lines

Year	Inflation	*Monthly Expenditure per Capita (Rs)*		
			Urban	
		Rural	Upper	Lower
1969-70		32	52	42
1979		99	156	125
1984-5		154	246	197
1987-8	Low	174	284	227
	High	191	312	250
1990-1		243	–	351
1992-3		344[a]	–	373[a]

Source: For 1969-70 to 1987-8, Ercelawn (1989) and for 1990-1, Malik *et al.* (1995), and for 1992-3. *Household Income and Expenditure Survey 1992-93*, pp.382-9.

Notes: a : Gives an urban inflation rate of 10% p.a. between 1987-8 and 1992-3 and a rural inflation rate of 13%.

In Table 4.5 an urban per capita consumption of Rs 373 per month corresponds to a *HIES* urban income group with a monthly household income of just under Rs 2,500. Similarly, a rural per capita consumption of Rs 344 per month corresponds to a *HIES* rural income group with a monthly household income of just under Rs 2,000. These income groups can therefore be defined as poor.

Two non-poor income categories have also been created to use as reference groups. For urban areas, Table 4.5 shows that groups with monthly household incomes between Rs 2,500-6,000 are defined as middle income, with a per capita consumption of Rs 373-547 per month, and those with incomes above Rs 6,000 are the upper income category who consume more than Rs 547 per month. Similarly, for rural areas, groups with household incomes between Rs 2,000-5,000 fall in the middle income category, and those above Rs 5,000 are in the upper income category. Based on these categories, we have re-estimated poverty estimates to report them by income.

Table 4.5 : Re-estimates of poverty lines and income categories for 1992-3

Urban Monthly Expenditure/ Capita[a]			Rural Monthly Expenditure/ Capita[a]			All Income Categories
Poverty Line	*HIES*	Category	Poverty Line	*HIES*	Category	
Consumption (Rs)	Consumption (Rs)	Income (Rs)	Consumption (Rs)	Consumption (Rs)	Income (Rs)	
373	< 373	≤ 2,500	344	< 344	≤ 2,000	Poor
	373-547	2,500–6,000		344-439	2,000–5,000	Middle
	> 547	> 6,000		> 439	> 5,000	Upper

Source: Calculated from *Household Income and Expenditure Survey 1992-3* (1996, pp.382-9).

Note: a = Monthly expenditure/capita on food, energy, rent, health, education, and apparel.

Table 4.6 gives us a headcount of 21 per cent urban poverty, and 29 per cent rural poverty based on the *HIES* grouped data for 1992-3. Our estimate of urban poverty for 1992-3 at 21 per cent is much higher than Malik's estimate for 1990-1 of 10 per cent. But there is some possibility that Malik may have underestimated urban poverty both for 1987-8 and 1990-1, at 9 per cent and 10 per cent, respectively, compared to Ercelawn's (1991) estimate for 1987-8 of at least 21 per cent, which our estimate approximates (see Table 4.2). Ercelawn has used a higher expenditure per capita to meet the RDA in urban areas compared to Malik, which accounts for a higher proportion of the urban poor in poverty. Therefore, if Malik were to re-estimate urban poverty both for *HIES* 1987-8 and *HIES* 1990-1, using Ercelawn's higher poverty line, he would get Ercelawn's figure of 21 per cent for 1987-8, and at least 21 per cent for 1990-1, given that he shows poverty to have increased between 1987-8 and 1990-1 in Table 4.1.

Table 4.6 : Estimates of size distribution of income for 1992-3

Income Group	Urban %		Rural %	
	Population	Income	Population	Income
Poor	21.2	10.1	29.7	17.6
Middle	51.1	39.0	54.9	49.5
Upper	27.8	50.9	15.4	32.8
All	100.0	100.0	100.0	100.0

Source: Calculated from *Household Income and Expenditure Survey 1992-3* (1996, p.274).

Our 1992-3 estimate for rural poverty at 29 per cent is higher than Malik's estimate for 1990-1 of 21 per cent and Ercelawn's estimate for 1987-8 of 23per cent. Since the urban and rural poverty lines have been inflated consistently between 1987-8 and 1992-3, our higher estimate can be attributed to both use of grouped data and an increase in actual poverty. However, the purpose of this exercise is not a precise estimation of poverty for 1992-3, which must await release of the individual household data, but to use available grouped data to profile the poor.

2.1. Profiles of the Poor

The idea of constructing an income-based poverty line is to determine the vulnerability of the households that fall below the poverty line. This is done by examining their demographic, occupational, and consumption attributes.

Here, too, the grouped nature of the data poses a problem since some variables of interest are not available in a grouped form. These include, in particular, a gender profile that could show the vulnerability of women in production and consumption, and an educational profile to show the weakness in skill endowments of the poor.

We start with the demographic attributes of the poor. First, we establish the relationship between poverty and family size, dependency ratios, and women's income. Second, we look at the relationship of occupational categories—manufacturing, agriculture, and services, capital versus labour income, and wage employment versus self employment—with the existence of poverty. Third, we show the distribution of food, energy, shelter, apparel, and savings in various income groups.

The results do not support a purely demographic explanation of poverty. While the gender structure of income is significantly linked to poverty, household size and dependency ratios are not. This is brought out in Tables 4.7-4.9. Table 4.7 shows that the poor have a significantly smaller family size compared to the middle and upper income categories.

Table 4.7 : Family size and income distribution

Income Group	*Urban* Adults Males	Females	Children	*Rural* Adults Males	Females	Children
Poor	1.2	1.1	2.4	1.1	1.2	2.4
Middle	1.7	1.7	3.6	1.7	1.7	3.8
Upper	2.4	2.2	3.7	2.3	2.2	4.2
All	1.7	1.7	3.3	1.5	1.6	3.4

Source: Calculated from *Household Income and Expenditure Survey 1992-3*, (1996, pp.81).

Both in rural and urban areas, the poor have approximately 2.3 adults per household, while the middle and upper income groups have between 3.4 and 4.6, respectively. Similarly, the average poor household had approximately 2.4 children, as compared with approximately 3.7 for the middle income, and approximately 4 for upper income categories. In adult equivalents, the family sizes of poor households are 4.2, compared with about 6.4 and 7.7, respectively, for middle and upper income groups. These results give rise to competing hypotheses about the relationship between household size and poverty. Contrary to the generally accepted view that a large household size leads to lower per capita income, the causal relationship may be reversed with household size adjusting for lower income as a survival strategy.

Dependency ratios, measured as the number of members per earner in a household in Table 4.8, support this hypothesis. If family size adjusts to income, it must be to keep the dependency ratio constant. This is broadly seen in Table 4.8, where the dependency ratio varies insignificantly between 3.89 and 4.3 for the urban income groups, and between 3.4 and 3.7 for the rural income groups.

Table 4.8 : Dependency ratios and income distribution

Income Group	*Urban* Mean per Household Earners	Members	Members/ Earners	*Rural* Mean per Household Earners	Members	Members/ Earners
Poor	1.2	4.6	3.8	1.4	4.7	3.4
Middle	1.6	6.9	4.3	1.9	7.1	3.7
Upper	2.1	8.2	3.9	2.4	8.1	3.4
All	1.6	6.7	4.2	1.7	6.3	3.7

Source: Calculated from *Household Income and Expenditure Survey 1992-3*, (1996, pp.160-1,175-6).

If the poor have insignificantly lower earners per household with the lowest incomes, then the reason must be the nature of their employment and associated remuneration. The bias against women's employment and remuneration is well acknowledged. Therefore, households reliant on women's incomes, especially female-headed households, are likely to fall into poverty. This is given limited support by Table 4.9, which presents female-headed and female-income reliant households as a percentage of the total in each income category.

Table 4.9 : Female-headed households and income distribution

Income Group	Female Head H.Hs	% of Earners Female but Non Head H.Hs	Total female Earning H.Hs
		URBAN	
Poor	2.1	6.3	8.4
Middle	0.9	7.1	8.0
Upper	0.5	8.3	8.8
All	0.9	7.6	8.5
		RURAL	
Poor	2.5	13.7	16.2
Middle	0.8	15.6	16.4
Upper	0.4	15.3	15.7
All	1.1	15.1	16.2

Source: Calculated from *Household Income and Expenditure Survey 1992-3*.

The poor have a somewhat higher proportion of female-headed households, over 2 per cent, compared to less than 1 per cent for the middle and upper income groups, in both regions.

The second set of attributes of the poor centre around their occupational structure. We estimated the share of income accruing to various groups from agriculture, manufacturing, and services. We also estimated income derived from different factors of production and from the nature of employment. The results are presented in Tables 4.10-4.12. We show in Table 4.10 that all three income groups are reliant on agriculture for about half their income. However, the contribution of the other half of rural income varies significantly across these income groups. The rural poor are over-represented in construction, with 17 per cent, compared to the global mean of 10 per cent. Not surprisingly, the poor have the lowest shares in the more remunerative sectors like trade services and finance.

Table 4.10 : Sectoral distribution of income

Income Group	Total	Agriculture	Mining	Manufacturing	Utilities	Construction	Trade	Transport, Storage, and Communication	Finance	Community and Social Services
URBAN TOTAL INCOME (million Rs)										
Poor	2,818.6	109.0	0.0	613.2	22.7	356.6	658.7	322.5	40.9	695.0
Middle	9,407.5	231.7	9.1	1,889.7	174.9	715.4	2,496.1	1,194.7	288.4	2,407.5
Upper	10,368.1	490.6	70.4	2,003.2	145.4	361.1	3,023.0	654.1	883.5	2,736.8
All	22,698.8	844.9	81.8	4,517.5	354.3	1,451.3	6,186.9	2,184.9	1,224.2	5,853.0
% INCOME										
Poor	100.0	3.87	0.00	21.76	0.80	12.65	23.37	11.44	1.45	24.66
Middle	100.0	2.46	0.10	20.09	1.86	7.60	26.53	12.70	3.06	25.60
Upper	100.0	4.73	0.68	19.32	1.40	3.48	29.16	6.31	8.52	26.40
All	100.0	3.72	0.36	19.90	1.56	6.39	27.26	9.63	8.52	26.40
RURAL TOTAL INCOME (million Rs)										
Poor	6,540.3	3,356.2	3.3	473.3	26.5	1,128.7	513.0	350.9	13.2	675.2
Middle	17,182.0	7,616.1	16.5	1,562.6	165.5	1,840.3	2,022.4	1,426.6	82.7	2,449.3
Upper	9,191.7	4,809.3	0.0	579.2	92.7	423.7	1,151.8	556.1	119.2	1,459.7
All	33,069.3	15,801.5	26.5	2,638.0	304.5	3,405.9	3,707.1	2,350.0	235.0	4,600.8
% INCOME										
Poor	100.0	51.31	0.05	7.24	0.40	17.26	7.84	5.37	0.20	10.32
Middle	100.0	44.33	0.10	9.10	0.96	10.71	11.77	8.30	0.49	14.25
Upper	100.0	52.32	0.00	6.30	1.01	4.61	12.53	6.05	1.30	15.88
All	100.0	47.78	0.08	8.00	0.92	10.30	11.21	7.11	0.71	13.91

Source: Calculated from *Household Income and Expenditure Survey 1992-93* (1996, pp. 205, 206).

Table 4.11 : Contractual distribution of rural income

Income Group	Total	Landlord	Self Cultivator	Share-cropper	Lessee Cultivator	Agricultural Labour	Self Cultivator/ Share-cropper	Self Cultivator Lessee	Share-cropper/ Lessee	Self Cultivator/ Sharecropper/ Lessee
TOTAL INCOME (million Rs)										
Poor	1,722.0	2.4	202.2	73.6	4.5	1,370.8	37.2	27.3	4.2	0.0
Middle	7,265.2	0.5	943.2	153.1	43.2	5,640.5	297.4	166.1	13.8	7.4
Upper	6,758.6	4.2	964.5	48.9	40.5	5,277.8	75.4	315.2	23.4	8.7
All	15,745.7	7.2	2,111.0	275.7	88.3	12,294.0	408.4	503.5	41.4	16.2
% INCOME										
Poor	100.0	0.1	11.7	4.3	0.3	79.6	2.2	1.6	0.2	0.0
Middle	100.0	0.0	13.0	2.1	0.6	77.6	4.1	2.3	0.2	0.1
Upper	100.0	0.1	14.2	0.7	0.6	78.1	1.1	4.7	0.3	0.1
All	100.0	0.0	13.4	1.8	0.6	78.1	2.6	3.2	0.3	0.1

Source: Calculated from *Household Income and Expenditure Survey 1992-3* (1996, p.463).

Table 4.12 : Occupational distribution of income categories

		% Income per month from:						
Income Group	Total	Wages	Self-Employment	Property	Owner-Occupied Houses	Pension and Benefits	Remittances and Gifts	Other
				URBAN				
Poor	100.0	61.1	20.5	1.1	16.3	0.9	1.5	0.8
Middle	100.0	53.5	26.0	1.7	12.4	0.9	5.5	0.1
Upper	100.0	43.3	31.2	4.3	13.2	1.3	6.4	0.5
All	100.0	46.3	29.4	3.3	13.0	1.1	6.4	0.3
				RURAL				
Poor	100.0	33.3	30.0	1.6	17.3	1.1	14.8	1.7
Middle	100.0	28.0	48.0	2.5	9.1	0.8	10.5	1.1
Upper	100.0	18.2	59.2	5.8	5.8	1.3	9.0	0.8
All	100.0	25.3	48.7	4.0	8.9	1.2	10.8	1.1

Source : Calculated from *Household Income and Expenditure Survey 1992-3* (1996, pp.249).

The results in table 4.10 can be supplemented with those presented in Table 4.11 which provides information on the distribution of land ownership and tenancy in rural areas. This shows that the poor are predominantly agricultural labourers, with 80 per cent of their income coming from this source, compared to the global mean of 75 per cent. They are under-represented in self-cultivation, with 11 per cent income shares from this source compared to the global mean of 13 per cent. Their access to land is also constrained as indicated by their reliance on the more onerous and subordinate contractual form of share cropping where they are over-represented, and their lower access to less constrained contractual forms like leasing where they are under-represented.

Table 4.10 shows that in the urban areas, the poor have a relatively high share of income from manufacturing, at 22 per cent compared to the global mean of 20 per cent; construction, at 13 per cent compared to the global mean of 6 per cent; and transport, at 11 per cent compared to the global mean of 9 per cent. As in the rural areas, the poor are also under-represented in more remunerative service sectors like finance and insurance, or trade and commerce. Since construction is part of the informal sector, with low wages, low upward mobility, job insecurity, and the use of casual labour, the disproportionate presence of the poor in this sector reflects not only their economic deprivation, but also that they confront uncertainty and insecurity.

The reliance of the poor on wage income in both urban and rural areas is supported further by information in Table 4.12 which reports occupational distribution. In urban areas, the poor have a much higher share of income from wages at 61 per cent compared to the global mean of 46 per cent. The urban poor earn virtually no property income and earn the lowest remittances. Also, the urban poor are significantly under-represented in self-employment at 21 per cent compared to a global mean of 29 per cent. The rural poor, like their urban counterparts, earn a significantly higher share of their income from wage employment at 33 per cent, compared to the global mean of 25 per cent. The rural poor are under-represented in self-employment at 30 per cent, compared to the global mean of 49 per cent, reflecting lower self-cultivation as well as lower engagement in other forms of entrepreneurial activities. Finally, the rural poor earn 15 per cent of their income from remittances, compared to the global mean of 11 per cent.

The third set of attributes of the poor centre around their consumption or expenditure. These are presented in Tables 4.13 and 4.14. As expected, the poor have the highest household budget deficits as shown in Table 4.13. The urban and rural poor have a monthly deficit of between Rs 420 and Rs 460, which is approximately 25 per cent of their mean monthly income. The urban middle income group also has a small deficit of Rs 80 per month, while the rural middle and upper income groups have surpluses. This is an important finding because it shows that the poor are extremely vulnerable to any macro-policy-triggered price changes. The poor already fail to consume 2,550 calories, and do not have any surpluses to absorb shocks.

Table 4.13 : Household budget surplus/deficits across income groups

Income Group	Average Surplus Per Month Urban	Rural
Poor	–529.0	–539.0
Middle	–2.0	–82.0
Upper	+1,833.0	+2,078.0
All	+458.0	+49.0

Source: Calculated from *Household Income and Expenditure Survey 1992-93* (1996, pp. 458).

Table 4.14 further underscores the importance of this result by showing the salience of the four essentials—food, rent, energy, and apparel—in the budgets of the poor. In both urban and rural areas, the poor spend approximately 82 per cent of their budgets on these items, as compared with 78 per cent and 72 per cent for the middle and upper income groups, respectively.

Thus, if macroeconomics policies raise the cost of essential goods, the poor only have 18 per cent of their expenditure from which to absorb the shock. If calorie expenditures are maintained, the high probability is that cuts would be introduced in contingency expenditures—such as births and deaths—or in social expenditures such as children's education and health.

We now turn to the incidence of taxation and public expenditure in Pakistan, which can have a major impact on poverty and income distribution.

Table 4.14 : Distribution of consumption by income groups

Income Group	Total	Food	Rent	Energy	% consumption expenditure on: Durables	Apparel	Transport	Laundry	Education	Leisure	Other
						URBAN					
Poor	100.0	49.6	17.0	7.1	1.5	8.2	3.4	5.0	1.1	0.4	6.8
Middle	100.0	47.8	17.1	6.0	1.8	7.9	3.6	4.8	2.1	0.7	8.2
Upper	100.0	39.0	20.0	4.7	2.5	7.7	6.3	4.8	2.7	1.5	11.1
All	100.0	42.7	18.9	5.4	2.2	7.8	5.2	4.7	2.3	1.0	9.9
						RURAL					
Poor	100.0	53.1	12.9	7.3	1.5	8.7	2.3	4.3	0.5	0.4	9.0
Middle	100.0	53.0	10.9	6.7	2.1	9.2	2.8	4.1	0.9	0.3	10.0
Upper	100.0	48.6	10.7	5.3	2.5	8.5	4.1	4.0	1.5	0.6	14.2
All	100.0	51.7	11.5	6.6	2.1	8.9	3.0	4.1	1.0	0.4	9.9

Source : Calculated from *Household Income and Expenditure Survey 1992-3*.

3. TAX INCIDENCE AND INCOME DISTRIBUTION

There have been very few studies done on tax incidence in Pakistan. Also, these studies differ in the time periods, the coverage of taxes, and the methodological framework employed to assess tax incidence. Irfan (1974) estimated the incidence of excise taxes only on tobacco and petroleum products for 1971-2. Alauddin and Naqvi (1981) considered the incidence of all taxes, except import duties for the year 1971-2. Both these studies computed the incidence of taxes on the basis of nominal tax rates rather than the actual tax collected.[10] Jeetun (1978), Qureshi (1988) and Malik and Saqib (1989) examine the incidence of all the federal taxes based on actual tax collections. Jeetun's study was for the 1972-3 fiscal year, Malik and Saqib's for 1978-9 and Qureshi's for 1984-5. All authors estimate the incidence of indirect taxes on the basis of consumption pattern derived from *HIES* surveys.[11]

On the basis of the data relating to the consumption pattern derived from the surveys, tax incidence for consumer goods can easily be ascertained. However, most of the indirect taxes in Pakistan are collected from intermediate and capital goods. In order to ascertain their incidence, the taxes on these commodities need to be allocated to various income groups as well. This is done on the basis of the probable increase in prices of different consumer goods due to a tax on the intermediate and capital goods. While Jeetun and Qureshi allocated taxes on intermediate and capital goods to various activities producing consumer goods on the basis of their knowledge and feel for the economy, Malik and Saqib used an input output table for apportioning taxes to various consumer goods. While Malik and Saqib use a superior method to that employed in the other two studies, their study is handicapped by having to use the only available input-output table based on the 1975-6 *Census of Manufacturing Industries*.[12]

Jeetun found Pakistan's tax structure to be slightly progressive in 1971-2; while direct taxes were highly progressive, the indirect taxes were only mildly progressive and bordered on proportional. Malik and Saqib also found Pakistan's tax structure to be slightly progressive in 1978-9 but, contrary to Jeetun, they found that indirect taxes were regressive. Qureshi concluded that Pakistan's entire tax structure, both direct and indirect, was slightly progressive in 1984-5.

While all the three studies report that Pakistan's direct tax structure was slightly or highly progressive, their conclusions differ in the case of indirect taxes. The difference may be attributed to differences in the method, time period, and coverage. In any case, further explorations of this issue and updated estimates were called for. Accordingly, we have estimated the tax incidence for the years 1987-8 to 1990-1 (the years for which data were available).

3.1. Tax incidence: 1987-8 to 1990-1

The incidence of excise duties, custom duties, and sales taxes have been estimated for the years 1987-8 to 1990-1 on the basis of consumption data obtained from *HIES* 1987-8. Unpublished disaggregated income tax data were obtained from the Central Board of Revenue.

Table 4.15 : Incidence of both direct and indirect taxes

Income Group (Rs/month)	Tax Paid/Income 1987/88	1988/89	1989/90	1990/91
Up to 600	7.08	7.90	8.42	7.81
601- 700	7.53	8.15	8.55	8.04
701- 900	7.87	8.36	8.79	8.24
901-1000	7.67	8.18	8.54	8.01
1,001-1,500	7.78	8.21	8.48	8.01
1,501-2,000	7.93	8.31	8.57	8.11
2,001-2,500	7.65	8.01	8.22	7.79
2,501-3,000	7.85	8.19	8.36	7.92
3,001-3,500	7.58	7.92	8.09	7.69
3,501-4,000	8.63	8.97	9.08	8.65
4,001-4,500	7.56	7.95	8.16	7.74
4,500-above	11.54	11.75	11.01	11.04

Source: Estimation by authors.

The estimation of tax incidence poses two problems. First, the commodity classification used in *HIES* and by the tax authorities is not the same. This problem is easily overcome through reclassification. Second, intermediate and capital goods account for a large proportion of taxes collected, and as such these had to be apportioned to various consumption goods for assessing their incidence on various income groups. As pointed out earlier, this problem can be overcome either by using an input-output table, or by making educated guesses as to where the intermediate and capital goods will be used. Since an input-output table for a recent year was not available, we have made use of information contained in the Input-Output Table of 1975-6.[13]

The tax incidence has been estimated for twelve income groups on the basis of tax collections, rather than the statutory rates of duty, and the *Household Income Expenditure Survey* for the year 1987-8. The survey provides data on average incomes by twelve income groups, and also the proportion of household's total expenditures allocated to different goods for these groups. The methodology we used to compute tax incidence is reported in Appendix 1.

Appendix 2, Tables I-IV show the incidence of sales taxes, custom duties, overall indirect tax, and income tax respectively. Based on these,

Table 4.15 gives the combined incidence of indirect and direct taxes. The numbers in the Table below represent the percentage of income paid by different income groups in both direct and indirect taxes.

These results show that Pakistan's tax structure is slightly progressive, but it is almost proportional if the last income group is excluded. This finding is consistent with the results obtained in the earlier studies cited above. A more notable finding is that, while the tax incidence increased the most for the lowest income group, it actually declined for the upper income group. This result is clearly evident from Table 4.16.

Table 4.16 : Increase in tax burden: 1987-8 to 1990-1

Income Groups (Rs/month)	
Up to 600	10.3
601- 700	6.8
701- 900	4.7
901-1000	4.4
1,001-1,500	3.0
1,501-2,000	2.3
2,001-2,500	1.8
2,501-3,000	0.9
3,001-3,500	1.5
3,501-4,000	0.2
4,001-4,500	2.4
4,501-above	–4.3

Source: Table 4.15.

Compared to a decline of 4.3 per cent in the tax burden for the richest, the tax burden on the poorest class has increased by 10.3 per cent. This pattern of the increase in tax burden is essentially a reflection of the emphasis on additional indirect tax mobilization, particularly sales taxes, under the Structural Adjustment Programme. The increase in sales taxes has been applied to those products which form a relatively higher proportion in the consumption bundle of the poorest.

4. INCIDENCE OF PUBLIC EXPENDITURES

Like taxes, public expenditures can be progressive, neutral, or regressive. Hardly any data exist to determine the distribution of benefits arising from public expenditures on social sectors, particularly education and health, accruing to various sections of society. The discussion which follows is therefore conjectural in nature.

4.1. Education

The fees charged by the government education institutions are quite nominal; only a very small proportion of the cost is recovered. The difference in cost of education per child and the fee charged is the subsidy per student. Estimates show that the absolute unit subsidy to post-graduate education is about 29 times the unit subsidy at the primary level.[14] Estimates also show that, relative to their representation in the population, the highest income group is highly over-represented in higher education whereas the lowest income group is under-represented.[15]

Table 4.17 : Distribution of educational expenditures by levels.

Level	Sixth Plan Expenditures	Seventh Plan Expenditures	Eighth Plan Allocations
Primary	23.6	46.6	47.5
Secondary	28.6	23.8	24.6
Teacher	1.4	1.2	4.9
Technical	6.7	3.6	3.6
College	9.2	7.5	3.7
University	10.3	5.9	6.0

Source: Khan *et al*. (1995, Table 3).
Note: Totals do not add up to one hundred since numbers are reported only for the major items of expenditure.

Primary education provided by the government benefits mainly the poor and the lower middle income class; the richer income groups send their children to more expensive private primary schools. Therefore, the subsidy to primary education is likely to accrue to the poorer income groups. By this reasoning, the changes in the pattern of educational expenditures over time would implicitly show changes in the benefits accruing to various income groups.

Table 4.17 shows that, between the Sixth and Seventh Plans, there was a major reallocation of expenditure away from the higher level to the primary level. This pattern of educational expenditure is expected to be sustained during the Eighth Plan period. This restructuring of the educational expenditure bodes well from an equity perspective.

Significant differences exist in the provision of educational services across the regions and gender. Table 4.18 below shows the provision of educational institutions by gender and the gender gap. While this gap has narrowed over time, female institutions are still about only one-third of those provided for males. This disparity is therefore reflected in participation rates and literacy ratios. Female literacy rate is currently estimated to be 24 per cent, which is less than half of the estimated 49 per cent male literacy rate. There are similar regional disparities in literacy rates, such that the estimated rural literacy rate of 28 per cent is less than half of the estimated urban literacy rate of 58 per cent.[16]

Table 4.18 : Gender gap in the provision of schools

Year	Primary			Middle			High		
	M	F	F/M	M	F	F/M	M	F	F/M
1959-60	17,901	3,260	.18	1,974	281	.14	1,069	203	.19
1969-70	41,290	11,170	.27	3,560	860	.24	1,995	520	.26
1979-80	57,220	17,771	.31	5,233	1,407	.26	3,361	924	.27
1989-90	110,522	29,966	.27	8,058	3,055	.38	7,184	1,895	.26
1994-5E	115,023	32,537	.28	10,255	3,870	.38	9,382	2,253	.24

Source: *Economic Survey 1995-96*, Statistical Appendix (1995, p. 209).
Note: E = estimate.

4.2. Health

Health facilities also show marked differences across urban and rural areas. Facilities per population in the rural areas are much more scarce than in the urban areas. For example, while there is one doctor per 2,330 people and one nurse per 5,823 people (statistics of relevance to urban areas), there is one rural health centre (with one health practitioner) for 203,109 rural people.[17]

In urban areas, the poor confront long queues with less than a minute of the doctor's time per patient. This is in contrast with airconditioned rooms, specialized doctors in waiting, and the availability of standardized medicine for the rich.

Gender and regional bias are once again considerable. The statistics which follow are taken from *Pakistan Integrated Household Survey, Final Results, 1991*. The percentage of children, five and under, reporting diarrhoea 30 days prior to the survey was 22 per cent in the urban areas, and 28 per cent in the rural areas. Similarly, a health practitioner was consulted in 90 per cent of the urban cases but 83 per cent of the rural cases. In both urban and rural areas, boys were about 7 per cent more likely than girls to consult a health practitioner. While 82 per cent of such children received some immunization in urban areas, 68 per cent did so in the rural areas. Overall, 72 per cent of boys and only 68 per cent of girls received any immunization. More telling about these disparities are infant and child mortality rates. Between 1986-90, these were 104 and 120 in urban areas, and 127 and 151 in rural areas, respectively.

Females and rural inhabitants have a higher probability of falling ill and less likelihood of consulting a health practitioner when they do. Thirty days prior to the survey, 24 per cent urban males and 34 per cent urban females, 15 years or older, reported having fallen ill. The corresponding numbers in the rural areas were 27 per cent and 36 per cent, respectively. Of those who fell ill, 82 per cent of rural males, but 74 per cent of rural females, reported having consulted a health practitioner.

5. SUMMARY AND CONCLUSIONS

This chapter portrayed a poverty map of Pakistan which characterizes the basic attributes of poverty. These characteristics yield some interesting alternative explanations of the causal mechanisms of poverty and the impact of government policy.

Poverty, defined as a headcount of those unable to meet a nutritional norm of 2,250 calories per day, shows a declining trend in the long run since the late 1960s, albeit with some interesting short-term fluctuations. Poverty increased over the 1960s, declined over the 1970s and much of the 1980s, to register a small but significant upturn by 1990. Income distribution improved over the 1960s, worsened over the 1970s, improved again over much of the 1980s, and worsened again by 1990. Poverty in the early 1990s is higher than it has ever been in the last three decades. Our explanation is that the two causal factors of GNP growth and explicit government policy towards the vulnerable have a complex relationship with poverty and income distribution.

GNP growth was high over the 1960s, low over the 1970s, high over much of the, 1980s, and dropped by 1990. Government policy towards the vulnerable was negligent over the 1960s, concessionary over the 1970s, and somewhat mixed over the 1980s. Therefore, poverty seems to have been affected by the combination of GNP growth and government policy in the following way. Over the 1960s, the high growth was not sufficient to decrease poverty, and a negligent policy towards the vulnerable actually increased poverty. Over the 1970s, poverty dropped, not because of growth, which was low, but because of a concessionary government policy towards the vulnerable. Over much of the 1980s, both growth and government policy supported the decline in poverty. However, by 1990, poverty increased again because of inflationary government policy which adversely impacted the vulnerable. Therefore, poverty seems to have a stronger relationship with explicit government policy rather than with growth.

Conversely, income distribution appears to have a close link with growth. Over the 1960s, government policy was negligent, especially towards income distribution, but the distribution improved, propelled by high GNP growth rates. Then over the 1970s, while government policy was explicitly directed towards improving income distribution, the distribution worsened due to low growth. Over much of the 1980s, high growth improved the income distribution again. By 1990, the hiatus in growth had worsened the income distribution. Therefore, our exercise shows income distribution to be more closely related to growth, while poverty is more closely associated with explicit government poverty alleviation policy.

The poverty map also brings out some interesting alternative explanations of the causal mechanisms of poverty. First, a demographic theory of poverty is not supported by the data, which shows a significantly lower mean family size of the poor compared to upper income groups. This suggests that family size adjusts to income rather than income adjusting to family size. A constant dependency ratio of earners to family size across income groups further supports this argument, showing that family size adjusts to income to keep the dependency ratio constant. Female-headed households are three times more likely to be in poverty.

Second, the poor are over-represented in particular economic sectors, which are remarkably consistent across both rural and urban areas. In rural areas, the poor are over-represented among the landless compared to higher income groups, which in turn leads them to be over-represented in the contractual employment of share tenancy and wage labour. The rural poor are also over-represented in manufacturing and construction, while being under-represented in the higher income sectors like trade and finance. Similarly, the urban poor are also over-represented in manufacturing and construction while being under-represented in trade and finance.

Third, the landlessness of the rural poor and the concentration of both the rural and urban poor in manufacturing and construction restricts them largely to low-wage employment. The poor are also significantly under-represented in self-employment.

The consumption profile of the poor shows them to be extremely vulnerable to pricing policy on food and essentials. Household budgets show the poor to be caught in permanent deficits of approximately 25 per cent of their mean incomes while the higher income groups run surpluses. Eighty per cent of the expenditure of the poor is on food, rent, energy, and apparel, which presumably exhausts their income, leaving health and education to be discretionary expenditure financed through deficits. They also earn 68 and 46 per cent of their income from wage employment in urban and rural areas, respectively. This makes them very susceptible to macroeconomics shocks.

Finally, we estimated the incidence of taxation across income groups. If the highest group, with incomes per month of above Rs 4,500 is excluded, the incidence of tax paid as a proportion of income is virtually constant at about 8 per cent across income groups. It is of concern that the incidence of taxation has become more regressive between 1987-8 and 1990-1, with the tax incidence increasing for the lowest income groups and decreasing for the highest income group.

APPENDIX 1 : Computing tax incidence

Let C_{ij} = Consumption expenditure on ith commodity as a proportion of total expenditure of jth household group;

h_j = The proportion of jth HH in total household;

E = Total expenditure;

E_{ij} = Expenditure on ith commodity by ith groups;

P_{ij} = Proportion of consumption of jth group in ith product;

and

T_{kij} = kth tax paid by jth group for ith product;

Then

$$E_{ij} = C_{ij}\ E_j$$

$$P_{ij} = \frac{h_j C_{ij} a E_j}{jhjC_{ij}E_j}$$

$$T_{ij}^{k} = P_{ij}\ TK$$

$$Tjk = \sum_j T_{ijk}$$

$$Tj = \sum_k T_j^k$$

To compute tax incidence, income accruing to each of the income class is estimated as following: Let Y_j be the income of jth household group, and m_j the share of ith group in GNP is

$$m_j = h_j\ Y_j$$

$$\sum_j k_j\ Y_j$$

Income accruing to each class, (I_j) is then $I_j = m_j$ GDP

Accordingly the incidence of tax (t_{ij}) is

$$t^k\ ij = t^k{}_{ij} / I_j$$

and,

$$t^k{}_j = \sum_i t^k{}_{ij}$$

$$t_j = \sum_k t_{ij}$$

APPENDIX 2 : Tax Incidence

Table I : Incidence of sales taxes

Income Group (Rs/month)	Taxes/Income 1987-8	1988-9	1989-90	1990-1
Up to 600	1.34	2.01	2.25	1.94
601-700	1.33	1.97	2.25	1.94
701-900	1.44	2.04	2.38	2.05
901-1,000	1.38	1.98	2.29	1.97
1,001-1,500	1.32	1.96	2.29	1.97
1,501-2,000	1.35	2.00	2.34	2.02
2,001-2,500	1.29	1.94	2.27	1.96
2,501-3,000	1.35	2.01	2.33	2.00
3,001-3,500	1.25	1.96	2.30	1.98
3,501-4,000	1.33	1.14	2.50	2.16
4,001-4,500	1.31	2.06	2.39	2.06
4,501-above	1.17	2.16	2.57	2.21

Source: Estimation by authors.

Table II : Incidence of custom duties

Income Group (Rs/month)	Taxes/Income 1987-8	1988-9	1989-90	1990-1
Up to 600	2.41	2.53	2.99	2.50
601-700	2.87	5.85	3.19	2.66
701-900	3.03	2.90	3.22	2.69
901-1,000	2.90	2.80	3.05	2.54
1,001-1,500	3.13	2.94	3.14	2.62
1,501-2,000	3.22	2.98	3.17	2.65
2,001-2,500	3.09	2.84	2.98	2.49
2,501-3,000	3.13	2.85	2.99	2.50
3,001-3,500	3.13	2.83	2.95	2.46
3,501-4,000	3.61	3.23	3.33	2.78
4,001-4,500	2.93	2.63	2.80	2.35
4,501-above	4.90	4.32	3.70	3.02

Source: Estimation by authors.

Table III : Incidence of income taxes

Income Group (Rs/month)	Taxes/Income 1987-8	1988-9	1989-90	1990-1
Up to 600	0.00	0.00	0.00	0.00
601-700	0.00	0.00	0.00	0.00
701-900	0.00	0.00	0.00	0.00
901-1,000	0.00	0.00	0.00	0.00
1,001-1,500	0.00	0.00	0.00	0.00
1,501-2,000	0.00	0.00	0.00	0.00
2,001-2,500	0.00	0.00	0.00	0.00
2,501-3,000	0.02	0.02	0.02	0.02
3,001-3,500	0.02	0.02	0.02	0.02
3,501-4,000	0.18	0.18	0.18	0.20
4,001-4,500	0.09	0.09	0.09	0.10
4,501-above	1.40	1.42	1.35	1.54

Source: Estimation by authors.

Table IV : Incidence of indirect taxes

Income Group (Rs/month)	Taxes/Income 1987-8	1988-9	1989-90	1990-1
Up to 600	7.08	7.90	8.42	7.81
601-700	7.53	8.15	8.55	8.04
701-900	7.87	8.36	9.79	8.24
901-1,000	7.67	8.18	8.54	8.01
1,001-1,500	7.78	8.21	8.48	8.01
1,501-2,000	7.93	8.31	8.57	8.11
2,001-2,500	7.65	8.01	8.22	7.79
2,501-3,000	7.83	8.17	8.34	7.90
3,001-3,500	7.56	7.90	8.07	7.67
3,501-4,000	8.45	8.79	8.90	8.47
4,001-4,500	7.47	7.86	8.07	7.65
4,501-above	10.14	10.31	9.66	9.50

Source: Estimation by authors.

NOTES

1. For details, see Kemal (1982).
2. This assumes that nutritional standards are both critical indicators of poverty and uncontroversial in themselves. For excellent reviews of this issue and its critique, see Osmani (1987) and Ercelawn (1989).
3. These include Naseem (1977), Mujahid (1978), Irfan and Amjad (1983), and Malik (1988).
4. See de Krujik and van Leeuwen (1985), Irfan and Amjad (1984), Ahmad and Allison (1990), and Malik (1991).
5. See also Ercelawn *et al.* (1991).
6. Note that the estimates of poverty of 16 for urban areas and 7 for rural areas in Malik (1991) differs from those in Malik *et al.* (1995) of 20 for rural areas and 9 for urban areas.
7. This view was shaped by Kuznet's inverted U-shaped hypothesis (1955).
8. The Gini coefficient is a measure of inequality. It varies between zero and one, with zero representing perfect equality and one representing complete inequality.
9. Other indicators of inequality, such as Theil's entropy measure, Sen Index, Pareto Curves, Takayama Index, Atkinson's Index also show similar trends and are, therefore, not reported here. For details, see Burney (1991).
10. Actual tax collections are a better measure of the total tax burden because various exemptions and statutory rates are not enforced. For example; compared to an average statutory rate of import duty of 59.8 per cent, the rate of import duty on the basis of revenues collected in 1989-90 was 28.8 per cent. (See Kemal 1991 for the impact of exemptions on the tax rates). Furthermore, tax exemptions may be specific to particular classes which would make the use of realized revenues necessary in a study of tax incidence by income group.
11. Jeetun's study is based on a 1971-2 survey, Malik and Saqib's on a 1979 survey, and Qureshi's on a 1984-5 survey.
12. Our update suffers from the same handicap.
13. The Federal Bureau of Statistics is expected to release an input-output table based on 1990-1 data soon.
14. Jemenez and Tan (1985, p.12). While these estimates are now dated, it is unlikely that the proportions have changed much, given the static nature of public education.
15. Khan (1991, p.1243). While these estimates are based on students of higher educational institutions throughout the country, they are drawn from a survey completed in 1982. More recent research done by the same author for the Quaid-i-Azam University (1994) shows a very similar picture.
16. *Economic Survey 1994-5* (1995, p.105).
17. *Eighth Five Year Plan* (1994, p.526).

5

The Policy Framework and Structural Adjustment

Tariq Banuri, A. R. Kemal, and *Moazam Mahmood*

INTRODUCTION

This chapter examines the economic policy-making framework in Pakistan. Three aspects of this framework are important and are discussed below: the nature of the constitutional system; the fiscal stance of the government of Pakistan; and the nature of policy regimes and their underlying determinants. The constitutional system and the tax structure represent the parameters within which policy regimes are examined. Our focus is on the populist policy regime of the 1970s and the structural adjustment programmes signed with the IMF and the World Bank in the 1980s and 1990s.

1. THE CONSTITUTIONAL SYSTEM

Pakistan is a federation of four provinces and so the allocation of functions and distribution of revenues between federal and provincial governments assume significance. The distribution of functions between federal and provincial governments in Pakistan is laid down in the 1973 constitution. The federal list places defence, external affairs, foreign aid, banking and currency, air, sea, and rail transport, national highways and strategic roads, communications, oil and natural gas as the responsibility of the federal government. A concurrent list which includes environment, law and order, labour legislation, and population planning is the joint responsibility of the two tiers of government. The residual functions are entrusted to provincial governments.

The provision that provincial and federal governments may entrust their responsibilities to each other through mutual consent has led to a considerable overlapping of functions. Nevertheless, the major responsibilities of provincial governments include education, health, agricultural support services, maintenance of the irrigation system, provincial and rural roads, and internal law and order. In particular, social sectors are in the domain of the provincial and local governments, rather than the federal government. Provincial governments have delegated or shared some of their functions with local governments, including the provision of basic rural and urban infrastructure such as roads, potable water, and sanitation.

Provincial governments have the power to raise land revenue, registration fee on motor vehicles, property taxes, stamp duties, certain minor taxes, and agricultural income tax. Nevertheless, major taxes such as custom duties, sales taxes, and excise duties are collected by the federal government. Provincial governments also receive a proportion of various taxes collected by the federal government.[1] Until 1990-1, any deficit in the provincial budgets was financed through special subventions made by the federal government to provincial governments.

The federal government meets its expenditure through tax and non-tax revenues, and any remaining deficit is financed through borrowing from outside and inside the country, and by resorting to deficit financing. Expenditures at the local level are financed through taxes and tolls raised by local governments and returns on remunerable projects and grants from provincial governments. Compared to the revenue heads allocated to the federal government, the share of total revenues raised by provincial and local governments are very small as shown in Table 5.1.

While local governments have run small surpluses in the past, provincial governments have run large deficits. These have been financed partly by the share of provinces in the divisible pool, but mainly through federal grants. Such a financing structure creates three problems. First, since provincial governments cannot chalk out their programmes independently, their priorities are not necessarily reflected in public expenditures. Second, uncertainty looms around implementation of the provincial programmes. Third, it creates incentives for overspending by the provinces.

The distribution of revenues between federal and provincial governments is governed by the recommendations of the National Finance Commission (NFC) to be convened every five years. Under the Constitution, the Commission is expected to announce an award which is sufficient to meet the entire non-development expenditures. However, even if the Commission met regularly and provided a mechanism which yielded sufficient resources to finance the non-development expenditures of the provinces, most of the problems enumerated above would continue.

In fact, the Commission has not met regularly. While the constitution stipulates the formation of a Commission every five years, there have been only three Commissions which announced their awards (in 1974, 1991 and 1997). The award of 20 April 1991, expanded the divisible tax pool, and allocated 80 per cent of it to the provinces, with

Table 5.1 : Public expenditures and revenues: 1984-5, 1990-1, and 1994-5

	1984-5				1990-1				1994-5			
	Expenditure		Revenues		Expenditure		Revenues		Expenditure		Revenues	
	Rs million	%	Rs million	%	Rs million	%	Rs million	%	Rs million	%	Rs million	%
Federal	90,074	73.8	73,105	88.4	198,801	77.7	172,206	91.2	318,056	72.3	302,499	94.6
Provincial	26,745	21.9	4,298	5.2	47,705	18.6	7,173	3.8	110,224	25.7	117,376	5.4
Local	5,177	4.2	5,294	6.4	9,039	3.6	9,346	5.0	–	–	–	–
Total	121,996	100.0	82,697	100.0	255,815	100.0	188,725	100.0	428,280	100.0	319,875	100.0

Source: *Economic Survey 1995-96*, Statistical Appendix (1996, p. 138).
Note : – means nil.

the share of each province determined by its population.[2] The 1991 award also provided for the payment of royalties on hydroelectricity and oil and the payment of a development surcharge (in addition to royalty) on natural gas to the provinces.

The award was expected to make the provinces self-sufficient in recurring expenditures. Development expenditures continue to be financed through federal grants. Moreover, since all development programmes entail corresponding non-development expenditures in subsequent years, the development of the social sector continues to be constrained. In the past, some provinces refused to accept development grants for the social sector on the grounds that they would not be able to meet the additional recurring expenditures. The problem can only be resolved by amending the Constitution to empower the National Finance Commission to provide resources to provincial governments for both development and non-development expenditures. The 1997 award has included wealth tax, capital value tax, and customs duty in the divisible pool. However, this enhancement may be offset by a reduction of the provincial government share in the revenue thus generated from 80 per cent to 37.5 per cent. Matching grants to the province have been introduced for provincial revenue generation, but this is subject to a ceiling of Rs 500 million.

Although local governments run small surpluses, these do not accrue from their resource mobilization efforts but from the low levels of their expenditures. This implies a low level of civic amenities delivery, including potable water, sewage and solid waste disposal. Accordingly, more and not less resources, and greater responsibility need to be placed at the disposal of local governments, and they should be required to work via communities (more on this in chapters 6 and 7).

2. THE TAX STRUCTURE

Pakistan relies heavily on indirect taxes, which accounted for three-fourths of tax revenues in 1994-5 (*Economic Survey 1995-6* 1996, p.139). Indirect taxes in the form of excise duties, sales taxes, and custom duties are generally imposed on manufactured goods. Since the manufacturing sector has grown rapidly, one would have expected a high tax elasticity with respect to GDP. Surprisingly, however, tax revenues have grown at a rate well below that of GDP. The paradox results from tax exemptions for the fastest growing manufacturing industries (Kemal 1986).

In this regard Pakistan's tax structure is peculiar, i.e. a very high rate structure but a very narrow base due to various tax exemptions. The exemptions are granted for each type of tax, including income tax, corporate tax, wealth tax, custom duties, import surcharges, sales taxes, and excise duties. These exemptions are not only a means of tax avoidance, but also a source of tax evasion. Rationalization of the tax rate structure, accompanied by the withdrawal of tax exemptions would lead not only to a significant mobilization of resources, but also to a more efficient and equitable economy. The Finance Supplementary Amendment Bill, 1997 has addressed this issue of exemptions and also attempted to expand the tax base in other ways. It is too soon to assess the impact of these measures, but much depends on assiduous implementation.

2.1. Personal and Corporate Income Taxes

Exemptions, full or partial, are granted to different types of incomes on the basis of dubious justifications. Sometimes they are granted to promote saving and investment, and sometimes just to maintain the status quo.

Agricultural incomes in Pakistan have traditionally been exempted from taxes, though without any economic rationale. Under the Constitution, only provincial governments are empowered to levy taxes on agricultural income. In the past, the provinces have not been too eager to do so due to the influence of landlords in provincial (and federal) legislatures. This is partly because, until the NFC award of 1991, the provinces had no incentive to raise resources through any means, let alone the politically difficult one of agricultural income taxation.

A start has been made in taxing agricultural incomes by using a wealth tax on agricultural land as a proxy for an income tax. Since the estimation of largely unrecorded agricultural income poses a technical problem in levying an agricultural income tax, an argument was forwarded for the imposition of a tax on land holdings, to begin with, as a proxy for agricultural income. The Benazir regime appointed a Task Force on agriculture in 1994 which recommended the levying of a tax of approximately Rs 2 per Produce Index Unit (PIU) above a floor of approximately 50 acres or 4,000 PIUs.[3] An agricultural income tax was levied by federal ordinance in 1993. So far, only the Sindh and NWFP assemblies have enacted this ordinance.

Opponents of agricultural income taxes maintain that, because agriculture is subject to heavy implicit taxation in the form of low output prices, there is no basis for taxing the income directly.[4] A couple of responses are possible to counter this argument. First, this is a political and not an economic argument. Since income taxes are borne by individuals and not the production sectors, it is not clear why high incomes should be exempt simply because they originate in a particular sector. Second, implicit taxation via price ceilings squeezes all the farmers, big and small, while agricultural income taxes would be paid by the rich only.

Economic logic supports the withdrawal of implicit taxation to improve resource allocation—irrespective of whether agricultural incomes are taxed or not. This withdrawal has no revenue implication; it is related primarily to the flow of resources between different production sectors rather than the flow between the government and non-government sector. However, the imposition of agricultural income taxes will yield about Rs 565 million per annum in revenues for the state.[5]

Apart from agriculture, tax exemptions were also allowed on a number of perquisites including accommodation, conveyance, medical bills, and entertainment allowances. The 1997 tax reform has brought perquisites into the tax net. Khan (1992) estimated that the withdrawal of these exemptions would increase tax revenues by Rs 1 billion.

In the early 1990s, the government imposed income taxes on certain specified types of incomes at low rates outside the purview of personal income taxes. Dividends are subject to a flat rate of 7.5 per cent, and a withholding tax at the rate of 3 to 4 per cent of the gross value of sales has been introduced on some businesses. Such withholding taxes are treated as the final settlement of the tax. No doubt, this has been done on the demand of the private sector which has problems in obtaining refunds. The significance of withholding taxes has been increasing, as is evident from Table 5.2.

Table 5.2 : Withholding taxes as a percentage of gross income tax collections (million Rs)

Years	Gross Tax Collection	Withholding Tax Payments Total	% of gross
1987-8	12,922	7,047	59.3
1988-9	14,827	8,467	59.3
1989-90	17,804	11,490	64.5
1990-1	21,814	13,988	64.1
1991-2	29,807	–	–
1992-3	37,803	–	–
1993-4	44,480	–	–
1994-5	62,618	–	–

Source: *Economic Surveys*, various years.

Tax relief and exemption is also provided to corporate and other industrial units to stimulate private investment in general, and investment in certain industries and areas in particular. Tax holidays for three years are available to all manufacturing units in Pakistan, and for 5 to 8 year for units in industrial estates and rural areas. Tax relief is also provided by operating tax credit schemes and accelerated depreciation allowances. All these exemptions significantly reduce the tax liability of the firms.

Fiscal incentives to stimulate investment have been found to be redundant. They only fuel excess demand for investment, since the demand for investible funds exceeds their supply significantly. On the other hand, such measures have generally been ineffective in shifting resources into priority sectors and less developed areas. This is because tax holidays and other tax concessions cannot increase profitability. The main impact of tax holidays has been to reallocate resources towards the fringes of developed regions.

This has, on the one hand, deprived the government of revenues and, on the other hand, produced gross inefficiencies in production. While hard estimates of revenue loss due to such exemptions is not available, it is likely to be in the range of Rs 5 billion annually.[6]

The withdrawal of all the income and corporate tax exemptions would yield tax revenue of about Rs 15 billion. If the revenue losses of other tax exemptions is also taken into consideration, the gain in revenues would be even higher. Estimates of the National Taxation Reforms Commission, even though highly exaggerated, suggest that only 28 per cent of taxable income is currently assessed, and that income tax collection would increase by Rs 75 billion through the control of tax evasion alone.

Tax evasion is a reflection of poor tax administration. There are three important forms through which it takes place: failure to file returns; under-reporting; and diversion of income. First, many persons earning more than the taxable income simply do not file returns; while the *Household Income and Expenditure Survey* shows about two million individuals with taxable income, only half this number file tax returns. Second, there are widespread cases of under-reporting of income by suppression of transactions, understatement of sales, overstatement of purchases and expenses, underinvoicing of exports, and overinvoicing of imports and bad debts. Third, there are also instances of the diversion of income through various methods.

Tax evasion can only be checked through an improvement in tax administration. The system of tax administration would improve if there were effective checks on the conduct of officials in the income tax department and their discretionary powere were curtailed. There is a need to develop a database to provide a basis for income assessment. Data on sales/turnover or input-output ratios can be used for this purpose.

2.2. Import Duties

Import duties are the main source of tax revenue, accounting for a fourth of total tax revenue in 1993-94 (*Economic Survey 1994-95* 1995, p.131). Tariff rates are still high in Pakistan; despite a series of reductions. The highest statutory rate of duty has been reduced from 65 per cent to 45 per cent through the New Economic Measures (1997). However, duties collected as a percentage of imports yield an average rate of over 22.4 per cent (see Table 5.3). The differential arises due to exemptions, partial or total, granted to various categories of imports. These exemptions are granted to specific users—such as a particular industry or public sector agency—with a view to promoting indigenization, developing poorer regions, or encouraging priority industries.

Such concessions have introduced major distortions in the structure of tariffs, leading to corruption, allocative inefficiency, and x-inefficiency. Naqvi and Kemal (1991) found that more than 80 per cent of Pakistani industries suffer from gross inefficiencies.

Thus, high rates of tariffs do not necessarily bring much revenues to the government due to the practice of granting concessional, or even zero, duty for some users. If some users are allowed tariff exemption, one can expect the dutiable imports of that product to fall to negligible levels. Another reason for the weak link between tariff rates and tariff revenues is the smuggling encouraged by high rates.

Tariff rationalization, including withdrawal of exemptions, would improve tax collection and lead to higher levels of efficiency. One estimate shows that if exemptions in tariffs are withdrawn, customs revenues would increase by 30 per cent (World Bank, 1987). The 1997 Tax Reform Act has reduced the maximum duty slab from 65 per cent to 45 per cent and suitably cascaded the duties on the different kinds of imports. The duty on smuggling-prone goods has been reduced to between 10 per cent and 25 per cent.

2.3. Sales Taxes

Until recently, sales taxes formed a very small proportion of tax revenues. In 1987-8, sales taxes formed only 9.3 per cent of tax revenues. Since then, however, the widening of the sales tax net has increased its share to 17 per cent of total tax revenue in 1994-5 (*Economic Survey* 1996, p.139).

Sales taxes are imposed on imported as well as domestically produced goods. At present, sales taxes are collected at the port of entry in the case of imports, and at the factory gate in the case of domestic production. In other words, sales taxes have simply become a device for enhancing tariffs on imports and excise duty on domestic output. Nevertheless, since sales taxes form a major part of the divisible pool, they assume special significance. Higher proceeds of sales taxes would place more resources with the provinces, and thus enable enhanced budgetary allocations for the social sector.

Sales taxes can be used as major revenue instruments. This is unlike tariffs, which serve a protective purpose, or excise duties, which can only help curb consumption. Therefore, there is an argument for broadening the coverage of sales taxes to all commodities (both domestic and imported), except those where there are strong equity considerations for not doing so—e.g. food and medicines. This argument, however, has to be weighed against the empirical evidence that the imposition of sales taxes during the last three to four years has placed a disproportionate burden on the poor. Therefore, the broadening of sales taxes must be accompanied with adjustments based on the consumption pattern of the poor.

2.4. Excise Duty

Only a very limited number of products are subject to excise duties; seven products account for as much as 85 per cent of the excise tax revenue. Since the basic objective of excise duty is to curtail the consumption of certain products, they should not be used primarily for revenue purposes. Moreover, since it is widely known that excisable commodities are being smuggled into the country in large quantities, a tough campaign against smuggling can raise revenues without the enhancement of rates. The campaign against imported cigarettes can be emulated in the case of other products for a substantive increase in revenues. The loss of revenue due to the smuggling of cigarettes alone is estimated to be more than Rs 5 billion.

2.5. User Charges

One of the main conditionalities under the Structural Adjustment and Stabilization Programmes has been the introduction of user charges. The argument is that the cost of services should be passed on to the beneficiaries. However, since this would lead to the erosion of real incomes of the poor, the government should be selective in the imposition of user charges. For example, primary education should not be in the net of user charges, although university education could be fully charged, subject to the provision of scholarships for the poor. Full cost recovery of social services assumes that there are no differentials in social and private profitability. When differences do exist—and they do in the case of social service—full cost recovery is sub-optimal.

The introduction of user charges presupposes complete revamping of the existing delivery systems, from centralized, supply-oriented structures to demand-oriented structures. Alternatively, services could be provided by the private sector or through community participation. Private sector provision would be possible, however, only if the activity is profitable—in other words, if providers can at least recover their full costs. This would depend on the nature of the service as well as on the underlying institutional arrangements.

Table 5.3 : Effective rate of import duty on important products (percentages)

	Share in Duty-Free Imports		Share of Duty-Free Imports in Total Imports		Average Rate of Duty			
					Including Duty-Free		Excluding Duty-Free	
Commodity Group	1987-8	1988-9	1987-8	1988-9	1987-8	1988-9	1987-8	1988-9
Tea, Coffee, etc.	0.1	0.1	0.83	1.68	32.00	31.51	32.00	32.00
Edible Oil	1.3	2.4	7.25	11.14	43.00	29.45	41.00	33.00
Sugar	0.1	0.0	2.37	2.47	92.00	88.74	104.00	91.00
POL Products	18.7	17.0	95.33	4.29	6.00	7.30	9.00	13.00
Chemicals	15.2	13.3	69.38	61.76	14.00	16.80	39.00	44.00
Fertilizer	12.2	8.3	100.00	100.00	–	–	–	–
Dyes, Paints etc.	0.4	0.1	10.71	2.79	44.00	53.39	52.00	55.00
Plastic Resins etc.	0.3	1.7	3.16	14.80	52.00	30.58	68.00	36.00
Rubber Products	1.0	1.5	26.57	41.12	33.00	32.71	49.00	56.00
Paper and Wood Pulp	1.2	1.6	15.67	26.63	20.00	26.63	31.00	36.00
Yarn and Fabrics	1.8	2.9	11.87	26.31	26.00	22.43	50.00	30.00
Iron and Steel	2.0	4.0	11.57	20.95	38.00	33.37	48.00	42.00
Metals other than Gold	0.5	0.7	8.02	14.05	15.00	22.50	26.00	26.00
Machinery	19.9	20.8	32.91	37.19	16.00	21.38	30.00	34.00
Vehicles	4.5	4.2	23.62	24.37	43.00	37.32	53.00	49.00
Sub-total	79.2	78.5	35.09	34.10	25.00	22.52	40.00	34.00
Others	20.8	21.5	45.34	62.94	27.00	21.59	65.00	58.00
Grand Total	100.0	100.0	38.53	37.82	25.00	22.40	42.00	36.00

Source : Central Board of Revenue.

Table 5.4 : GNP and population growth rates

Years			*Growth Rates*		*Population Growth (%)*	
	GNP (Rs million)	Per Capita GNP (Rs)	GNP (per cent)	Per Capita GNP (per cent)	Population (million)	Population (million)
			(1959-60 Constant Factor Cost)			
1959-60	16,803	373.0	6.5*	3.7	45.03	
1964-5	23,299	450.1			51.76	2.8
1969-70	32,339	542.0			59.70	
1974-5	40,188	574.0			69.98	
1976-7	43,696	588.0	5.0	1.9	74.33	3.1
1977-8	48,354	631.0			76.60	
1979-80	54,888	675.0			81.36	
1984-5	75,586	798.0	6.1	3.0	94.73	3.0
1987-8	88,887	856.0			103.82	
			(1980-1 Constant Factor Cost)			
1987-8	402,516	3,877.0			103.82	
1990-1	458,845	4,033.0	4.4	1.3	114.00	3.1
1991-2	485,362	4,137.0			117.00	
1992-3	495,059	4,097.0			121.00	
1993-4	514,826	4,136.8	3.9	3.1	124.45	3.0
1994-5R	540,499	4,222.3			128.01	

Source: *Economic Surveys*, various years.

Notes: * = The years for which growth rates are presented represent terminal years. The base year is the year for which the earlier growth rate was reported or for which no growth rate was reported e.g., 6.5 is the growth rate for the period 1959-60 to 1964-5.

R = Revised estimate.

The government's inability to raise revenues has played a big role in the change of policy regime in Pakistan as will become clear in the next section.

3. POLICY REGIMES AND THE STRUCTURAL ADJUSTMENT PROGRAMME: 1978-9 to 1987-8.

The decades of the 1970s and the 1980s provide an example of two contrasting economic regimes, the Keynesian-populist (KP) regime of Zulfikar Ali Bhutto (1971-1977), and the structural adjustment (SA) regimes that followed—including the regimes of Ziaul Haq (1977-1988), Nawaz Sharif (1990-1993; 1997-) and Benazir Bhutto (1988-1990 and 1993-1996). The KP regime broke with the past pattern of economic policy-making, and oriented it specifically towards social development and poverty alleviation. However, the SA regimes revoked the populist stance and introduced various shifts away from populist goals.

Pakistan's growth and distribution policies since independence in 1947, and particularly over the decade of the 1960s, had a distinctly inegalitarian flavour. Although growth was high, it was widely believed to have been accompanied by increasing regional and functional inequalities, a growing concentration of wealth and stagnation of real wages (Amjad, 1982). The KP regime is believed to have been brought in mainly because of an expanding and violent reaction to the perceived injustice of the economic policies of the 1960s.

The KP regime transformed the private and concentrated structure of the economy into a mixed economy through two populist reforms: nationalization of manufacturing assets and land reforms. Approximately 30 per cent of manufacturing assets and all banking and insurance units were nationalized, and a new sub-sector of long gestation capital goods was begun within the public sector.[7] Land reforms halved ownership ceilings to 300 unirrigated acres and 200 irrigated acres; however, only 2 per cent of the total area was redistributed (Herring 1983).

The impact of these asset redistribution policies on growth was disastrous. Table 5.4 shows that real annual growth of GNP per capita declined from 3.7 per cent in the 1960s to only 1.9 during the KP period. While a slowdown in agricultural growth was partly responsible, private industrial expansion also slowed down so that GDP growth rate was only 1.3 per cent above the population growth rate of 3.1 per cent.

There was also a massive expansion in state expenditure on public sector investment, employment creation, consumption and production subsidies, and social services. The KP regime inherited a balanced budget and plunged it irrevocably into Keynesian deficits, reaching 9 per cent of GDP by the end of its tenure as shown in Table 5.5.

A significant component of the additional expenditure was for development. The share of development in total expenditure rose from a negligible level to 38 per cent as indicated in Table 5.6.

Other areas of increased expenditures were subsidies, social services, and, given the increasing deficit, debt servicing. A new experiment in the form of state subsidies was introduced, which rose to 8 per cent of total expenditure by 1978-9. Similarly, expenditure on social services rose from negligible levels to 5 per cent of public spending in 1977-8. As a result of the deficit financing, debt servicing expanded on the exchequer.

Two-thirds of the state subsidies were for production. These included agricultural input subsidies and a subsidy on petroleum to cushion the oil shock. Besides this, subsidies on wheat and sugar to support urban consumption were introduced along with a national rationing system. As a result of this shift in policy, inflation increased to double digits for the first time in the country's history, public debt expanded quickly, and the current account deficit rose to above US $ 1 billion in 1984-5 and reached US$ 3.6 billion in 1992-3.

The KP regime left behind a growth crisis as well as fiscal and payments crises. The successor military regime called in the IMF for assistance in 1978-9. Since then, some form of conditionality in return for loans has become a permanent feature of the economic landscape of the country. Pakistan and the IMF signed a Trust Fund Loan for 1979-80. In the following year, Pakistan negotiated a 3-year Extended Fund Facility (EFF) for 1980-1 to 1982-3. In 1983-4 the IMF offered another Structural Adjustment Loan (SAL) which the government refused, presumably to avoid conditionality, but also because its foreign exchange reserves had recovered to over $2 billion. As an alternative, a series of sectoral loans—for agriculture, industry, energy, and the financial sectors—were negotiated with the World Bank (WB). Each loan was conditional upon reforms in the specific sector with no cross conditionality across sectors.

In November 1988, the government signed another agreement with the IMF just before the election of a democratic regime. The World Bank (WB) and the Asian Development Bank (ADB) loans were also secured against IMF conditionality. The agreements were subsequently ratified by succeeding elected regimes.

Table 5.5 : Budget deficits and deficit financing (Rs million)

Years	Revenues	Expenditure		Deficit/	Financing			Deficit
		Total	Development	Surplus	External	Domestic		% of
						Non-Bank	Bank	GDP
1959-60	1,978	1,847	15	131	–	–	–	–
1969-70	6,665	5,109	4	1,556	–	–	–	–
1971-2	6,926	7,165	117	–236	–	–	–	0.5
1975-6	19,264	32,329	13,404	–12,480	6,769	1,810	3,901	9.5
1976-7	21,910	35,171	15,958	–12,838	5,860	969	6,009	8.6
1977-8	26,482	40,898	15,353	–13,893	6,129	2,817	4,947	8.0
1978-9	30,704	48,994	18,494	–17,315	6,711	2,108	8,502	8.9
1979-80	38,502	54,629	19,082	–14,663	6,951	1,407	6,305	6.3
1980-1	47,002	63,639	23,321	–14,618	6,977	5,286	2,355	5.3
1981-2	51,937	71,013	24,463	–17,174	5,345	6,313	5,516	5.3
1982-3	59,181	87,121	27,435	–25,654	5,162	14,368	6,124	7.1
1983-4	72,290	100,002	36,591	–25,174	5,001	12,280	7,866	6.0
1984-5	77,403	116,819	33,050	–36,777	5,169	12,873	18,735	7.8
1985-6	89,877	134,463	39,777	–41,644	8,584	26,962	6,098	9.1
1986-7	103,873	152,402	36,160	–46,710	8,424	27,371	10,915	8.2
1987-8	117,021	180,373	46,728	–57,563	12,691	30,931	13,941	8.5
1988-9	139,108	201,176	48,110	–56,879	18,195	37,865	819	7.4
1989-90	158,805	221,645	56,050	–56,060	24,592	29,581	3,534	6.5
1990-1	163,857	260,970	65,293	–89,193	21,149	23,724	43,368	8.7
1991-2	216,570	321,474	91,354	–89,970	18,022	515	72,464	7.4
1992-3	239,528	348,654	76,196	–107,525	24,340	19,972	63,219	8.0
1993-4	270,734	364,913	71,453	–92,179	25,210	55,048	12,507	5.9
1994-5R	319,875	428,280	81,900	–103,405	30,600	47,626	18,551	5.5

Source: *Economic Surveys*, various years.
Note : R = Revised estimate.

Table 5.6 : Percentage distribution of total government expenditure

Years	Total Expenditure	Development Expenditure	As % of Current Expenditure						
			Total	Defence	Interest	Subsidies	General Administration	Social Services	Other
1975-6	100	38.3	61.8	25.1	7.6	9.2	4.5	1.3	14.1
1976-7	100	42.8	57.3	23.1	7.9	6.9	4.5	1.6	13.3
1977-8	100	37.5	62.5	23.7	8.2	8.0	5.7	5.2	25.5
1978-9	100	37.7	62.3	21.0	8.1	12.3	5.4	2.0	12.0
1979-80	100	34.9	65.1	23.2	8.8	12.0	5.5	2.2	11.8
1980-1	100	37.3	62.7	24.5	9.4	7.7	4.6	2.6	14.4
1981-2	100	34.7	65.3	26.2	10.7	6.1	4.8	3.7	16.4
1982-3	100	33.7	66.3	26.7	12.6	5.5	4.7	2.4	16.6
1983-4	100	28.0	72.0	26.8	14.1	6.1	6.1	2.8	17.6
1984-5	100	28.3	71.7	27.3	14.1	5.9	5.6	9.0	11.1
1985-6	100	29.6	70.4	26.5	14.7	6.0	5.5	9.2	10.3
1986-7	100	23.7	76.3	27.1	15.7	4.5	6.8	10.1	12.8
1987-8	100	25.9	74.1	26.1	18.4	5.6	4.7	9.6	10.9
1988-9	100	23.9	76.1	25.4	18.9	7.8	5.1	9.6	10.5
1989-90	100	25.1	74.9	26.5	20.7	4.6	4.7	9.0	8.9
1990-1	100	25.6	74.4	25.7	22.3	4.4	4.8	8.1	9.9
1991-2	100	26.4	73.6	24.0	20.2	3.6	5.3	14.1	6.8
1992-3	100	21.9	78.0	28.4	21.1	2.3	6.1	15.4	4.5
1993-4	100	19.6	80.4	25.2	29.9	1.5	7.0	15.5	6.5
1994-5R	100	19.1	80.9	23.8	23.8	1.5	7.6	16.5	8.2

Source: *Economic Survey*, various years.
Note : R = Revised estimate.

Table 5.7 : Current account balance, remittances, and reserves (US$ million)

Years	Net Current Account Balance	Remittances	SBP Reserves	Merchandise	
				Exports	Imports
1969-70	–469	101	229	829	1,399
1970-1	–663	64	287	–	–
1971-2	–443	93	199	–	–
1972-3	–131	145	285	–	–
1973-4	–549	150	463	–	–
1974-5	–1,168	212	403	978	2,114
1975-6	–948	334	486	–	–
1976-7	–1,051	578	614	–	–
1977-8	–605	1,156	431	1,283	2,751
1978-9	–1,114	1,397	1,010	–	–
1979-80	–1,140	1,748	904	2,341	4,857
1980-1	–1037	2,095	2,019	2,799	5,563
1981-2	–1,534	2,225	1,866	2,319	5,769
1982-3	–517	2,886	1,460	2,669	5,616
1983-4	–997	2,737	2,758	2,457	6,009
1984-5	–1,680	2,446	2,489	–	–
1985-6	–1,236	2,595	1,190	2,942	5,984
1986-7	–719	2,279	1,638	3,498	5,792
1987-8	–1,682	2,013	1,784	4,362	6,919
1988-9	–1,934	1,897	1,320	4,364	7,202
1989-90	–1,891	1,942	1,227	4,926	7,411
1990-1	–2,171	1,840	1,402	5,902	8,385
1991-2	–1,346	1,468	–	6,762	8,998
1992-3	–3,688	1,562	–	6,782	10,049
1993-4	–1,965	1,886	–	6,685	–8,685

Source: *Economic Surveys*, various years.

A comparison of economic performance under the two regimes gives some paradoxical results. While growth has been higher under SA than under KP (Table 5.4), no enduring success was achieved in reducing the twin deficits until 1990-1.[8] Between 1979-80 and 1982-3, the budget deficit dropped from 9 per cent to 5 per cent of GDP, but rose again to 8.5 per cent by 1987-8, as indicated in Table 5.5. At the same time, apart for a few good years, the net current account deficit has remained above $1 billion throughout the decade, as evident from Table 5.7. Foreign exchange reserves also increased initially to $2.7 billion in 1983-4, but halved by 1990-1. The main tool for domestic adjustment was a decrease in expenditure, because revenues had not risen as a per cent of GNP. The major source of decrease in expenditure was development expenditure, which declined from its peak of 43 per cent of total outlays in 1976-7 to 26 per cent in 1990-1.

Another important reversal has been the cutback in subsidies, which peaked at 12.3 per cent of total expenditure in 1978-9 and then declined steadily to 1.5 per cent in 1994-5 (Table 5.6). Expenditure on social services also declined dramatically from 5 per cent of the total in 1977-8 to 2 per cent in 1978-9, and remained between 2 and 3 per cent in the following five years. In 1984-5, however, the WB sectoral conditionality itself directed investment into social services, increasing the allocation to 9 per cent in 1984-5, the level at which it remained until 1990-1, when it subsequently shot up to 16.5 per cent in 1993-4. Conversely, the share of defence in total expenditure rose from a trough of 21 per cent in 1978-9 to approximately 28 per cent by 1992-3, and then declined to 24 per cent in 1994-5 (Table 5.6). General administration expenditure at over 7 per cent in 1993-4 and 1994-5 was unusually high.

4. THE STRUCTURAL ADJUSTMENT PROGRAMME 1988-1994

4.1. The Fiscal Crisis in the Late 1980s.

After the first period of structural adjustment (EFF) in the early 1980s, the economy did well for a few years. The annual GDP growth rate rose to 6.4 per cent by 1987-8, the current account deficit fell below 4 per cent of GDP in the first half of the 1980s, presumably because of flexible exchange rate management and import reforms. However, the budget deficit was about 8 per cent of GDP (Table 5.8). Even so, there was a lid on monetary expansion, and inflation remained in single digits. However, a series of shocks disturbed this equilibrium.

The crisis was triggered in 1984-5 by a bad cotton crop. Cotton exports plummeted, dropping revenues with them. Remittances, having peaked in the first half of the decade, now dropped as Table 5.7 shows. There was an external current account deficit of $1.7 billion, which resulted in a 60 per cent decline in the foreign exchange reserves to $1.2 billion.

By 1987-8, the macroeconomic picture had worsened. The external current account deficit was still high at 4.4 per cent as Table 5.8 shows, foreign exchange reserves had stagnated at $1.8 billion, the external debt servicing burden had risen from 21 per cent of receipts (in 1984-5) to 39 per cent, and the fiscal deficit had risen to 8.5 per cent of GDP (Table 5.5). The rising fiscal deficit can be accounted for by stagnant revenues which stayed around 17 per cent of GDP, while expenditures rose from 23 to 27 per cent of GDP between 1980-81 and 1987-8, as can be seen in Table 5.8.

4.2. The Adjustment Programme 1988-9 to 1994-5

Towards the end of 1987-8, when elections were pending and the military regime was on its way out, the government signed a three-year agreement with the IMF, for a structural adjustment facility of $ 2.1 billion, to be accompanied by a package of structural reforms. The terms of the agreement were later ratified by successor governments after some renegotiations. The assistance was to be divided between the IMF's general purpose loan of $ 0.8 billion, the WB's $ 0.5 billion sectoral loans, and the ADB's, 0.4 billion sectoral loans.

Pakistan signed a Stabilization Programme with the IMF and a Structural Adjustment Programme with the World Bank in 1988, which, besides other conditionalities, called for a substantial reduction in the budgetary deficit from 8.5 to 4.8 per cent of GDP over the period 1987-8 to 1990-1. To meet these objectives, the growth of public expenditures was to be contained below the growth of GDP, and the revenue-GDP ratio raised to 20 per cent by 1990-1. The resource mobilization measures proposed by the programme included the introduction of a generalized system of sales taxes, withdrawal of exemptions from the custom duties, imposition of user charges, and improvement in tax administration.

The objectives of the 1991-4 structural adjustment programme were set down in a memorandum at the time of the agreement. The broad objectives to be achieved over a three-year period, have largely remained consistent with the earlier agreement. They are: an annual growth rate of GDP of at least 5.5 per cent of GDP; increase in foreign exchange reserves to at least four weeks of imports; decrease in the external debt ratio from 31 to 25 per cent of GDP; decrease in fiscal deficit eventually from 8.5 to 4.5 per cent of GDP; increase in domestic savings from 9 to 10 per cent of GDP; increase in gross investment from 16 to 19 per

Table 5.8 : Internal and external imbalance (percentages)

Key Indicators	1980-1	1984-5	1985-6	1986-7	1987-8	1988-9	1989-90	1990-1	1991-2	1992-3	1993-4	1994-5[R]
GDP Growth Rate	6.4	8.7	6.4	5.8	6.4	4.8	4.6	4.6	7.7	2.3	4.5	4.4
Debt Service/Receipts	4.7	20.9	27.2	34.6	39.1	41.3	42.8	44.8	44.5	46.3	49.7	–
Debt Service/GDP	3.1	4.0	5.4	4.2	4.8	5.1	5.7	4.9	8.0	8.3	9.2	8.4
Gross I/GDP	17.2	16.5	17.0	17.5	16.5	17.3	17.3	17.4	18.6	19.1	17.9	17.2
Domestic S/GDP	6.3	4.7	7.0	10.5	9.2	10.1	13.0	14.4	–	–	17.4	16.4
Revenue/GDP	17.3	16.6	16.9	18.1	17.3	18.1	18.6	16.1	17.9	17.9	17.2	17.2
Expenditure/GDP	22.5	24.2	24.6	26.6	26.7	26.1	25.9	25.6	26.5	26.0	23.2	23.0
Deficit/GDP	5.2	–7.8	8.1	8.2	–8.5	7.4	6.6	8.7	7.4	8.0	5.9	5.5
Exports/GDP	10.5	8.0	9.6	11.1	11.6	11.6	12.4	13.5	14.2	13.2	13.1	13.5
Imports/GDP	19.3	19.0	17.9	16.1	16.7	17.6	17.4	16.7	19.0	19.2	16.5	17.2
Current Account/GDP	–3.7	–5.4	–3.9	–2.2	–4.4	–4.8	–4.7	–4.8	–2.8	–7.1	–3.9	–4.0
Debt/GDP	20.9	–	–	–	43.4	43.0	43.3	44.6	43.3	45.3	44.6	42.0

Source : *Economic Surveys*, various years.
Note : R = Revised estimate.

cent of GDP; reduction in domestic borrowing for budgetary support to 4 per cent of GDP, bank borrowing of no more than 1 per cent of GDP; decreased reliance on taxes on international trade, especially import duties; and an expansion of the tax base.

The situation in 1994-5 was more difficult than that in 1988. The Gulf War led to a drop in remittances from overseas Pakistanis to $1.4 billion, while the disruption of trade with Middle Eastern countries jacked up the total loss in foreign exchange earnings for this reason to approximately $ 2 billion. In addition, political differences led to the winding down and termination of bilateral aid from the USA, which made the generation of additional revenues more important.

4.3. Revenue measures

Between 1988-9 and 1991-2 the government took a number of initiatives to raise annual public revenues by 2.7 per cent of GDP (Table 5.9). This effort needs to be examined to assess the actual increase in revenues as well as the incidence of increase in taxes by income groups.

Table 5.9 : Resource mobilization: 1988-9 to 1991-2
(New Tax Measures)

Years	Proposed Additional Taxation	
	Rs million	% of GDP
1988-9	7,695	1.0
1989-90	6,689	0.8
1990-1	7,679	0.8
1991-2	13,923	1.2
1993-4	21,655	1.5
1994-5	45,500	2.7

Source : Central Board of Revenue.

The revenue impact of the new measures is presented in Table 5.10, which compares the actual increase in revenues with the projected growth of revenues in the absence of new measures. This exercise will make it possible to determine the implied actual increase due to the new measures. It is then compared with the increase expected at the time of the budget announcement.

We estimated the growth of revenues on the assumption of a tax elasticity with respect to GDP of 0.81.[9] This calculation shows that the new taxation measures increased revenues by only 1.4 per cent of GDP compared to the envisaged increase of 2.7 per cent (see Table 5.9). The budgetary announcement of the additional measures seems to have been exaggerated. Accordingly, the need for more and effective resource mobilization remained.

Table 5.10 : Envisaged increase in tax revenues: 1988-89 to 1991-92 (Rs million)

Years	Actual Increase (1)	Increase Projected in Absence of New Measures (2)	Increase Implied Due to New Measures (3) = (1) - (2)
1988-9	16,882	10,576	6,306
1989-90	9,097	10,764	–708
1990-1	10,205	17,444	–7,239
1991-2	34,668	18,175	16,493

Source : *Economic Survey 1995-96*, Statistical Appendix (1996, p. 139).

The resource mobilization effort between 1988-89 and 1991-92 focussed mainly on indirect taxes which were to generate 82.5 per cent of the additional revenues.[10] Within indirect taxes, the focus in the first two years was on the sales taxes, and in the last two years on the excise and custom duties as shown in Table 5.11.

Table 5.11 : Increase in revenues envisaged at the time of the budget through additional tax measures (Rs million)

		Additional Revenues from:			
Years	Total	Income taxes	Custom duties	Excise duties	Sales taxes
1988-9	7,695	1,124	575	2,800	3,466
1989-90	6,689	1,015	2,190	24	3,460
1990-1	7,679	828	4,196	2,116	540
1991-2	13,923	3,335	5,255	4,650	683

Source: Central Board of Revenue

The other main proposal was to increase resources through increases in user charges and in the prices of electricity, gas, and petrol. This is also the main instrument of energy policy. Petrol and gas prices were to be raised to border levels, and the declining trend in the real price of electricity was to be reversed. A major problem with this policy is its regressive impact on incomes (see chapter 4). Another problem may be additional inflationary pressures because of the increase in the cost of production. Table 5.12 reports the price trends for domestic electricity.

Table 5.12 shows that price increases over the mid-1980s were very low. From 1988 onwards, there have been much larger annual increases in the rate structure. At the lowest rate of electricity use, there has been a total increase of about 61 per cent between 1988 and 1994 and there were two further major increases in 1995.

Table 5.12 : Domestic electricity prices

Year	Minimum < 50 units Rs/KW	% annual increase	Minimum > 600 units Rs/KWH	% annual increase
1980	0.34	–	0.50	–
1985	0.37	1.7	0.77	8.6
1987	0.39	2.6	0.89	7.2
1988	0.49	22.8	0.99	10.6
1989	0.51	4.0	1.24	22.5
1990	0.56	5.7	1.24	0.0
1991	0.61	12.2	2.17	56.0
1993	0.76	11.0	2.47	6.5
1994	0.80	5.1	3.18	25.3

Source : ENERCON

Again for gas, Table 5.13 shows that the mid-1980s had negligible increases in prices. But from 1987 onwards, there have been four upward jumps. At the lowest rate of gas consumption, there has been a total increase of about 66 per cent.

Table 5.13 : Domestic gas prices

Year	Slab 1 Rs per 1,000 m^3	Slab 1 % annual increase	Slab 2 Rs per 1,000 m^3	Slab 2 % annual increase
1982	14.0	–	21.0	–
1983	16.0	13.4	24.0	13.4
1984	18.0	11.8	27.0	11.8
1985	4.0	0.0	27.0	0.0
1986	18.0	0.0	27.0	0.0
1987	22.5	22.3	27.0	0.0
1991	31.0	32.0	46.5	54.4
1993	35.7	7.1	55.8	9.1
1994	37.5	4.9	63.3	12.6

Source : ENERCON

Petrol prices displayed the same trend as shown in Table 5.14. The mid-1980s had no increases in petrol prices, but between 1989-90 and 1994-5, they increased by over 75 per cent.

The price of kerosene, which is of critical importance as fuel for the poor, has risen in tandem with petrol prices, as shown in Table 5.15. The price has increased in the last four years by 71 per cent.

Table 5.14 : Domestic petrol prices

Year	Price Rs/Litre	Increase %
1980-1	4.83	–
1985-6	7.14	7.8
1987-8	7.16	0.1
1988-9	7.16	0.0
1989-90	7.16	0.0
1990-1	10.16	35.0
1991-2	11.85	15.4
1993-4	13.13	10.3
1994-5	15.30	14.6

Source: *Economic Surveys*, various years.

This increase in energy prices, with its effect on basic necessities, partly explains the increase in poverty between 1987-8 and 1990-1, documented in Chapter 4. The SA policies followed in SAL2 in the late, 1980s and early, 1990s, have therefore been qualitatively different from the polices of SAL1 of the late 1970s and early, 1980s. SAL1 concentrated on demand management policies of expenditure reduction, which had an adverse impact on the access of the poor to public services, but did not increase poverty as measured by headcounts. SAL2 concentrated on supply response policies and on revenue generation by increasing user charges which have directly increased the burden on the poor.

Table 5.15 : Domestic kerosene oil prices

Year	Prices Rs/Litre	Increase %
1980-1	3.14	–
1986-7	3.66	16.56
1987-8	3.64	0.33
1988-9	3.66	–0.55
1989-90	3.78	0.55
1990-1	5.14	3.28
1991-2	5.80	–35.98
1992-3	5.96	12.84
1993-4	7.10	19.12
1994-5	7.30	2.82

Source: *Economic Survey 1995-96*, Statistical Appendix (1996, p. 152).

Another main instrument of revenue generation has been the introduction and expansion of a General Sales Tax (GST). This GST is likely to be regressive in its incidence, as indicated in chapter 4.

4.4. Expenditure

The main brunt of expenditure cuts has not been on social services, as in the early 1980s. In Table 5.6, we showed that development expenditure has been reduced from the 30 per cent level in the mid-1980s, and has now evened out at about 29 per cent. There is to be a two-pronged strategy. Primary education, basic health, water supply, and sanitation expenditures are to be increased as part of the Social Action Plan which is accompanying the SALs (see chapter 6). These are commendable goals. However, we will argue further on in this study that the quality of education and health care deserves as much priority as their simple extension.

In current expenditure, the main cuts have been in subsidies. Table 5.6 shows these to have been reduced by more than half from about 8 per cent in 1988-9 to 1.5 per cent 1994-5. Table 5.16 shows that, in consumption subsidies, the cuts have come in wheat and edible oils, which are a large portion of the consumption basket of the poor.

In absolute terms, subsidies rose until 1988-9, and have declined steadily since then. The subsidy to wheat and edible oil has also declined dramatically to 43 and 5 per cent compared to the peak of 61 per cent and 24 per cent in 1989-90 and 1983-4, respectively.

The main policy instrument of the SA economic philosophy for industry is privatization. There is now a considerable debate and literature on this. Management rather than ownership appears to be more critical for profitability (see Vicker and Yaroow 1988). Also, if subsidies to public industry are to be cut, then by the same logic, subsidies to private industry should also be cut. The 1997 Nawaz Sharif regime appears to be experimenting with restoration of management incentives in some public sector corporations for energy generation.

4.5. The external sector

The government has liberalized the exchange rate regime by permitting foreign currency accounts and the holding of foreign assets by citizens and by issuing dollar bearer certificates with a spread of a quarter per cent over LIBOR. In addition, it continues to maintain a managed float exchange rate system.

Table 5.16 : Subsidies

Year	M.Rs Total	Distribution of total subsidies (percentages)								
		Wheat	Sugar	Edible Oil	Fertilizer	Tubewell	Pesticide	Exports	Petrol	Other
1972-3	0	–	–	–	–	–	–	–	–	–
1973-4	2,243	–	–	–	–	–	–	–	–	–
1975-6	2,981	39.7	–	–	20.4	0.8	12.8	–	8.3	18.0
1976-7	2,428	45.0	0.2	–	15.7	2.0	20.0	–	0.2	16.9
1977-8	3,290	49.1	0.6	–	18.8	0.6	15.9	–	12.2	2.8
1978-9	6,030	41.7	0.2	9.6	28.1	0.4	4.4	8.3	7.0	0.3
1979-80	6,544	25.0	0.3	12.5	34.9	0.3	3.1	7.8	6.8	8.9
1980-1	5,378	19.6	1.5	10.8	45.7	0.4	–	13.1	8.4	0.5
1981-2	4,333	30.1	–	–	41.4	0.6	–	26.6	–	1.3
1982-3	4,779	23.5	0.8	–	40.8	0.5	–	28.9	–	5.5
1983-4	6,134	20.7	0.2	24.2	23.9	–	–	27.6	–	3.4
1984-5	6,861	18.7	–	21.6	21.8	–	–	24.7	–	13.2
1985-6	8,130	47.0	–	–	29.6	0.2	–	22.5	–	0.1
1986-7	6,933	40.2	–	16.2	–	–	–	22.2	–	1.1
1987-8	10,130	38.7	–	21.4	0.1	–	–	19.2	–	7.5
1988-9	15,700	46.4	–	18.5	15.4	–	–	–	–	1.6
1989-90	12,315	61.0	–	9.5	10.4	–	–	–	–	7.7
1990-1	10,183	37.0	–	13.2	12.3	–	–	2.9	–	12.5
1991-2	10,653	45.2	–	1.8	11.5	–	–	1.3	–	–
1992-3	8,215	56.8	–	–	9.9	–	–	6.2	–	–
1993-4	8,756	43.2	–	5.2	9.2	–	–	9.1	–	–

Source: *Economic Surveys*, various years.

In Pakistan, the main obstacle to private foreign inflows is not currency restrictions, however irksome these may have been, but the absence of a secure base for large-scale private capital. As long as this complex but necessary condition is not met, private inflows will be constrained. If inflows are not forthcoming at a higher rate than before, exchange rate liberalization can only lead to increased debt as in the case of Latin American countries in the late 1970s (see Banuri, ed. 1991). Also, Khan and Aftab (1996) show that, based on the past experience of the Pakistani economy, exchange rate liberalization is not likely to be an effective tool in improving the trade balance.

The second policy instrument in the external sector is trade liberalization. It has proceeded on three fronts. Import license requirements have been reduced or cut for a number of commodities; maximum tariff barriers have been reduced from 125 to 45 per cent in the 1997 tax reform; and non-tariff barriers are being dismantled. This raises concerns in the business sector about de-industrialization. The PPP government (1993-6) has refused to reduce the maximum tariff rate to 45 per cent in the 1995-6 budget as called for in the SA conditionalities and had thus provoked the ire of the IMF.

4.6. The impact

The reform package carried out so far indicates a qualitatively different impact from that experienced in the early 1980s. During the first experience of SA, expenditures on social services were the primary targets. Moreover, there were other factors accompanying SA. Principally, Gulf migration and remittances increased domestic wage rates. As a net result, poverty in terms of income and expenditure decreased. However, poverty in terms of public access to social services increased.

During the second round of SA, the government has actually increased social sector allocations under the Social Action Programme. It has instead relied on increasing user charges and imposing sales taxes for revenue enhancement. The increase in user charges, sales taxes, and cuts in subsidies, that were critical to the consumption pattern of the poor, will all increase poverty in terms of income and expenditure. In a paper examining the impact of structural adjustment on labour and the poor, Khan and Aftab (1995) argue that public sector employment has decreased while public sector wages have been frozen. Also, overall unemployment in occupations with a high incidence of the poor has increased dramatically. This time round, the mitigating impact of Gulf remittances has also dropped significantly. On balance then, apart from greater social sector expenditure that is designed to make the poor better market players, the direct impact of the second round of SA on the poor appears to have been very harsh.

5. SUMMARY AND CONCLUSIONS

This chapter on economic policy had two objectives: first, to establish constitutional and fiscal parameters within which economic policy has come to be formulated, second, to examine and characterize the policy regimes of the last two and a half decades. The policy regime of the 1970s is seen to be Keynesian Populist (KP) in character while the regimes of the 1980s and onwards have been based on Structural Adjustment Programmes (SA) signed with the IMF and World Bank. We have contrasted the impact of these two kinds of regimes on growth and welfare.

The constitutional parameters result in the expenditure share of the federal government in total expenditure at about 75 per cent; the expenditure shares of the provincial government at about 20 per cent; and those of local government at about 5 per cent. An even greater contrast is that the major revenue heads are allocated overwhelmingly to the federal government, giving it a revenue share of about 95 per cent, and the share of the provincial government of about 5 per cent. This creates a disincentive for provincial fiscal responsibility and, not surprisingly, provincial governments have run large deficits. Provinces may also lack interest in federal development grants, since they imply future provincial recurring expenditure commitments. Further, since the level of provincial expenditure and deficit is not guaranteed by the National Finance Commission's sporadic awards, provincial programmes are jeopardized. Local governments run small surpluses because of very low expenditures. Expenditures in fact need to be much higher to improve scarce social services like water, sanitation, health, and education. These constitutional parameters militate against provincial and local responsibility and decentralized delivery systems.

Pakistan's tax structure, rather than being transformed by policy, has in fact constrained it. The tax structure is characterized by a large (two-thirds) share of indirect taxes, a high rate structure with a narrow base, and a low tax elasticity with respect to GDP. Revenue as a share of GDP has remained consistently below 20 per cent. These tax constraints are attributed to widespread exemptions and avoidance. The most notable exemption, which lowers the share of direct income and wealth taxes, is the recalcitrant agricultural sector. Avoidance results in a narrow tax base of one million individuals filing tax returns. At least another million escape the tax net because of lax tax administration. The major sources of indirect taxes are import tariffs (riddled with exemptions); sales taxes (whose revenue potential is considerable but which are currently structured to be regressive); and excise duties (meant to curtail specific consumption but which are significantly evaded). The 1997 tax reforms have attempted to address some of these problems.

It is within these constitutional and tax parameters that the contrasting KP and SA regimes have been fashioned. The KP regime of the 1970s attempted to change the past inegalitarian policy by significantly increasing the role of the public sector in production and consumption. Populist nationalization of one-third of the large-scale manufacturing sector and the entire financial sector significantly raised public sector commitments and expenditure on production. A significantly enhanced share of the development budget added to public expenditure. Subsidies for production and populist subsidies for consumption of essentials further enhanced public expenditure. This vastly increased share of public expenditure in GDP, relative to a stagnating revenue share, generated a large domestic deficit rising to about 10 per cent of GDP from virtually zero at the beginning of the decade.

Nationalization drove down private investment and growth, while public sector investment raised imports and expanded the external deficit, and drove down foreign exchange reserves. Finally, the large deficits fuelled inflation leading to stagflation. The major causal factor in the failure of the KP regime appears to be that it lacked the revenue base to launch public sector led growth and welfare polices.

The twin deficits and inflation ushered in the SA regimes which are based on IMF conditionality of ESAF loans. Deficit reduction has been based on demand management policies of reducing public expenditures, raising taxes and user charges, and supply response policies of increasing producer prices. Public expenditures have been cut by reducing development expenditure, subsidies for production and consumption, and initially, the social service recurrent budget shares. Cuts in subsidies, user charges, and supply response policies raised the price structure of the economy with an adverse impact on the poor. Growth picked up in the 1980s and early 1990s, as did foreign exchange reserves, although both have been subject to exogenous fluctuations brought on, for example, by floods, pests, and oil price increases. However, the revenue share has almost stagnated below 20 per cent of the GDP, which has implied that the deficit has fluctuated with good and bad years but stayed high on an absolute level. The high deficit has kept inflation stubbornly in double digits. Meanwhile, a belated social sector catch-up scheme, SAP, has raised public sector expenditures. Again, the SA regime is foundering on its inability to raise revenues, and consequently, to reduce deficits and inflation and to deliver welfare.

NOTES

1. Until the 1991 award, the provinces received a share of income tax, export duty on cotton, excise, and royalty on natural gas, and gift tax.
2. The divisible pool now includes income and corporate taxes, sales taxes, export duty on cotton, and excise duty on tobacco products and sugar.
3. The PIU makes equating lands of differential fertility possible.
4. Hamid, Nabi, and Naseem (1990) estimate that between 1960-1 to 1986-7, the mean total transfer from the agricultural sector was 2.4 per cent of GNP.
5. Estimate by Mahmood (1995). This represents about 0.2 of one per cent of the estimated total annual revenues of Rs 290 billion but 3.1 per cent of the estimated total provincial revenue of Rs 18 billion in 1993-4 (*Economic Survey 1994-95*, Statistical appendix, p.131). Reviewing the literature, Ul Haque (1993, p.66) points out that yield estimates from a direct income tax on agriculture vary from Rs 2.5 billion to Rs 6 billion.
6. This is estimated from a common belief that at least 10 per cent of new investment over the last ten years has gone to tax exempt areas.
7. These were primarily light engineering units. The country's largest manufacturing goods sector, textiles, was not touched (Amjad 1982).
8. Feroze (1986) attributes this pick up in growth not to economic policies, but to better weather leading to improvement in agriculture and the cotton-based industry.
9. Elasticity of tax revenues to GDP has been taken from *Economic Survey 1986-7*. Malik and Saqib (1989) report an elasticity of 0.97.
10. In the first three years, the proportion of indirect taxes in total additional revenues from the new tax measures was as high as 87.8 per cent.

6

Accelerating Human Development in Pakistan

Giovanni Andrea Cornia

INTRODUCTION

Over the past three decades, a number of contributions to economic analysis have focused on human development, human needs, and the 'human factor' in overall development. Most prominent among these were the 'human capital' and the 'basic needs' approaches. In spite of advances made, health, nutrition, and education (as well as other fundamental 'public goods', such as good administration, law and order, participation, and justice) in most countries have remained peripheral to the theory and practice of most academics, policy-makers, and development planners. A number of enduring biases and more contingent factors have been at the base of such neglect.

First, while it is generally accepted that health, nutrition, and particularly education are desirable because of their contribution to the welfare of the population, most conventional economists still do not view them as a *sine qua non* of development. Rather, they see them as a kind of lower-priority 'welfare-oriented consumption' which ought to yield precedence to investment in power, transport, telecommunication, and industrial infrastructure. Though countries such as the Republic of Korea, Taiwan, Costa Rica, China, Chile, Sri Lanka, and Jamaica have represented important exceptions to this rule, the majority of developing nations and today's developed countries during their take-off phase, have in fact, insistently under-invested in human development. In several respects, Pakistan is only an extreme case in a fairly general pattern.[1]

Second, in a number of countries, the lack of real political democracy and justice have inhibited the effective and spontaneous support and participation of communities in the design and execution of social sector activities, thus reducing the effectiveness of already inadequate government interventions.

Third, in the 1980s, the re-establishment of macroeconomic balance prevailed over any other development objective, whether human-focused or not. With governments facing severe fiscal constraints, health, education, and social welfare came to be seen—even more than previously—as luxuries which could be afforded in good times but not in bad times. However, due to donor urging and financial backing, but mainly due to its own corresponding effort, Pakistan's expenditure on social development as a percentage of GNP gradually increased.[2] In Pakistan, and elsewhere in developing countries, when adjustment efforts were at their peak, it started to become clear that the pendulum had swung too far and the neglect of the social sectors was exacting too high a cost in both political and development terms.

1. ARGUMENTS FOR JUST DEVELOPMENT

Four closely interrelated factors may have contributed to the greater awareness in Pakistan and elsewhere, of the role and importance of human capabilities and effective political participation for overall development. First, the large and growing dissonance between economic growth and human resource development is itself a major source of concern. Second, empirical evidence, as well as theoretical reasoning, suggests strong linkages between human development and growth in the short as well as the long run. Third, this is particularly true for an increasingly open economy in the 1990s. And finally, the growing recognition that rapid and sustainable development will be impossible without a substantial improvement in public participation in decision-making.

To start with, there was the stark, unambiguous, and tragic realization that forty years of steady and sustained economic growth (averaging 5.5 per cent a year) and the quadrupling of GNP per capita over the 1950-90 period (see Table 2.1) had brought Pakistan only modest improvements in adult literacy, primary and secondary education, infant mortality, and nutritional status. In certain areas, such as female literacy—key to overall improvement in human welfare—change was negligible. In 1992, there were only 9 countries (out of 173), all of which were much poorer, with female literacy rates as a percentage of male literacy rates lower than those of Pakistan (*HDR* 1994, p.146-7).

Theoretical reasoning as well as empirical results have added to the recognition of the importance of education in general and female education in particular. During the past ten years, the importance of education has emerged via various approaches. These include Sen's human capabilities approach, the new growth theory approach, and, to some extent, the approach implicit in UNICEF's *Adjustment With a Human Face*.[3] The centrality of the human factor as an end and means of development, both in the short term and the long term, have gradually gained greater acceptance. This has probably been facilitated by the ever-expanding empirical evidence of the positive effects of appropriate health and nutrition interventions on growth, equity, and family planning. This evidence may be summarized in terms of the short-term and long-term positive effects.

1.1. Short-term effects

First, calorie and micro-nutrient supplementation have been found to have an immediate positive impact on the labour productivity of malnourished manual workers, the attention span and learning ability of schoolchildren, and in reducing pregnant women's chances of giving birth to LBW (low-birth-weight) babies. Several nutritional supplementation programmes have shown that labour productivity increased rapidly following their introduction. A study of rubber plantation workers in Indonesia, for instance, found increases in productivity equal to 15-20 per cent of magnitude in only 60 days. Given the low cost of nutritional interventions (particularly micro-nutrient), the benefit to cost ratio of such programmes range from the 4 to 40 interval (Cornia, 1989).

Second, the establishment of a network of preventive and primary health care reduces the number of lost working days and the demand for expensive hospital staff. A 1985 survey covering several developing countries shows that hospitalization and/or hospital treatment are more expensive than out-patient preventive care by a factor of 2 to 20 (Robertson 1985).

Third, similar effects are obtained through water and sanitation interventions. For instance, a WHO analysis of the health impact on diarrhoeal morbidity rates from the introduction of cost-efficient water pumps in 28 developing countries found an immediate 37 per cent decline in the incidence of diarrhoea. In addition, there were considerable reductions in the incidence of other water-borne diseases such as cholera, typhoid, and amoebiasis (Esrey *et al.*, 1985).

1.2. Long-term effects

First, the elimination of malnutrition at an early age—particularly for the 0-3 age group—has also been found to generate enormous beneficial effects on labour productivity by alleviating the risk of physical and mental growth retardation. Adults who have suffered malnutrition at an early age are generally shorter, have a lower body mass and aerobic capacity, and, because of these reasons, have lower labour productivity. The negative effects of malnutrition at an early age are even more dramatic in terms of cognitive development, school performance, skills acquisition, and consequently, the ability to perform a productive activity. Thus, cost-effective nutritional interventions at an early age are an efficient means of avoiding future losses of output. In a highly-quoted study, Selowsky and Taylor (1973) found that providing nutritional supplements during the first two years of life to the 25,000 children who become malnourished in Chile every year would generate a lagged benefit in excess of 1 per cent of GNP a year.

Second, early interventions in health and nutrition are also generally more efficacious and avoid substantial outlays in the long term. For instance, the often large costs borne by households and governments for the treatment of permanent impairments (such as blindness, deafness, mutism, cretinism, and paralysis) can be avoided with more expenditures on preventive and primary care together with micro-nutrient supplementation for children. In the USA, it has been shown that each dollar spent on child immunization saves 10 dollars in subsequent medical costs.

Third, the greatest (and most readily measurable) impact on economic performance is probably that of education. Without delving into the vast literature on this theme, it is sufficient to emphasize that literacy, numeracy, and the capacity to think and learn—all necessary requirements for the acquisition of those modern technical skills essential to the industrialization of Pakistan—cannot be increased without a prior massive expansion of primary and secondary education. In addition, primary education and basic literacy have been shown to be important factors in raising productivity levels among small farmers.[4] Education brings about higher productivity in agriculture through two complementary paths. Education accelerates the identification and adoption of new inputs and farming practices. Also, education itself is a crucial complementary input in the technological package, since the productivity levels obtained with new technology have been shown to be dependent on farmers' education. The empirical evidence available also shows that the effects of schooling are stronger in regions where (as in the irrigated plains of Pakistan) new seeds and new fertilizers are being introduced rather than in remote regions where technology is stagnant and where farmers are isolated from markets.

Fourth, the effects of education on industrial and agricultural productivity only start to become evident at a given threshold, corresponding to 3-4 years of schooling for activities utilizing relatively simple farming methods, to complete primary education for more complex activities. The effects of 'some schooling' (i.e., of intermittent attendance during the first two or three years of elementary school) seem to have only a limited impact on productivity.

Finally, in countries such as Pakistan, the biggest impact of increases in female education and literacy is felt through the reduction of persistently high levels of fertility and infant mortality. Data from the

World Fertility Survey and various demographic and health surveys have unambiguously demonstrated that the average number of children per woman at child-bearing age declines with an increase in her level of education. While women with elementary education have lower fertility levels than those with no schooling, the sharpest drop in fertility occurs for women who have attended lower-secondary school (age bracket 11-14). The same data also show that age at marriage and contraceptive prevalence rates are strongly correlated to the level of female education. If the persistently high population growth rate of Pakistan is to be reduced, the immediate efforts to set up family planning programmes need to be accompanied by a massive effort in improving female education and literacy. Higher levels of female literacy also have a powerful effect on infant mortality and malnutrition. Education enables the mother to make a far more efficient use of whatever household, community, and public resources are available to the family.

1.3. Factors specific to Pakistan

The two points made above—a wider acceptance of more human-focused development theories and growing empirical evidence of the positive growth and income-distribution effects of appropriate social investments—are all the more important at this juncture in Pakistan's economic development. Indeed, the structural adjustment efforts initiated in Pakistan (see chapter 5), and likely to continue for several years, are de facto necessitating a far higher degree of openness, export orientation, and competitiveness from the Pakistani economy than in the past. The relatively low wages currently prevailing in Pakistan will no longer be sufficient to ensure the success of an 'open economy' approach to economic development. Considerable improvements in agricultural productivity will also be needed (to keep real industrial wages low), while major improvements will also be required for the 'widening' and 'deepening' of industrial skills, physical infrastructure, and good governance (all factors which, as discussed in chapter 7, have a strong wealth-creating effect).

Furthermore, it will not be easy to achieve the goals of modernization posited by the structural adjustment efforts without substantial improvement in effective participation by people in public matters. Real democratic control and a socially acceptable distribution of income are, indeed, necessary conditions for social consensus, a commodity in short supply in Pakistan today.

2. SOCIAL DEVELOPMENT TARGETS FOR THE 1990s

Faced with an unsatisfactory social development record, conscious of the 'emergencies' the country faces on the demographic and environmental front, and confronted with the new challenges posed by the structural adjustment programme, the federal and provincial governments in Pakistan have developed a comprehensive and ambitious social development plan. It should be noted that this projected expansion of the government in the public goods sector is likely to be accompanied by its gradual withdrawal from the industrial sphere, a withdrawal which, it is hoped, should free substantial human and financial resources.

Although the federal government has explicitly stated that economic and social goals will be pursued in a mutually reinforcing way, clearly articulated targets for the time being have been formulated for major social indicators as part of the Social Action Plan cited as *The Eighth Five Year Plan* (1993-1998), Perspective Plan. The main quantitative targets for the years 1993-2008 are summarized below.

Table 6.1 : Trends in selected main social indicators 1951-2008 (actual and planned)

	1951	1961	1972	1980	1990	1992 /1993	1997 /1998	1998 /2003	2003 /2008
Infant mortality rate	178	142	145	125	106	86	65	40	30
Access to potable water:									
Rural	–	–	–	20	45	47	70	80	85
Access to sewerage:									
Urban	–	–	–	42	55	60	80	85	90
Rural	–	–	–	2	10	13	32	55	75
Adult literacy rate:									
Male	17	27	30	35	41	47	71	80	85
Female	9	8	12	16	22	22	34	49	80

Source: *National Programme of Action*, for numbers up to 1990 and *The Eighth Five Year Plan 1993-8*, (Government of Pakistan 1994, p.427) from 1992-3 onwards.

It is possible to do a simple exercise to assess how realistic target setting is in the social sectors, by seeing how consistent targets are with past achievements in comparable periods. Though accelerated growth rates in the achievement of social sector targets are possible with the requisite commitment (as we will show below), it is still instructive to see how closely past achievements approximate future targets. Table 6.2 represents such an exercise for selected indicators for which we had the needed data.

Table 6.2 reveals that the targets for the ten years following 1992-3 are very ambitious compared to the achievements of the prior decade.

The last column of Table 6.2 shows that, except in the case of access to potable water in the rural areas, the targets imply an increase in achievement from two to five times more than that achieved in the 1980s.

Table 6.2 : Actual and implicit average yearly rates of progress for four main social indicators

	a 1950-90	b 1980-90	c 1992-3-2003	c/b
Infant mortality rate	2.3	1.9	4.6	2.4
Access to potable water:				
Rural	–	2.5	3.3	1.3
Access to sewerage:				
Urban	–	1.3	2.5	1.9
Rural	–	0.8	4.2	5.2
Adult literacy rate:				
Male	0.6	0.6	3.3	5.5
Female	0.2	0.6	2.7	4.5

Source: Based on Table 6.1

The next set of tables looks at actual achievements to date for a broader range of social sector indicators. Pakistan has been a very late starter in improving its social sectors, but its growth record shows a very interesting trend. This is evident from Tables 6.3 and 6.4 which report indicators for health, nutrition, water supply and sanitation, and education. Table 6.3 reports the indicator levels over time from 1951 to 1995 and Table 6.4 presents the growth rates of these indicators.

Table 6.3 shows that progress has been made in social sector development. On an absolute level, the average of Pakistan is better than the average for all developing countries. For example, consider the first three social indicators reported in the Table 6.3. Pakistan's infant mortality rate, child mortality rate, and maternal mortality rates for the last reported year of 91, 137, and 340, respectively, are much above the average of 92, 144, and 717 respectively, for all developing countries.[5]

The initial decade of 1951-61 shows relatively high rates of improvement of Infant Mortality Rates (IMRs) of 2 per cent and male literacy rates of 5 per cent. The decade of 1961-72 shows deterioration in the IMRs and low growth in male literacy, while female literacy growth is high only because of a low base. So this decade of high economic growth was not accompanied by high social sector development.

Table 6.3 : Social sector achievement levels

	1951	1961	1972	1980	1990	T
Infant Mortality Rate	178	142	145	125	106	91(1993)
Under 5 Mortality Rate	–	–	–	193	162	137(1994-6)
Maternal Mortality Rate	–	–	–	600	500	340(1993)
Incidence of Malnutrition among Children (<5)	–	–	–	52	43	40(1993)
Coverage of Safe Water Supply:						
Urban	–	–	–	72	80	96(1990-5)
Rural	–	–	–	20	45	71(1990-5)
Coverage of Sanitary Facility:						
Urban	–	–	–	42	55	62(1990-5)
Rural	–	–	–	2	10	19(1990-5)
Primary Enrolment Ratio: (Class 4)						
Male	–	–	–	63[a]	83	89(1995-6)
Female	–	–	–	32[a]	48	57(1995-6)
Completion Rate						
Male	–	–	–	53	43	55(1988)
Female	–	–	–	41		45(1988)
Adult Literacy Rate:						
Male	17	27	30	35	41	50(1995)
Female	9	8	12	16	22	24(1995)

Source: *National Programme of Action*, *Pakistan Demographic Surveys*, various years, *World Development Report 1996*, (1996) *Human Development Report 1991,1996* (Government of Pakistan 1991, 1996), *Economic Survey*, various years.

Note: a = Data for 1983 drawn from *The Sixth Five Year Plan 1983-88* (nd, p.551).

T = Terminal year or period.

The following period of 1972-80 has high rates of improvement of IMRs and literacy for both males and females. Chapter 4 shows this period to be one of low economic growth but one characterized by populist social policies. While these social policies of redistribution of assets through nationalization and land reform were not effective in reducing income inequalities (chapter 4), the focus on social policies did improve social well-being as reflected by these social indicators.

Data are available for a larger number of social indicators for the 1980s than for the earlier decades. However, the previous indicators of IMRs and male adult literacy show a drop in their trend growth rates in the 1960s. This was a period of high growth accompanied by major structural adjustment programmes. In chapter 5, we showed that in the first half of the decade, these programmes accompanied a cut in social services. Subsequently, a conscious policy of adjustment with a human face is seen to significantly improve social sector indicators.

Finally, the half decade up to 1995 also shows high rates of improvement in these social indicators. This period witnessed a downturn in economic growth but a high priority on the social sectors in the form of a Social Action Plan (SAP). SAP represented an acceleration of development expenditure of an annual average rate of 43.5 per cent between 1992 to 1995 in the sectors of education, health, water supply, and sanitation.[6] Again social sector policy is demonstrated to be a necessary condition for social sector improvement, while economic growth is demonstrated to be an insufficient condition. Table 6.5 summarizes this and other policy corollaries. Table 6.4 shows growth rates of social sector indicators.

Table 6.4 : Social sector growth rates

	Annual Growth Rate (%)				
Indicator	1951-61	1961-72	1972-80	1980-90	1990-T
Infant Mortality Rate	20	−0.2	1.7	1.6	1.0
<5 Mortality Rate	–	–	–	1.6	1.2
Maternal Mortality Rate	–	–	–	1.7	2.5
% Children with Malnutrition (<5)	–	–	–	1.9	0.5
Safe Water:					
Urban	–	–	–	1.1	1.6
Rural	–	–	–	12.5	4.6
Sanitation:					
Urban	–	–	–	3.1	1.0
Rural	–	–	–	40.0	7.2
Primary Enrolment Ratio:					
Male	–	–	–	4.5	1.4
Female	–	–	–	7.1	3.8
Completion Rate:					
Male	–	–	–	–	0.5
Female	–	–	–	–	1.2
Adult Literacy Rate:					
Male	4.6	1.0	1.9	1.7	4.3
Female	−1.1	3.7	3.6	3.8	1.8

Source: Based on Table 6.3.
Note: T = Terminal year reported in Table 6.3.

Table 6.5 reviews the change in four outcome indicators, i.e. economic growth, poverty, inequality, and social sector improvement over the last four and a half decades. In the 1950s, economic growth was high, but from a low initial base, just as social sector growth was high due to a low initial base. The 1960s had high economic growth which reduced income inequality. However, social sector policies were not given high priority during this period and, as a result, social sector improvement was low and poverty also increased.

Conversely, over the 1970s, economic growth was low but the social sectors were given high priority. Social sector indicators improved and poverty also decreased. Increased income inequality accompanied low growth. Over the 1980s, economic growth was high, but the social sectors were given high priority only in the second half of the decade. While income inequality decreased, social sector growth was not remarkable. Finally, in the first half of the 1990s, while economic growth has slowed down, high social sector priorities have produced high social sector improvements.

Table 6.5 : Policy impact on social sector development

Indicators of Change	Time Period 1951-60	1960-72	1972-80	1980-90	1990-5
Economic	High	High	Low	High	Middle
Poverty	na	Increase	Decrease	Decrease (end year increase)	na
Income Inequality	na	Decrease	Increase	Decrease (end year increase)	na
Social Sector	High (from low base)	Low	High	Middle	High
Social Sector Priority	Low	Low	High	1st half low 2nd half high	High

Source: Based on evidence reported in chapters 2 to chapter 5.
Note: na = Not available.

Several policy corollaries emerge from Table 6.5. First, that economic growth appears to be directly associated with income equality and not necessarily associated with a reduction of poverty or improvement in social sector indicators. Second, and this is the main message of this chapter, that improvement in social sector indicators requires an unambiguous high policy priority given to the social sectors. Third, a decrease in poverty, though not in income inequality, appears to accompany improvements in social sector indicators. Finally, a result not evident from Table 6.5, but one we nevertheless assert because of evidence from other countries reported earlier in the chapter, long-run growth is positively associated with a high policy priority given to the social sectors.

Notwithstanding the direct and indirect gains from social sector development, realism in target setting is called for. In addition to Table 6.2, Table 6.4 also provides a hint about the realism of selected SAP targets. The achieved average annual growth rate in primary enrolment ratios of 1.4 per cent for males and 3.8 per cent for females between 1990-5 can be contrasted with the SAP target of 2.5 and 8.8 per cent for roughly this period for males and females, respectively.[7] Similarly, the

1990-5 annual average growth in rural water supply and sanitation of 4.3 per cent and 7.2 per cent can be contrasted with the SAP targets of 15.1 and 31.2 per cent for 1991-5. Finally, in the health sector, the target of 4,666 Basic Health Units by 1995 can be contrasted with the achieved number of 4,274.[8] The first two targets seem to be very ambitious, and this is consistent with what we concluded from Table 6.2. This does not however, mean that they cannot be achieved. The next section provides examples from various countries, including Pakistan, of remarkable achievements in social sector development when the political will and accompanying financial commitment was present.

3. SUCCESSFUL SOCIAL SECTOR EXPERIENCES

Social progress of the scale envisaged in the years ahead in Pakistan in SAP I and the planned SAP II has, in fact, been achieved in the recent past in a number of developing countries characterized by economic and social conditions, which are not too dissimilar from those of Pakistan. Three of these experiences are reviewed briefly below in order to document the main features of the approaches and policies, the volume of the resources mobilized, and the progress attained. Such experiences could provide a valuable source of inspiration for Pakistan.

3.1. Zimbabwe: Increasing school enrolments and reducing illiteracy in five years

Zimbabwe—a country with a 1992 per capita GDP of 2,100 in PPP $ terms (lower than $2,160 for Pakistan)—became independent in April 1980.[9] Until then, the education system comprised of two kinds of schools, those for whites, which followed the Anglo-Saxon system, and those for Africans, based on the same model but short on ideas, resources, and teachers. While primary and secondary enrolment and completion rates for white children were close to 100 per cent, those for black children were only 57 and 4 per cent respectively. It is evident from these numbers that black school dropout rates were extremely high. On the last days of the month, as many as one-third of school children went hungry since parents saved on food to pay school fees. Half of the black adult population was illiterate.

With independence, the government embarked on a massive literacy and enrolment programme. The school system was unified, school fees for primary education were abolished, new teacher training colleges were established, and a mass literacy campaign was launched. The communities were mobilized to revitalize the school system. The cost of building new schools, for example, was (and still is) borne by the communities, though in elementary schools, books were free for everyone. The government mobilized its resources too. The share of the budget allocated to education increased from 10 per cent in 1979 to 15 per cent in 1980, to 20 per cent in 1981, and to 22-24 per cent for the rest of the decade. This was achieved mostly by cutting the military budget. In terms of GNP, the increase was from 3.5 in 1978-9, to 5.2 in 1980, to 9.6 (on average) for the rest of the decade. No less than 67 per cent of the overall education expenditure was allocated to primary education in 1980. With the achievement of full enrolment in primary education, and with the rapid expansion of secondary education, the primary allocation declined to 56 per cent of the total education allocation by 1988.

The results of these efforts were startling. In the first five years, the total number of children enrolled in the seven grades of primary school had almost tripled, increasing from about 820,000 in 1979 to 2,150,000 in 1984. Since then, their number has stabilized at around 2.2 million. The primary gross enrolment ratio (which includes under-age and, especially, over-age children who had not entered school) increased from 57 per cent in 1979 to 135 per cent in 1984. In addition, the completion rate rose to 80 per cent. Girls represented half of the children enrolled in primary education and 40 per cent in secondary education.

The increase in secondary and tertiary enrolment was equally phenomenal, or even more so. The number of adolescents in secondary education increased, in fact, ten times between 1979 and 1989, and the corresponding enrolment rate rose (for the white and black population combined) from about 7 per cent in 1979 to 46 per cent in 1989. Meanwhile, the university population grew from 8,000 to 50,000.

These achievements are all the more remarkable given that they occurred during a period of slow and unstable growth in GDP per capita (averaging only 1.2 per cent a year over the 1980-9 period) and of stringent macroeconomic and fiscal adjustment. Despite these constraints, and after the large increases of 1980-2, government expenditure on education continued to rise at 4-5 per cent a year in real terms. Additional resources were mobilized from the communities, and some expansion in private secondary enrolment also took place. With the adjustment process still going on, books are free only for schools in poorer areas, but fees for (compulsory) elementary education have not been introduced since, as the Minister of Education herself noted, this would result in an increase in school dropouts, particularly for female children. This, the Minister remarked, is a price Zimbabwe is not prepared to pay. Instead, the introduction of taxes earmarked for education and fees for children of well-to-do families in high-income areas was preferred.

3.2. Thailand: Eradicating severe and moderate malnutrition in a decade[10]

Since the late 1960s, Thailand has experienced a rapid growth of GDP and household incomes. Such growth, however, was not trickling down to most rural households. During this period, health care resources were largely concentrated in the Bangkok Metropolitan Area and a few other big cities. In addition, during the first three five-year National Economic and Social Development (NESD) plans, from 1961 to 1976, nutrition represented only a small part of the health sector activity. During the fourth NESD plan, 1976-81, a national nutritional surveillance system was finally set up. When the first national nutritional data were released in 1981, it became apparent that no fewer than 55,000 infants and pre-school children died annually due to protein energy malnutrition (PEM). The surveillance system also showed that the prevalence of PEM in pre-school children was over 51 per cent and that the nutritional activities included in the fourth NESD plan were only partially implemented. This partial implementation was due to the lack of intrasectoral collaboration, limited involvement of the communities, inadequate and poorly targeted government expenditure, and the persistence of pronounced income inequality and widespread poverty. The latter occured despite the remarkable economic performance and in spite of the long-achieved food self-sufficiency of the country. This situation is not too dissimilar to that of Pakistan.

Since 1982, with the inception of the fifth NESD plan, the government's health policy has undergone profound modifications. The major shifts concerned health strategies, poverty alleviation, and nutritional interventions. In the health sector, there was a determined shift towards primary health care. By 1989, about 600,000 village health communicators and 62,000 village health volunteers (VHV) had been trained and were present in practically every village. Health facilities were created all the way down to the *tampon* (sub-district) level, to which the VHV referred those cases they could not take care of by themselves. By 1989, 98 per cent of the approximately 53,000 Thai villages were involved in PHC. In addition, the proportion of families with access to clean water increased from 32 per cent in 1982 to 78 per cent in 1989.

This massive effort was sustained by a considerable increase in the resources allocated to PHC by both the government and households. First of all, the overall tax ratio increased from 15 to 18 per cent of GDP. Second, despite the growth in public debt service payments, the Thai Government gradually increased the share of public expenditure allocated to health and social services from 10.5 per cent in the early 1980s to 11–11.5 per cent at the end of the decade. Overall, real public health expenditure rose by 52 per cent between 1982 and 1989. Cuts were made, instead, in the military budget and in economic subsidies. Third, the share of public health expenditure assigned to preventive and primary health care increased gradually from 34 to 37 per cent with the share allocated to rural areas growing from 70 to nearly 80 per cent. Community and household health expenditure increased at an even faster rate.

In the fifth NESD plan, it was recognized that malnutrition was a symptom of poverty, ignorance, the lack of an appropriate monitoring system, and co-ordinated action among the various government agencies. The main thrust of the nutrition policy was therefore to combine a poverty alleviation programme (see later) with stop-gap measures to relieve the most severe forms of malnutrition until systematic solutions could be introduced. Such measures included regular nutritional surveillance using a growth chart to cover every child; nutrition information and education; community production of nutritious foods; supplementary feeding programmes at the village level; a school lunch programme covering 5,000 schools in poor areas; and food fortification.

The poverty alleviation plan (PAP) was a major innovation introduced with the fifth NESD plan in 1982. The creation of a Rural Development Organization, responsible for all development policies, led to a remarkable improvement in integration and co-ordination among the various ministries at both the central and the local level. A set of minimum basic needs indicators was introduced and subsequently used for problem identification and for the targeting of government interventions. Under the new PAP, 32 development projects were implemented with the participation of the communities of 12,500 poor villages (about a quarter of the total), while a rural job creation programme was also introduced. Between 1982–6, the yearly cost of PAP was a modest US $ 68 million, equivalent to only 1 per cent of public expenditure, or 0.16 per cent of GDP. During the sixth NESD plan for 1987-91, a similar approach was continued, with PAP expenditure strongly focused on 5,800 backward villages. Some government input was also received by 35,000 villages, while 12,000 better-off villages were encouraged to work with the private sector.

The results of this three-pronged approach were remarkable. To start with, the combined incidence of mild, moderate, and severe PEM malnutrition in under-five children declined drastically, from 51 per cent in 1982 to 21 per cent in 1989. Severe malnutrition, in particular, was completely eradicated while moderate malnutrition declined from 13 per cent to 1-2 per cent. The reduction in malnutrition was particularly pronounced in the first three years of the programme, indicating the speed with which even acute nutritional problems—not dissimilar to those experienced by Pakistan—can be tackled in just a few years, provided the right approach is followed. In parallel, the infant mortality rate declined from 41 per thousand in 1981 to 28 per thousand in 1989.

3.3. Reducing IMRs by more than 5 points per year over a decade: The case of China and Costa Rica[11]

In the post-World War II period, a number of developing countries, including China and Costa Rica, have reduced IMRs at very rapid rates. China, for instance, was able to reduce its IMR from 121 to 61 from the early 1960s to the early 1970s. Costa Rica engendered an even greater relative decline in IMR, from 75 per thousand in the mid to late 1960s to only 22 to the mid to late 1970s. Were there common features in the phenomenal achievements of these two countries which were so fundamentally different in terms of economic structure, level of development, degree of urbanization, and political organization, let alone in terms of culture, religion, and social values? Despite these deep differences, the approaches followed in the field of social development present startling commonalities. First, in both countries, emphasis was placed equally on economic and social development. Second, the approach to health improvement was a broad-based one, and included activities in the field of environmental sanitation, housing, and education. During the respective decades under consideration, both countries achieved universal primary enrolment and secondary enrolment rates of about 40 per cent. Third, there was a deliberate attempt to remove any remaining sex discrimination in access to health and other public services. Fourth, in the health sector narrowly defined, there was a strong emphasis on rural primary health care. This programme was implemented and financed by a National Health Programme in Costa Rica, while it was predominantly organized and funded at the 'commune' level in China.

In both cases, the rural PHC programme included the development of sanitary infrastructure, mobilization of the communities, periodic home visits (in Costa Rica) for immunization against the main vaccine-preventable diseases, deworming of the population, promotion of nutrition and health education, including prenatal care and family planning. In Costa Rica, these broad-based efforts were sustained by increasing allocations of public funds. Health expenditure per capita more than doubled (while GNP per capita increased by only about 50 per cent). In China, too, there was an increase in the allocation of state and commune resources for PHC, though the increase varied substantially from county to county.

The overall decline in IMR in both countries was largely due to the sharp decline observed in the incidence of and fatality due to diarrhoea, respiratory infections, and immuno-preventable disease (only in China;

in Costa Rica their contribution to IMR was already fairly low). Smaller declines were observed for infant deaths due to complications in pregnancy and malnutrition.

4. SUCCESSFUL EXPERIENCES FROM PAKISTAN

Pakistan has also been able to realize similar accelerations in the rate of progress in specific social programmes. The Expanded Programme of Immunization (EPI) and the provision of potable water in Azad Jammu and Kashmir (AJK) are two such cases. These are briefly described below.

4.1. Improving immunization services during the 1980s

Improvement in the delivery of immunizations during the past decade is one example of how Pakistan has been able to expand public access to essential services in the social sector. As shown in Table 6.6, immunization coverage increased steadily during the 1980s. In addition, the establishment of a solid managerial foundation for the expansion of Primary Health Care (PHC) related health services has been a major contribution of the Expanded Programme on Immunization (EPI) during the 1980s.

Table 6.6 : Immunization coverage in Pakistan in 1980-90

	BCG	BPT	Polio	Measles	TT
1980	8.0	3.6	3.8	1.0	—
1985	77.2	80.2	89.4	54.7	—
1990	95.4	87.0	87.0	85.6	37.5

Source: UNICEF (1986).

The success of EPI is based on a combination of factors, including enlightened community involvement, promulgation of clear objectives, implementation of continuous training, creation of managerial supervision, availability of logistical support, consistent communications activities, and high levels of government/donor co-operation. In general, the goals of EPI have succeeded in reducing preventable mortality and morbidity from the six target diseases by: (1) increasing the coverage of fully immunized children 0-11 months of age to 80 per cent by 1990; (2) providing two doses of tetanus toxoid to 80 per cent of pregnant women by 1990; and (3) establishing a reliable logistic system for sustaining high coverage levels.

As one of the key elements of the Accelerated Health Programme (AHP) from 1982-5, EPI soon became a high-priority for provincial and district health services in the early part of the decade. Considerable emphasis was given to recruitment and training of large numbers of vaccinators, estimation of the targeted numbers of children and pregnant women, and the initiation to training programmes for supervisors as well as vaccinators. Frequent field visits and regular coverage surveys, using a standard methodology, insured constant monitoring of programme implementation.

In the mid-decade, efforts were made to refine the training being provided to EPI staff, to implement specific training courses in supervisory skills, to automate data systems, and to initiate expanded communications activities. Outreach services were supported from health centres and mobile teams provided services to remote populations. Disadvantaged urban slums were prioritized. Female vaccinators were appointed to improve access to pregnant and child-bearing-age women.

This massive effort required concerted political will and substantial donor co-ordination. Social mobilization efforts succeeded in creating demand for services and in capturing the support of community leaders. Emphasis on continuous monitoring and flexibility in modifying strategies were critical. EPI's achievements during the 1980s provided major impetus to other PHC-oriented initiatives being planned for the 1990s.

4.2. AJK: A case of rapid rural water supply coverage in the 1980s

The AJK case has some interesting features of rapid and increased coverage in the 1980s. The population of AJK was estimated to be 2.4 million in 1988, of which 90 per cent is rural. There were altogether 5,232 settlements (population up to 500) in the state, which created difficulties for provision of services. The average annual precipitation is about 1,500 mm.

The coverage of rural population with access to potable water increased from less than 200,000 in 1981 to over 1 million or nearly 50 per cent of the population in 1990. AJK now has one of the highest percentages for rural water coverage in Pakistan, estimated at about 40 per cent (1988), although with considerable variation among districts. Poonch and Mirpur are high at 52 and 55 per cent, while Bagh, Muzaffarabad, and Kotli are lower at 28, 34, and 36 per cent respectively. The bulk of the increase came after 1986. A major contributor to the rapid expansion of coverage was the involvement of local NGOs and community organizations in project implementation and management.

Although the process of rapid expansion took off in the mid-1980s, it had started around a decade earlier with the introduction of four crucial elements: (1) the demonstration of appropriate design and technology (primarily gravity-fed systems with reasonable cost and socio-economic compatibility); (2) the establishment of institutional links to obtain full acceptance of the technological approach from the political, technical, and administrative systems (i.e., Local Government and Rural Development Department [LG&RDD]); (3) capacity-building (human, technical, and infrastructural) to carry out the programme, including the formation of a rural water supply (RWS) cell at LG&RDD; (4) development of mechanisms for community participation and self-help; (5) and involving women from the early stage of the programme (1981).

Increased awareness generated high demand by the rural population at the beginning of the 1980s, compelling politicians and government agencies to enhance the provision of development funds from the budget and inducing increased donor assistance. From the strategic point of view, this experience can certainly be replicated in other areas/provinces, whereby coverage from 5-8 per cent can be increased to 40-45 per cent in a time-span of barely 5-8 years.[12]

4.3. The Cost of Inaction

Before making serious commitments to the social sector, Pakistani authorities may want to assess the cost of inaction, i.e., the cost which would be incurred by all segments of the Pakistani society. While the resistance encountered in mobilizing or reallocating resources and in altering traditional approaches and values in the health, education, and nutritional fields should not be underestimated, it is evident that the cost to Pakistani society of limited action on the social front will be extremely high. This price will comprise not only the unwarranted human cost of child deaths, illiteracy, illness, malnutrition, and unacceptable human degradation and suffering, but also a considerable economic cost due to the environmental problems induced by uncontrollable population growth, the lack of competitiveness associated with limited skills and lack of education, and the huge health costs borne later in life by households whenever early preventive measures are not introduced in childhood. Finally, the lack of determined action could also entail considerable political costs, as the failure to achieve minimum services and living conditions for the population, and the erosion of law and order and good governance could lead to unstable and unsafe political and personal conditions. In the case of Pakistan, a massive acceleration in the investment in human resources would indeed be a positive-sum game, in which everybody—the poor, the industrialist class, the agricultural producer, and the state itself—would gain substantially.

5. MAIN FEATURES OF THE SOCIAL STRATEGY PROPOSED

This section describes the main features of a strategy which, if properly implemented, would allow Pakistan to reach objectives being contemplated under SAP II. The main discussion of required institutional arrangements that would underpin this strategy is in chapter 7.

Before proceeding, we make two observations. First, a strategy discussing transformations as profound as those proposed here must necessarily be very holistic and should include, therefore, an examination of changes not only in social policies, but also in macroeconomic and growth policies and in values, attitudes, and behaviour. Such a broad approach, however, is not followed in this chapter, partly because several of these issues are dealt with at length in other chapters of this study, and partly to avoid too cumbersome a treatment of the policy changes required.

Second, that the benefits which ought to derive from the development strategy presented will extend well beyond those concerning human conditions, living standards, and social service coverage. The economic and political costs of the strategy proposed ought to be juxtaposed therefore not only with social sector improvements, but also with improvements in economic conditions, civil society, and political participation that will accompany them.

The strategy proposed here is more women-focused, egalitarian, community-based, and proactive than any of those adopted after Partition in 1947. It includes the following six main components, each of which is discussed in detail below.

i. First and foremost, a strong focus on women.
ii. The adoption of cost-efficient approaches in the delivery of basic social services to the entire population.
iii. Greater equity (by class, gender, region) in the distribution of the benefits of public expenditure.
iv. Greater emphasis on decentralization, community participation, and good governance.
v. A rapid increase (when compared to the past) in public and private expenditure on health, education, family planning, potable water supply, and nutritional support.
vi. The launching of a parallel poverty alleviation programme to sustain the incomes of the poor.

5.1. Focusing social policy on women

To a very large extent, the unsatisfactory social and economic development record in Pakistan depends on the low status of women in society, on their low level of literacy, on their restricted access to basic services, and on a pervasive gender bias in the access to economic resources which is a source of severe intra-sex and intra-household income inequality. Women are married at an early age, have shorter lives, work longer hours, remain mostly illiterate, and have minimal opportunities for schooling, training, and gainful employment. Their low/secondary status precludes any significant decision-making even in fertility control.

While it is the main ethical and development problem per se, the low status of women in Pakistan is a main cause of a much larger set of development problems, be it the population explosion (with its attendant negative effects on the labour market, poverty, and pollution); the insufficient supply of industrial skills; the high levels of infant mortality and malnutrition; and even the inadequate increase in farm productivity.

The pervasive gender bias affecting the country, with only very modest changes over the last few decades, contrasts sharply with the key role of Pakistani women in productive, reproductive, and welfare activities. In addition, as at least 75 per cent of all health care takes place at the family or individual level, women have the greatest responsibility for promoting family health and nutrition (Levin *et al.* 1984). Their role in supporting the cognitive development of children is also fundamental. It is, therefore, paramount that with the new strategy, adequate resource opportunities, and access to health, education, and other welfare services are ensured to all women.

Past policy approaches have been universal in nature and, in most cases, have been gender-neutral. In a context where culture and tradition placed women in an ancillary position, such a gender-neutral policy approach has failed to compensate for the existing gender bias, and has perpetuated the traditional problems of gender discrimination.

The social development plan proposed here must therefore deal head on with this issue and introduce specific provisions for women's education, women's health, training, credit, and welfare. If this approach is espoused fully, a number of concrete measures ought to follow. In the education sector, for instance, there is a need to expand schools for girls, literacy campaigns for rural women, and teacher training colleges for women at a rate at least twice as high as that for boys and men (see Table 4.18). In addition, support and motivational campaigns focusing, for instance, on the need for girls to attend school and to reduce phenomenally high dropout rates among girls are necessary.

Similarly, two-thirds of the new trainees for Community Health Workers should be women, and health programmes specifically aimed at women (such as TBA training, pregnancy control, immunization against tetanus, and more generally, MCH services) should be developed on a priority basis. It is important, however, that women are also adequately represented in the upper echelon of the medical profession, and particularly in specific branches such as obstetrics. These examples could be easily extended into the economic field (where a given share of credit, extension services, and inputs should be targeted specifically at women), and the field of labour-saving household technologies. These examples would only reiterate, however, the same general point: given the unique role of women in production, reproduction, and welfare activities, the highest social and economic returns to public (and private) investment are obtained by focusing first and foremost on women.

5.2. Adopting cost-effective approaches in service delivery

Even rapidly growing allocations of budgetary (and private) resources to health, education, and social welfare in the years ahead—an issue which will by itself face considerable resistance (see point 5.5)—will not automatically ensure that the targeted coverage of basic social services is achieved.

This objective will be achieved only if important shifts towards more cost-effective approaches take place in a number of sectors, particularly in rural water supply, health care, and education. Pakistan is no exception to a more general rule prevailing in several (but certainly not all) developing countries where the provision of social services is affected by a series of biases in favour of expensive, urban-based, capital and skill-intensive activities, often modelled on those of industrialized countries. While the source of this bias can be found in Pakistan's (now remote) colonial heritage and in donor policies (which favour the financing of capital costs and the practice of tied aid), domestic policies also deserve blame. For instance, as noted in a study on the effectiveness of aid to Pakistan, the 'GOP in the past has favoured capital-intensive investments in the health sector, which carry high running costs, and are therefore unlikely to be cost-effective' (Cassen *et al.* 1990). A stronger case along these lines can be made for rural and peri-urban water supply. In this sector, the technology adopted is often capital and foreign inputs intensive, and hence too costly and limited in the access it provides. In addition, the pricing policies of water supply services tend to favour a relatively small group of (generally well-off) households. Finally, the 'brick and mortar' approach adopted in school construction costs more than twice that of indigenous approaches which rely more heavily on local materials.

In economic terms, the preference accorded to high-tech, high-cost approaches represents an incongruence. The 'choice of techniques' does not reflect factor prices. It is important, therefore, to shift to more appropriate, less skill-intensive, and more community-based approaches to the delivery of social services. In the health sector, the recent shift by GOP towards preventive and primary health care (and particularly towards EPI) should be continued and expanded through a rapid extension of the network of Basic Health Units (BHU) and Rural Health Centres (RHC). In addition, the recruitment of Community Health Workers (CHW) should continue. These measures ought to allow substantial saving on expensive hospital equipment, highly qualified (and costly) doctors, certified nurses, and other health specialists normally employed to deal with common health problems. Such staff should instead be used for more complex tasks.

Considerable advances in training for providing basic skills at very low costs have been, and will continue to be, the key to the success of primary health care. Worldwide, the cost of basic training for CHWs is in the range of US $ 100 and US $ 500. By contrast, the cost of training a fully qualified doctor is at least US $ 60,000 (Cornia and Stewart 1990).

Arguments in favour of the adoption of 'appropriate technologies' can be developed for other specific health activities: at the modest expense of about 10 cents (US) per episode of diarrhoea, Oral Rehydration Therapy can replace the expensive intravenous rehydration, which costs about US $ 20 per episode; the Essential Drug Programme can allow savings of up to 50 per cent in the drug procurement budgets. In the subcontinent, appropriate low-cost approaches have also been successfully tested for rural and peri-urban water supply. The total annualized per capita cost of providing 40 litres of water per person per day through hand pumps, rainwater catchments, and piped water with communal standposts vary between US $ 1 and about US $ 5 (in 1987 US $) as opposed to US $ 150-200 typical of western-style water systems.

5.3. Improving distribution of benefits of public expenditure

The extension of social service coverage which would follow from the adoption of appropriate low-cost approaches would automatically entail a better and wider distribution of the benefits of public expenditure. The literature on 'expenditure incidence' in South-East Asia shows consistently, in fact, that basic services benefit the poor more than they do the rich.[13] In this regard, substantial results have been achieved during the last five years through the EPI programme.

Much more can be done to correct the existing class, gender, and geographical inequality in the distribution of services. In addition to some of the specific measures discussed (in section 5.1) to correct the existing gender bias in the provision of social services, three measures are proposed here. First, in Pakistan there is still considerable scope for reallocating part of the public expenditure from universities and central hospitals to elementary education and primary health care. The short-fall in resources in the former sectors could be covered by raising means-tested cost-recovery. Similar measures are needed in water supply where extremely low levels of cost-recovery for piped water services contributes to the fiscal deficit, and prevents the extension of potable water services to grossly under-served areas (Altaf *et al.* 1991). The initial steps taken by GOP under SAP are encouraging and need to be thoroughly implemented and extended.

Second, the distribution of the benefits of public expenditure can also be improved through improved targeting of food subsidies, and regular monitoring-evaluation of the equity-efficiency of this policy.

Third, greater decentralization in the provision of (most) social services can reduce the historical distortions in the geographical distributions of social services, particularly if the federal government agrees to provide additional financial support to acutely underdeveloped areas with weak tax and resource potential.

While decentralization is much needed for government legitimacy, good governance, and democracy (see section 5.4), poor communications and transport systems, and population dispersion (particularly in the western, north-western and northern regions) require greater decentralization of many (but by no means all) social service tasks in Pakistan. Such decentralization is also called for because it involves easier supervision of personnel, resource distribution, and operations at lower levels of administration.

5.4. Good governance, decentralization and local-level democracy

As mentioned in chapter 1, a central obstacle to the achievement of comprehensive social development in Pakistan is the crisis of governance, i.e., of the government's inability to design and implement policies, particularly policies which require targeting, selection, or judgement. Such a crisis manifests itself in excessive centralization of the GOP over the years; in the erosion of participatory institutions such that they are virtually non-existent today; in the hostility towards participatory institutions and local-level democracy; in the gradual erosion of the self-confidence, skills, and the system of grassroots institutions needed for organizing collective action; in the breakdown in professional standards, lax supervision, and growing corruption of large sections of the civil service (including those dealing with education, tax administration, and law and order); and in the arbitrary procedures of government institutions which are no longer perceived as acting in the public interest.

In view of these fundamental problems, some quarters have argued (and justifiably) for massive programmes of privatization not only in industry, but also in the social sector. The privatization of public goods, however, is no solution to the crisis of governance for very well-known reasons. Particularly in countries like Pakistan, where primary income distribution is highly skewed and 'market failures' are more likely, privatization would preclude the access of low-income groups to those public goods (such as basic health and education) which have been shown to have high rates of both private and social returns.

There is no alternative, therefore, to what will be a painful and difficult reform of the state apparatus, and to greater participation of civil society in the design and execution of social sector activities. The following measures are among those most urgently needed: First, institutional reform ensuring that some of the basic functions of the state such as public security, fair judicial recourse, and enforcement of contracts are actually being fulfilled. A few measures are specifically required for the social sector. They include the re-establishment of competitive criteria in the selection of CBS and PAS cadres; equal career opportunities for specialist cadres; reform of civil service training (which actually neglects many branches of public administration, including health and education); and clarification of frequent overlapping responsibilities between local and provincial government departments.

Second, the pervasive influence of the central government should gradually be reduced through a gradual decentralization of tasks to the provincial and, even more, to the district and union levels. The rationale for decentralization is that the closeness of public administration to the problems of society allows for faster and more relevant and efficient decisions concerning local needs. In addition, decentralization allows for more genuine democratic control from the beneficiaries of the services (through school boards, parent commissions, and user associations). Such informal bodies should provide support to teachers and health workers, oversee the attendance to the quality of services, decide on the site of new facilities, and provide additional resources (see point 5.5). The management of primary and secondary education, CHWs, BHUs, RHCs, and local water and sanitation projects should be among the first functions to be devolved. It must be clear, however, that this process of decentralization must be accompanied by a devolution of tax revenue or tax power, and by the gradual but sustained strengthening of district and union administrative cadres.

Third, and finally, there is a need for far greater community participation and democratic control in social sector activities. The past discussion on social development has often ignored this aspect of reform, largely because the debate has been dominated by orthodox economists who tend to recognize only two decision-makers—the individual and the state—and tend to ignore civil society, community organizations, and NGOs.

The case for far greater reliance on communities, their local representative bodies, and NGOs in Pakistan is a strong one. Greater reliance on community participation and social mobilization in the design, delivery, and monitoring of social activities ensures in the first instance a greater relevance of these programmes to the actual needs of the population, and greater internalization of their benefits by the poor. In addition, community participation also facilitates the mobilization of additional cash resources and of other resources in kind—such as labour and locally available material—which have a low opportunity cost but intrinsic productive value. And, finally, the active involvement of the community enhances the sense of self-reliance and responsibility of people and their ability to take care of their lives.

5.5. Increasing the flow of public and private resources to social sector activities

By any measure, Pakistan's investment in human resources appears grossly inadequate. Data for 1960 and 1990 on public expenditure on education and health for the larger South Asian countries, including Pakistan, as well as all developing countries, are reported below in Table 6.7.

Table 6.7 : Public expenditure on education and health as a percentage of GNP for Pakistan, selected other South Asian countries, and all developing countries.

	Education		Health	
	1980	1992	1960	1990
Pakistan	2.0	2.7	0.3	1.8
India	2.8	3.7	0.5	1.3
Bangladesh	1.5	2.3	na	1.4
Nepal	1.8	2.9	0.2	2.2
Sri Lanka	2.7	3.3	2.0	1.8
All developing countries	3.8	3.9	0.9	2.1

Source: *Human Development Report 1996* (1996, pp.160-1)

Except for Bangladesh, Pakistan lagged behind all South Asian countries in its educational effort in 1992. However, since Pakistan is trying to catch up, its level of effort is very low compared to Sri Lanka where the literacy rate is twice as high as that that of Pakistan.[14] While cost-effectiveness is clearly important, the example of Zimbabwe's successful educational transformation was also based on a massive infusion of resources into the education sector. This lesson is also true for the health sector as evident from Costa Rica's example. Once again, though its educational expenditure matches that of other South Asian countries and that of all developing countries, it needs to make a special effort given its lagging health indicators. For example, Pakistan's infant and under-five mortality rates at 89 and 137 per thousand far exceed those of all developing countries at 70 and 101 respectively.

It will certainly take a formidable effort to generate additional resources. The constraints imposed by the structural adjustment programmes underway will further complicate this task. Without these additional resources, however, the social development targets projected for SAP II will not be met. Four options for the mobilization of additional resources are therefore presented below and there are further details in chapter 7.

5.5.1. *Improving the intersectoral allocation of government expenditure*

Pakistan spent 6.9 per cent of its GDP on the military in 1994. This was much higher than that of any other South Asian country and about twice the average of all developing countries (*HDR* 1996, p.175). A slightly larger amount is absorbed in interest payments (*Economic Survey* 1996, p.140). Considerations regarding the security environment and monetary stability reduce the scope for reallocating part of these excessive expenditures. Nevertheless, the proposed freezing of military expenditure at their 1991 levels in all SAARC countries could have freed a substantial sum. The privatization programme may also gradually reduce the expenditure on production subsidies to state-owned companies. However, as in most countries undergoing adjustment programmes, the 'peace and privatization dividends' might well be absorbed by further reduction of the budget deficit and by the projected increase in interest payments.

5.5.2. *Increase tax revenue at the central and local level*

In view of the above discussion, a target of generating, say, an additional 5 per cent of GDP for investment in the social sector requires that the overall revenue ratio as a percentage of GDP be raised from the 17.1 per cent in 1994-5 (*Economic Survey* 1996, p.138). The need for increasing tax yields in Pakistan is accompanied by that of improving both horizontal and fiscal equity. As discussed in chapter 4, the burden of taxation has been increasing on the lowest income groups due to an increasing reliance on indirect taxes. Another characteristic of Pakistan's tax system is its excessive centralization. The federal government raises close to 80 per cent of total tax revenue, the provincial governments about 20 per cent, and local authorities close to nothing (see Table 5.1).

Given the present distribution of tax power, most of the increased taxation would have to take place at the federal level. However, the acute legitimacy problems faced by the federal government may render this objective difficult to achieve. Increased taxation might be feasible instead, if it is accompanied by greater administrative transparency and control, greater devolution of tax power at the provincial and local level, and by earmarking the increase in tax yields to specific social sector activities.

Given these two considerations, increases in tax yield would be more feasible if the levy and expenditure were linked regionally and/or sectorally. This will require a major devolution of tax power, and the establishment of a federally-funded regional development fund for very poor areas.

5.5.3. *Increasing contributions from households and communities*

Households will also have to increase their direct expenditure on the social sector. It is important, however, that due consideration is given to the different paying abilities of various types of households in order not to preclude access to basic services for the poorest.

To start with, greater recourse to means-tested cost-recovery is advisable in higher education, certain types of hospital treatments, and private piped water installations. It is also possible to divert part of the demand for high-income social services to the private sector. Finally, the emphasis on community participation will also generate additional resources, both in kind and in cash.

5.5.4. *Increasing the level and appropriateness of foreign aid*

In view of the very ambitious targets set by the GOP, it would be reasonable to count on additional flows of aid resources to the social sector, particularly if this additional aid is 'matched' by equivalent amounts of domestic funds as under the Social Action Plan. The increased allocations of aid resources, however, will have to be accompanied by a lessening of the biases characterizing it, i.e., its bias for excessive capital and import intensity, its instability over time, its excessive tying, and its preclusion of financing of recurrent costs.

5.6 Introducing poverty-alleviation and income-support measures

The final component of the alternative strategy proposed, concerns measures aimed at ensuring a floor for the incomes of the poor. The theoretical argument for this prescription is that the satisfaction of health and nutritional needs does not depend on interventions in these specific sectors alone, but also on the satisfaction of other social needs (e.g., literacy), and on the preservation of minimum levels of income for all households. Indeed, most needs have joint causal factors. So, unless all these joint causal factors are dealt with, no particular need can ever be satisfied. A child's learning ability depends not only on the local availability of elementary schools and teachers, but also on his/her health and nutritional status, on his/her parents' degree of literacy, and on the ability of his/her family to bear the indirect costs of education (uniform, books, and stationery).

The case for ensuring minimum levels of income as a supportive measure to the achievement of given health, nutritional, and educational targets rests in particular on three arguments. First, even the utilization of free public services entails considerable costs to the users, for transport, for inputs (teaching material, drugs, uniforms, meals consumed outside of the household), and often for 'gratitude money'. It has been estimated that for poor families in rural areas in NWFP, the indirect costs of utilizing free health care facilities can be as high as 30-40 per cent of their income. Second, utilization of free services also entails foregoing a certain amount of income or productive time. The children, and in particular the girls, of poor families are often not allowed to attend school because of the loss of services or income this entails for the household (chapter 3, section 2). Third, the growing trend towards the introduction of fees for services (even when these fees are relatively low), and the demand for various kinds of contributions from the communities, cannot succeed if household incomes do not reach minimum subsistence levels. Adequate family incomes should, therefore, be seen as a necessary complementary input for the achievement of social goals.

6. SUMMARY AND CONCLUSIONS

This chapter introduces human development as an alternative, or as just development. The focus in this chapter is on establishing the case for this approach. Both theoretical reasoning, and short-term and long-term empirical evidence are cited in support of such an approach.

Under the first Social Action Plan (SAP I), Pakistan set what appeared to be a very ambitious plan for its social sector development. While a formal evaluation of SAP I has not been released, case studies from other developing countries and for Pakistan show that what may appear as very ambitious social sector targets for attaining human development are actually attainable with the requisite political and concomitant financial commitment. Examples illustrating this include the case of Zimbabwe for education, of Thailand for malnutrition, and of China and Costa Rica for health. In addition, examples of successful social sector interventions in Pakistan include the expanded programme of immunization throughout the country, and rural water supply coverage in AJK.

Pakistan has shown some progress in improving social sector indicators between 1951 and 1995 on an absolute level. However, it still lags far behind the average for all developing countries on social indicators like literacy, educational attainment, and infant, child, and maternal mortality rates. For this reason, the political and financial commitment to the social sectors implicit in SAP I and SAP II are very welcome. Our review of the material in chapters 1-5 reveals that human development does not automatically accompany economic growth. Indeed, in the past, the greatest gains in social sector indicators in Pakistan occurred when there was a definite policy commitment to human development. Interestingly, we found that reductions in poverty have overlapped with periods of higher human development.

This chapter concludes with a concrete proposal on a strategy for human development. The proposal includes a discussion of appropriate technology for the delivery of social sector services, appropriate restructuring of social sector expenditure, resource mobilization, and decentralization of service delivery to the community level. Detailed discussion of the institutional underpinnings of implementing such a strategy is left to the next and concluding chapter. Indeed, the next chapter also encapsulates our vision of moving beyond adjustment with a human face.

NOTES

1. For an analysis of such under-investment, see Behrman and Schneider (1994).

2. Pakistan's combined expenditure on social development (education and health) gradually increased from 2.0 per cent of GDP in 1981-2 to 2.9 per cent in 1991-2. Thereafter, it rose to 3.3 per cent in 1995-6 (*Economic Survey 1995-6*, Statistical Appendix, pp.6-7).

3. See for example Dreze and Sen, 1989, and the Symposia on *New Growth Theory* in *The Journal of Economic Perspectives*, Vol 8, No. 1, Winter 1994.

4. See among others, Lockheed *et al.* (1980), Cotlear (1989), and Azhar (1991) who used Pakistani data.

5. All developing country averages are taken from the *Human Development Report 1996* (1996, p.159).

6. Government of Pakistan, *Social Action Programme 1992-95* (1992, p.47).

7. All SAP targets are taken from the Government of Pakistan, *Social Action Programme 1992-95*.

8. This represents the actual number of Basic Health Units in place by 1994 reported in *Pakistan Economic Survey 1995-96*, Statistical Appendix (1996, p.238).

9. *Human Development Report 1996* (1996, pp. 136-37). PPP represents purchasing power parity.

10. This section borrows from Kiranadana and Tontisirin (1992).

11. This section borrows from Mata and Rosero (1988) and from UN (1988).

12. For a recent description of the success of this programme and the determinants of this success, see Government of AJK (1995).

13. See e.g. Ailailima (1984) on Sri Lanka and Meerman (1979) on Malaysia.

14. Pakistan's estimated adult literacy rate is reported to be 38 per cent, while that of Sri Lanka's is 94 per cent for 1993 as reported in the *Human Development Report 1996* (1996, pp.150-4).

PART THREE

CONCLUSIONS

7

Learning From Failure : Institutional Reform for Human Resource Development

Tariq Banuri and *Moazam Mahmood*

INTRODUCTION

This chapter describes the institutional bases of specific policy measures. Broadly speaking, these are measures for employment-creation, skill-augmentation, and for increasing access to productive inputs and income transfers. These measures specifically include government and NGO supported land redistribution schemes, rural-work programmes, training and credit facilities in urban and rural areas, and even simple social security provisions for the unorganized poor, such as those successfully implemented in Tamil Nadu (Guhan 1992). In view of the expected increase in income inequality which will accompany the process of liberalization and adjustment over the medium term, such measures are likely to be required on a growing scale.

The objective of human resource development policies is to provide the population with guaranteed access to basic social services and social welfare. Two interim objectives are important for most southern countries: a massive transfer of financial and human resources into the social sector, and improvements in the efficiency, equity, and quality of these services. As is argued below, the increase in public and private expenditure on the social sector is itself constrained by the efficiency and perceived equity of the system. Moreover, the prospects of efficiency gains through traditional financial and physical reforms are generally viewed as being limited. This means that a non-traditional mechanism of institutional restructuring must be a major element in the pursuit of human resource development.

This does not mean that institutional reform must be the only item on the agenda. Indeed, the prescriptions in chapter 6 were derived from success stories in Pakistan and other southern countries working within existing institutional constraints. The suggestion is that similar successes might be achievable in other areas as well. In this chapter, however, we will look not at success stories, but at instances of the failure of earlier approaches. We begin by asking why these policies did not work in some countries or in certain fields, and why they have not been adopted universally despite demonstrated need and feasibility. The focus on past failures can help in the identification of obstacles to successful implementation and thus in the removal of these obstacles.

Although simply providing more money is not a sufficient condition for improvement, it may well be a necessary condition. However—and this is one of the obstacles to be reviewed here—the fact is that governments have found it very difficult to raise additional financial resources. A practical solution would seek to address the institutional and other causes of this inability.

Even when governments sought to introduce social programmes—the expansion of primary education, primary health, water and sanitation programmes, and population control programmes—the quality and the coverage of the programmes have remained inadequate. There has been a generalized inability to go beyond simple statistical targets. The management and supervision of the personnel—whether in public or private employment—providing the services has proven to be far more complicated than had been anticipated. Also, these programmes have been criticized not only for being wasteful and inefficient, but also for being inequitable, arbitrary, and self-defeating.

Thus, primary education in rural areas and urban slums suffers from neglect, inattention, and poor motivation. Teachers are often absent, teaching is poor, schools lack essential supplies, buildings are poorly maintained and poorly designed, extra-curricular activities are virtually non-existent, syllabuses are of poor quality and often irrelevant to perceived societal concerns, and children are encouraged to memorize rather than understand. Many of these problems exist at higher levels as well. At the college and university level, curriculums as well as syllabi are centrally designed, hence leaving little room for teacher creativity or for the introduction of emerging ideas and problems into the course content. Education is generally seen only as a diploma-granting activity, thus encouraging indifference towards quality concerns.

Conditions in health care, social welfare, environmental conservation, and population welfare programmes are broadly similar. Rural hospitals and dispensaries lack staff and facilities, and do not have effective systems of supervision over the dispensation of medicines provided by the government. The hygienic conditions of even some of the best hospitals are inadequate. The staff, even where they choose to be present, are poorly motivated and poorly managed. Neglect and malpractice are common, with very little legal recourse available to the victims.

Social welfare and income support schemes, of which there have been a few, suffer from problems of identification and targeting. The programmes are also simplistic, in that they are not based on a proper understanding of the causes and dangers of poverty and destitution. In addition, the personnel managing the programmes are again poorly motivated and often interested only in fulfilling their assigned quota, rather than in following the spirit of the programme. Most programmes suffer from considerable leakages.

In general, population welfare programmes have tended to fluctuate between authoritarianism and indifference. Very little effort has been made to integrate the programmes into the concerns of the supposed beneficiaries. Thus, the personnel of the population welfare department are devoted exclusively to proving that they have distributed the requisite number of contraceptives. These programmes are simplistic because they do not even seek to exploit the interconnections between socio-economic change and fertility behaviour.

In short, while there is an argument for expanding the range and coverage of existing systems of service delivery, there is an even more imperative argument for improving the functioning of such systems, of making them more responsive to broader social needs as experienced and articulated by the supposed beneficiaries, of improving the motivation and professionalism of the personnel providing the services, and of integrating qualitative as well as quantitative targets into the programme. This requires an agenda for institutional reform.

1. AN AGENDA FOR INSTITUTIONAL REFORM

Such a programme will require action along five closely related dimensions: decentralization, community development, integration of needs, accountability, and the provision and strengthening of judicial recourse.

1.1. Decentralization

The first, and most important, component of institutional reform is a systematic programme of decentralization. This stems from the recognition that centralized state agencies have proven to be inefficient as well as inequitable in the provision of social services and welfare. There is a growing consensus in the development literature that appropriate and sustainable social change will not be possible in most Southern countries without massive decentralization of the economy and the polity. However, the full implications of this recognition have often not been worked out.

It is widely conceded that the existing highly centralized states in Southern countries are poor managers of economic systems (and even worse of social systems) in volatile environments. This is a simple systemic argument. Centralized systems are not simple aggregates of more decentralized systems, and can often be weaker than the latter.

Even if the speed of processing information were to be identical in both systems, the very quantum of information which flows to and from the centre requires more time and better management. Moreover, if, as it is reasonable to assume, the quality of information depends inversely on the distance travelled, then centralized systems will receive poorer information and will become less efficient than decentralized ones.

In general, centralized management of social services is not likely to be responsive to the problems of vulnerable groups. Galbraith (1990) sums up the problems of leviathan systems simply as the lack of flexibility to respond. To this can be added the lack of empathy to respond. This is not out of volition. It is simply that the larger the system, the greater the unknowable. The geographical, cultural, and conceptual distance that separates programme managers from focal groups creates deficiencies in the information base and time lags in analysis and response. All this is widely conceded.

However, a major strand of thinking has used this as an argument to roll back the state entirely. But this extreme position fails to recognize that some social services—most prominently primary education. health, and income distribution—must continue to be provided through collective social action. Our view is that the state cannot abdicate its responsibility of being the primary guarantor of social development. Abdication of this responsibility is likely to hurt vulnerable groups in the population—mothers, infants, primary school age cohorts, particularly girls, and the poor. This will cause not only human damage, but also impair the productivity of present and future generations, thus causing economic damage (see chapter 6). There are high economic and social returns to continued state financing of social services.

The state's role in managing distribution is determined by domestic imperatives. Domestic institutions articulate the value attached to welfare and equity, and their role in the growth strategy. At some level, these values emerge from a shared recognition in society of the interdependence between the welfare of various groups in the population. The strength of institutions, the degree of consensus, and the level of articulation will determine the strength of the popular constraints placed on the state's actions.

In industrialized countries, attempts since the 1970s to roll back welfare programmes—on the grounds that they lower efficiency and productivity—have been constrained by opposition from dissenting voices and institutions. In other middle and low income countries that may lack explicit civic institutions, states have often been restrained from privatizing welfare and social services by the fear of mass-based political alternatives. In Pakistan, however, the absence of either of these possibilities has encouraged the state to move towards the privatization of welfare with virtually no constraints. As a result, the Pakistani state is rapidly abdicating its responsibilities. It has a comprehensive agenda for privatizing social sector development, and it will not redistribute income through increasing direct taxes.

The alternative vision for maintaining the priority of collective social provision of basic services and welfare depends on the vision of a decentralized economy and polity. This scheme, which is developed below in some detail in the context of the education sector, would involve the strengthening of local government institutions and transferring the management and provision of social services to the lowest possible level of the state—primary education, health, and environmental care to the community level, and secondary and tertiary care to town/city or district levels, and to higher levels only where necessary.

However, such decentralization would neither be possible nor effective unless the first step—namely, the recognition of the sovereignty of the decentralized units—is taken. This means that society has to begin the process of creating and legislating local rights, obligations, and responsibilities in a manner that cannot be tampered with arbitrarily. In other words, the problem of decentralization can be described as a process of forging a consensus over a local charter.

Just as the federal Constitution and the National Finance Commission Awards (see chapter 5) have created the possibility for provincial governments to focus their attention exclusively on the governance of the province, there is a need for institutions and awards that would create the possibility for lower tiers of government—at the district, city, town, and village levels—to shift their attention exclusively to the governance of their particular territory. In the absence of such explicit agreements, the primary incentive will continue to be the manipulation of, and negotiations with, higher echelons of government.

While this is not the place to go into the details of what a new decentralized structure will look like, a few comments are necessary.[1] First, the idea that social services be managed at the lowest possible level of aggregation may translate into many possible tiers of government—in addition to the federal and provincial, district, metropolitan, town, and village level management is called for. In addition, other administrative and political units—divisional, *tehsil*, and union council—may also have justifiable claims in this regard. Second, the recognition of sovereign rights of such institutions means that the rights of federal and provincial governments to shift administrative and political boundaries will have to be made less arbitrary. Third, there will have to be a mixture of participatory, representative, and managerial forms of governance depending on the need. Fourth, every attempt must be made to create macro-level stability for each unit of governance in order for there to be incentive for each unit to focus on its micro-level concerns.

This also provides an alternative way of perceiving the debate between the state and the market (Israel 1990). While there are global and efficiency grounds for the state's abdication of the role of managing growth, there are domestic imperatives for the state's retaining the role of management of income distribution and the provision of social services.

1.2. Community development

If the state is an imperfect manager of social services, then a lower level of aggregation has to be found for their creation and management. This is the second necessary condition in conceptualizing an alternative strategy for social sector development. In addition to the theoretical argument that local communities are the best protectors of their interests, there are strong empirical arguments to support this view.

The theoretical argument is as follows: Define a community on the basis of relative spatial proximity, like a village or an urban *abadi*. This very largely also defines the community in terms of common requirements for social services, like education, health, housing, water, sanitation, roads, energy needs, and the environment. It may also define the community in terms of basic classes, and therefore employment and income needs. If the community has a set of common social service requirements, then its perception of the problem is likely to be the most accurate, and its solution to the problem will be the most relevant and useful under any given set of constraints. Finally, the community's response to the problem will also be the fastest.[2]

There are two other empirical arguments. The first is the new system of production, based on flexible specialization, uses labour re-skilling, worker innovation incentives, and quality circles. This system finds that the immediacy of labour to the problems of production makes it a better innovator than the R&D engineers in their remote laboratories (Kaplinsky 1990). The second argument is based on a few successful experiments by Non Governmental Organizations (NGOs) such as the Orangi Pilot Project (OPP) in Pakistan. These NGOs operate at the community level by encouraging the community to identify and prioritize its problems and define its solutions. The success of these programmes in terms of their expansion and impact has been very high (see Appendix).

Thus, a major element of the alternative strategy for social sector development is to define the community as the principal agent of change. This means that the community decides what services to demand under a given set of constraints. This establishment of a clear responsibility with the community gives the system an endogenous dynamic, which is not immediately obvious in traditional development strategy. Traditional development strategy is premised on the assumption that exogenous agents of change are essential to progress since they are more technically advanced. The alternative argument is that the demonstration effect of change in other communities and the democratic articulation of needs within each community will lead to an endogenous development motivation.[3] Autonomy of choice will also minimize conflict across communities.

Focusing on the community also brings out the need to integrate various possible structures of collective decision-making—participatory, representative, and managerial. At some level, supervision and accountability will be ensured through the institutionalization of participatory decision-making. This will have to be complemented, in appropriate cases by other forms of decision-making (Banuri 1991a).

However, identifying the community as the principle decision-maker is not sufficient to produce harmonious social development. In order to become operative, the programme requires an institutional basis of action, as well as financial and technical support from the government. As mentioned earlier, the first step is to legislate on the rights and powers of various tiers of government. In addition, there is a need for providing support to NGOs engaged in community development. In some cases, as in the NWFP, the government itself has to set up an NGO for this purpose. In other cases, existing NGOs could be supported by the provision of funds, training, and requisite legislation.

1.3. Integration of needs

The third necessary condition for an alternative strategy for social sector development is the integration of needs. This is again both a theoretical and an empirically-observed argument. The basic argument is that the long-term solution to one need does not lie in fulfilling that need alone. As pointed out in chapter 6, most needs have joint causal factors. So unless all these joint causal factors are alleviated, that particular need can never be satisfied. For example, Sen (1991) argues that, in the case of food security systems, since malnutrition is caused jointly by the lack of caloric intake, health care, shelter, potable water, sanitation, and income, meeting only one of these needs will not resolve the problem. Successful NGOs like OPP in Pakistan, SEWA, in India, and BRAC (Bangladesh Rural Advancement Committee) have discovered the problem of joint needs and have had to evolve an integrated multi-sectoral approach through their experience (Cornia 1987a).

1.4. Accountability

The fourth necessary condition for an alternative strategy for social sector development is that the community organization should be accountable to the users of its services; that is, the community organization should be accountable to the community itself. This is necessary for the community as both a defensive and an offensive measure.

As a defensive measure, the community must be able to hold the community organization accountable for carrying out its mandated work. This principle must be embodied in the legal charter that creates the community organization as an instrument of the community. The community organization's failure to meet its obligations should be covered by civil and criminal law. Breach of contract should represent a clear and effective threat.

As an offensive measure, the community must be able to hold the community organization responsible for its social service development lagging behind that of other similar communities. A demonstration effect, leading to competition between communities in similar conditions, will provide an impetus for development of social services. This offensive accountability must be embodied in the charter of the community organization in the form of periodic elections to the organization. The community's ability to sack and re-elect the organization leadership frequently will create more dynamic organizations.

1.5. Judicial recourse

The fifth necessary condition for institutional restructuring is the community's access to judicial recourse. If defensive and offensive accountability of the community's organization is to be practised, the community should be able to sue for breach of contract. Therefore, judicial recourse must first become an obvious social choice for the individual or community by being perceived as fair. Then it must also become convenient, cheap, and fast. Judicial recourse is important not only in its own right, but also because the absence of strong, independent, and effective judicial institutions can become an obstacle to the pursuit of any social objective whatsoever. This is especially the case for the institutionalization of decentralization and community management.[4]

In Pakistan, community-level judicial institutions (and some higher ones as well) have suffered from over-burdening, and, therefore unconscionable delays, poor support services, poor career prospects, and poor motivation. There are increasing concerns over the weakening of supervision. These problems need to be examined and redressed. However, the answer is not to introduce ad hoc measures, such as speedy courts, that lead to the undermining of the very principles of justice but to strengthen the existing system (Jahangir 1991).

Judicial recourse will facilitate not just micro-level community development but also the entire growth and development process as argued above. If growth and distribution are to be based largely on the development of private capital, then it is necessary to provide security for private capital. Ultimate security of private capital rests in judicial recourse for breach of property rights and contracts.

2. MOBILIZING RESOURCES FOR HUMAN DEVELOPMENT

One reason for the inability to raise resources is that the existing system is perceived as providing unequal access to the services created by the government. The sense of injustice this produces can result in an unwillingness to pay for the services. In other words, the system itself is a constraint on generating private expenditure at the lower end of the income scale. Moreover, if taxes are viewed as bearing no relation to the service, which is arbitrarily and unjustly distributed in any case, then there would be no incentive to pay. Lastly, the possibility of evading taxes, either by colluding with tax officials, or by seeking personalized amendments in the regulations, also creates a disincentive for complying with legal obligations. This is especially so in competitive industries where relative profitability may be determined almost entirely by the ability to manipulate the tax situation.

This suggests action along three fronts: first improving the equity and accessibility of the services provided by the state;[5] second, linking the services more closely with the revenues; lastly, reforming the system of tax administration itself, to make it less arbitrary, more universal, equitable, and legitimate.

Linkages between services and revenues can be provided through a number of mechanisms. Thus, instead of asking for a general increase in the tax revenue base, it may be more feasible, as pointed out in chapter 6, to increase the tax yield if it were earmarked for specific social service expenditures. Classic examples are linking vehicle taxes to the improvement of municipal roads and gasoline taxes to the improvement of highways. In general, the quality and quantity of the service could be linked directly to resource generation. For instance, direct and indirect taxes could be levied for the provision of secondary or tertiary levels of education and health. As discussed, direct income taxes could even be levied on untaxed sectors like agriculture.

This tax yield would become more legitimate if the levy and expenditure were to be linked regionally, or in smaller territorial units. The lower the level of disaggregation and the more explicit the link between the revenue and the service, the more legitimate the tax burden. For instance, the typical village population of 200-400 households would be more willing to pay a tax for draining and sanitation in their own village, but less willing to pay the same tax if it goes into the provincial (or even district) coffers before being allocated for the same purpose. For example, as Altaf *et al.* (1991) have shown, there is a high level of willingness to pay for predictable and high quality water supply in rural as well as urban areas.

The existing system of unequal access constitutes another major impediment to the accumulation of private investment funds for social services at the lower end of the income scale. However, when the poor can be organized to provide their own social services, they have been observed to generate their own investment (see Appendix).

The experiment of providing counterpart public funding to private institutions has also been very successful. The government has expanded rural production infrastructure considerably in this manner. Village water channels have been traditionally unlined, which has led to wastage of land and water due to seepage and salinity. To line these channels, the government has offered material inputs if matched by village labour. As a result, approximately 10-20 per cent of the water channels have been lined in the Punjab over a few years through participatory action by local villagers. Similarly, villages that were allocated public road access are willing to provide land (or where necessary, the money to purchase it) for this purpose; the burden is shared on an equitable basis of owned area, and has been observed to work well. It is of interest in these cases that the government acted not as the sole source of funding and management, but as a successful NGO by orchestrating the voluntary actions of various civic groups and by bringing in institutional restructuring to improve the efficiency of the system. The extension of these experiments of counterpart funding and community management to social service provision would be straightforward.

However, the kind of disaggregated responsibilities envisaged here can be generalized only if they are linked with proposals for redistribution across regions. In other words, a broad societal consensus on the need to transfer funds to poorer communities—to support their local effort at providing social services—would be necessary. As mentioned earlier, such redistribution must be done in a predictable and transparent manner.

Another source of resources is the improvement in the functioning of existing institutions. In education, the most glaring example is that many rural schools have been found to exist on paper only (SAHE 1989). In sanitation, urban municipal corporation funds are frequently diverted to officials' homes, so urban waste remains uncollected and visible. In health care, hospital stocks of medicines are sold on the black market. The degree of misappropriation became evident when hospitals attempted to block pilferage by differentiating the packaging of their drugs from that of the private sectors. The result was that the private sector developed serious shortages in critical drugs. In housing, under the Seventh Five Year Plan (1988-93) the government attempted to build a very limited number of rural 7 *marla* (200 square yards) houses which lay unoccupied and derelict.

There is the possibility of introducing financial cum physical measures to increase the capacity utilization of existing institutions. This is based on the constancy of fixed costs. If fixed overhead costs are large, relative to the variable running costs of a facility, then the number of users can be increased. A school can add an afternoon shift, and even a night-time adult literacy shift, to its regular morning shift. This reduces the fixed costs of the building by one-half or two-thirds, and only the variable running costs increase. Similarly, a hospital can entertain more patients, and as long as it increases its working hours proportionately, the quality need not deteriorate up to some optimal use of its fixed facilities.

The third issue is of direct reform of tax administration. It may well be that work incentives, organizational structures, and the nature of internal and external supervision have led to the creation of significant leakages. Not only does this reduce revenue collection, it also adversely influences the willingness to pay taxes. There is an urgent need to examine this issue in all its complexity.

3. A CONCRETE EXAMPLE OF AN ALTERNATIVE EDUCATION STRATEGY

The abstract conditions for social sector development delineated above can be illustrated using the concrete example of one sector, i.e., education. This will apply by analogy to other critical sectors like health, sanitation, housing, and income generation.

3.1. School Education

In the education pyramid, we can begin at the base with the largest enrolment in primary schools and work up to the apex of the smallest enrolment in universities and professional colleges. Define a community as a group of relatively contiguous households whose children should be in primary school. Assume three problems in this community. There is no public primary school. Boys have access to a primary school at a one-hour distance from their home. Girls' enrolment in an equally distant school is much lower.[6] These three problems imply a school supply and demand problem. Because facilities are low, some households withhold boys and even more households withhold girls. For a significant increase in coverage, especially for girls, both supply and demand problems have to be tackled.

The community can elect a school board from within itself to establish, monitor, and guide the running of a primary school. To meet the demand problem for girls, the board needs to be more sensitive and responsive to girls' enrolment problems. Survey results show that, for the most part, girls' and boys' non-enrolment result from similar causes.[7] These include work at home and on the farm, expense, and negative attitudes of parents and the child. However, an earlier survey of the literature indicates that rural girls may have special needs, meeting which would enhance their enrolments (Khan 1993). These could include boundary walls, toilet facilities, women teachers, child-care, and flexible timings. Responsiveness to these enrolment needs would be facilitated by a school board consisting of a majority of women.

The school board can be created by a charter which mandates it to establish the school. Given the charter, the state should recognize the school board as the competent authority as well. The school board should estimate minimal requirements for boys and girls of the community. It should then estimate costs. The board can then negotiate with the state for whole, part, or counterpart public funding. The board has to generate the community's share of the funding. It can experiment with a variety of cost distributions across the community. These can range from minimal fixed contributions, based on the ability to pay, to payments based on land and asset ownership.

After generating this funding, the board can then contract out the construction of the school premises and monitor the construction. The board will also be responsible for managing the school, monitoring its running, and providing guidance. Four areas critical to a school's running are teachers' employment policy, school pricing policy, syllabus policy, and a specific enrolment enhancement incentive policy.

Teachers' employment policy must be designed to minimize absenteeism which plagues remote primary schools. It must encourage local employment and so create an incentive for education. It must encourage women's employment, and so motivate girls to get education. To meet these requirements, local employment and women teachers should be given top priority. Finally, employment policy must offer permanent contracts. This will be critical for increasing the vested interest of teachers in their school.

School pricing policy has to balance low fee incentives for attendance against high fee for growth. To meet both these needs, a two-tier structure could be introduced. Local children's fees could be kept low and children from other localities could pay more. The higher fee would reflect use of facilities by those who had not contributed to establishing them. It would also reflect better facilities in some localities attracting children from other localities.

School pricing policy could also differentiate morning, afternoon, and evening shifts. Local children could be preferred for morning shifts.

Children from other localities could be given afternoon shifts. The school premises could also be used for adult literacy programmes, or other social sector programmes like health and nutrition care in the evenings.

Syllabus policy has to balance standardization with local innovation and incentives. Standardization can be checked through periodic province level exams at the end of primary, middle, and high schools. This leaves the policy fairly free for innovation and incentives. Syllabi must be approved by both the teachers and the board. In fact, teachers must form a majority on the syllabus committee. The syllabi must also create an incentive to increase enrolments. Some skilling courses which increase employment and income generating prospects should be included. Regional languages, literature, and history must also be prioritized.

Finally, a specific incentives policy must be designed to increase enrolment. The school board will best understand the nature of the incentives which the community needs to send its children to school. An important constraint on children's schooling is that education is found to be too expensive, both directly and indirectly in terms of the non-availability of the children to do household and farm chores.[8] The school then needs to offer some material incentive to compensate at least partly for this opportunity cost.

One generally agreed form of compensation is the provision of a simple hot meal and milk. This could also be combined with a nutrition policy for vulnerable children. For girls, the provision of a creche for sibling children under their care would be a major incentive. In each case, with the local school board in charge, incentives could be provided locally at cheap rates. For example, elder women with a low opportunity cost of labour could provide meals and creche services cheaply.[9]

3.2. Post-school education

The case of post-school education is analogous to that of primary education once a community is defined. Since college enrolment is lower, the community will be larger and spatially more spread out. But the community will still be defined by the college that serves it. The community should elect a college board similarly recognized by the state.

In pricing policy, the board can charge lower local fees and higher fees for students from other regions. It can expand its facilities, attract students from other regions, and so finance its growth. In syllabi policy, the faculty should have sole authority over courses. College syllabi must contain a high proportion of vocational skilling for employment and income generation. College syllabi should meet the regional demand for employment as well as the more global demand.

The college board must have an additional specific growth policy. For this, the board should liaise with both the state and the private sector, which can endow chairs and faculties. The board can also apply parental means testing to determine students' fees. This will also help generate funding for growth.

4. SUMMARY

The argument of the previous section is not intended as a prescription for the education sector alone, but as the basis for finding a more general alternative for human resource development. Thus, we believe that the responsibility for supervising and arranging primary health care must be transferred to local communities, that secondary and tertiary care must be supervised by local boards of governors at the appropriate levels, and that the salaries and perquisites of the providers of such services must be linked to the assessments of their effectiveness and worth by the beneficiary populations.

Similarly, income support and welfare programmes in general need to be routed through local communities. These communities must be encouraged to take over the primary responsibility for providing such services. Whether they are in the forms of loans, grants, scholarships, or training schemes, the expanded participation of the community will enhance both the targeting and the liquidity of the programmes. Similarly, programmes of nutrition, school lunches, nutritional support to pregnant and lactating women, support for infants and children, particularly girls, need to be more efficiently targeted. This can be done better at the community level through a proper system of governance that is open, transparent, participatory, and democratic.

Lastly, population welfare programmes need to be focused on the needs of the communities, providing jobs for women, encouraging female literacy, reducing macro-level uncertainty, and enhancing predictability in the social, political, and economic environment. This means that the focus of the programme must shift from the statistical objectives of the agency to the felt needs of the community which induce people to have many children.

This chapter then contains our vision of just development. To summarize, in this chapter we identified a model for development of the social sectors based on abstract necessary conditions. We argued that there are two necessary conditions for significantly increasing the proportion of the population covered by the social sectors. These are an increased share of the expenditure on social services and increased efficiency of these sectors. Significant generation of expenditure in both the public and private sectors is constrained by the efficiency of the social sector. Efficiency gains in the social sectors are small, using traditional, financial, and physical administrative reforms. Efficiency gains are arguably higher using institutional restructuring. This institutional restructuring in turn is based on five necessary conditions. These are decentralization from state management, community control, an agenda of integrated needs, accountability of the community's organization, and the judicial recourse required for instituting accountability. We demonstrated our vision of just adjustment and just development, based on these necessary conditions, by giving a concrete example of the organization and financing of community-based schooling. We argued that such a social experiment has wide applicability for the attainment of our vision of just development and moving beyond adjustment with a human face.

NOTES

1. For one example of a detailed account, see Banuri (1991a).
2. Findings of an SDPI (Sustainable Development Policy Institute) study of community rural water supplies, supported by the Multi-Sectoral Support Unit, suggests that a catalyst in the form of a community mobilizer may be needed to induce successful collective action. See Khan *et al.* (1996).
3. Once again, we do not preclude the possibility that the process of change can be initiated by an external agent or that an external agent can have a qualitative impact on the process and pace of change. What matters is that the community owns and internalizes the transformation process.
4. For a detailed argument, see Banuri (1991a).
5. Some of the recommendations made earlier regarding decentralization and community management are pertinent in this regard.
6. Distance from school is now not as great a problem but still not an insignificant one. Final results of the 1991 *Pakistan Integrated Household Survey* (1992, pp.67-8) show that 11.4 per cent of males, and 13.7 per cent of females aged 5-25 mentioned 'school too far away' as the first reason for not attending school. For males, this ranked as the fourth, and for females, the third most frequently mentioned cause of not attending school.
7. *Pakistan Integrated Household Survey, Final Results, 1991* (1992, pp.67-8).
8. Combining the direct cost and the indirect cost (children not being there to do chores), the cost factor is the first and second most important reason, respectively, for boys' and girls' non-enrolment. *Pakistan Integrated Household Survey, Final Results, 1991* (1992, pp.67-8).
9. See Azfar (1994) for an account of a SAP-funded community schooling programme which has several features similar to the community schooling model we delineated here.

8

NGOs in Pakistan : An Overview

Khawar Mumtaz

INTRODUCTION

Chapters 6 and 7 presented community or participatory development as an alternative model for attaining human-centred development or just development. In this Appendix, we review the experience of the NGO sector, particularly the component engaged in grassroots participatory development in Pakistan. After an overview, successful experiences are reviewed, lessons highlighted, and problems identified. As will become evident from reading this Appendix, the progress of participatory development in Pakistan does lend hope to it representing an alternative approach which can, in due course, substantially complement mainstream development efforts.

1. BACKGROUND

In a 1991 study, UNDP compiled a list of 4,833 NGOs (56 per cent of which were in the Punjab and 36 per cent in Sindh) of which and contacted 1,035 (10 per cent randomly) for the study (UNDP 1991b). Most of the NGOs sampled were registered under the 1961 Welfare Ordinance, 70 per cent were rural CBOs, 11 per cent were led by females, 84 per cent were welfare organizations, 54 per cent operated at the community level, 5 per cent at the national level, and 56 per cent had a membership of less than 100. 87 per cent of sampled NGOs felt they would benefit from training and 55 per cent found the lack of funds a major obstacle, although only about one-third were not receiving any government grants.

The TVO (Trust for Voluntary Organisations) commissioned a study in 1994 to update the existing information base generated by UNDP. Thus all NGOs registered under the Companies Ordinance 1984, Societies Registration Act 1860, and the Voluntary Social Welfare (Registration and Control) Ordinance of 1961, were initially considered part of the universe. This identified 8,547 NGOs, which suggested a very rapid growth rate of NGOs. However, after excluding religious organizations, professional and commercial associations, employees unions, housing societies, urban health and sports clubs, and private clinics and hospitals, 4,545 organizations remained. Of these, 1,998 were found non-existent or not found at all. Even so, this represents a very rapid growth rate over a three-year period. Once again, most of the NGOs were found to be community-based organizations (CBOs) engaged in charity, relief, and welfare work.

The NGOs may be categorized as:

i. Welfare-oriented: providing social services to the poor and the underprivileged.
ii. Grassroots development-oriented: geared towards organizing targeted communities for participating in development activities.
iii. Issue-oriented: women's NGOs focus on improving the economic and social status of women. Activities include social service and delivery, research and information dissemination, advocacy, and development. Similarly, there are environmental, health, population, and research NGOs.

The roles and perspectives of NGOs have grown and evolved over the years. From being limited to charitable and philanthropic organizations at the time of independence, NGOs stepped into welfare-oriented roles as the state system increasingly failed to deliver. After the 1970s, there has been a shift towards development and community-based initiatives. The number of women NGOs in particular has expanded rapidly in the post-1970s period. Most NGOs are supported by community contributions, local donors, and/or receive funds from the government. In recent years, support from international donors has also become available.

2. SCOPE OF OPERATIONS

2.1. Welfare-Oriented NGOs

As reported above, the great majority of NGOs in Pakistan have a social welfare orientation. They operate in neighbourhoods or villages and are involved in the provision of civic amenities such as basic health, education, library facilities, vocational training, youth programmes, and credit. According to a 1982 survey, only 50 per cent of the registered NGOs could actually be located. Of these, 40 per cent were involved in the provision of education, 11 per cent in health, and over 45 per cent in social community services. Again, according to the 1991 UNDP survey, welfare orientation was dominant. The major services provided included medical aid, vocational, and industrial skills, formal education, assistance to poor students, and adult education.

Among the welfare-oriented NGOs, the Abdus Sattar Edhi Welfare Trust is outstanding. The organization's activities include humanitarian assistance, attending to those affected by civil strife in the cities of Sindh (Karachi, Hyderabad, Sukkur), and running homes for destitute women and children, organizing feeding programmes for the poor rehabilitation of drug addicts, and providing relief in emergency situations. There is now a network of Edhi Homes throughout the country.

2.2. Grassroots Development Organizations

Organizations with the specific objectives of mobilizing and organizing targeted communities for development activities have emerged over the last decade or so. Though few in number, these have provided models for dealing with socio-economic issues at the community, neighbourhood, or lane level.

Among NGOs working with agriculture and rural development, three types are significant. First, there are the national level capacity-building and/or funding organizations. These include TVO (Trust for Voluntary Organizations), SPO (Strengthening Participatory Organizations), and NGORC (NGO Resource Centre). Second, there are implementing support organizations such as Pattan and Sungi that work directly with CBOs and, in the process, attempt to transform their orientation from a welfare-oriented one to a participatory development one. Third, there are the Rural Support Programmes that have followed the AKRSP (Aga Khan Rural Support Programme) model of forming village or community organizations. The Rural Support Programme Network (RSPN) is a network of 16 such rural support programmes, which, as of December 1994, had 4,464 organizations with a membership of 115,636 and over a million estimated beneficiaries.[1] While the RSPs do have a specific model, they are open to working with existing community organizations: for instance, Sungi sometimes initiates a community organization.

AKRSP is perhaps the largest NGO in the country in terms of its budget and beneficiary base. AKRSP operates in five of Pakistan's northern mountain districts. Institution-building and community participation are the keys to AKRSP's work. It has encouraged the establishment of broad-based village organizations (2,809 in 1993) to generate capital through savings, upgrade human skills to increase productivity, and alleviate hardships. The AKRSP's *Thirteenth Annual Review* (p.16) reports that as of December 1995, there were 854 women's organizations with a total membership of 23,010. They are involved in collective production and income-generating activities, which include producing vegetables, poultry farming, and running plant nurseries. The objective is to organize women and to equip them with information, technology, savings, and credit for income generation, and to improve their status and quality of life (further details in section 3.3).

In urban areas, the major grassroots non-government development initiative is the Orangi Pilot Project (OPP) in Karachi. It was sponsored by an international financial organization in 1980 and received support from other international donor agencies. OPP's entry point was sanitation and its activities revolve around broad-based lane organizations managed by local inhabitants. It has developed physical infrastructure for sanitation with community participation. This has later been followed by activities in education, health, and income generation for women. An offshoot of the OPP is the Rural Pilot Project which began work in 1990 with middle farmers in rural areas surrounding Karachi (further details in section 3.4).

Busti is another community oriented organization formed to deal with the problems of *katchi abadis* of Karachi. Saiban, also in Karachi, is patterned on the Khuada Ki Basti experience in Hyderabad (discussed below). Anjuman Barai Taleem and SAHE are among the NGOs in Lahore that are experimenting with innovative methods to bring education to children in low-income neighbourhoods. Both started work on the basis of self-help and self-reliance; SAHE, however, now accepts donor funding for some of its activities.

Adult Basic Education Society (ABES), operating from Gujranwala, is an NGO which develops and produces basic education and adult literacy material. It organizes adult literacy programmes in low-income urban and semi-urban areas with active community participation. Unless the community is willing to work in partnership with ABES, programmes are not started. In the late 1980s, it developed the Health Education and Learning Project (HELP), which works on the principles of intense community interaction.

2.3. Women's NGOs

There was a proliferation of women's NGOs in the 1980s. This period coincided with the institution of repressive measures against women in Pakistan and the increased support of WID programmes from international development agencies. Thus, the growth of women's organizations received an impetus from the availability of donor funding for Women-in-Development projects. Women's NGOs fall in the same broad categories as all NGOs in Pakistan, i.e., they are either welfare-oriented or grassroots development organizations. Most of these are based in urban areas with a few having outreach to rural communities. A number of women's NGOs that started in the last decade are concerned with advocacy of women's rights and legal aid.

Among the organizations with a relatively large outreach are APWA, Family Planning Association of Pakistan (FPAP), Behbud Association, and the Girl Guides Association. APWA, established in 1949, was one of Pakistan's first women's organizations. It established a network of industrial homes and girls' schools and colleges. It runs mother and child care clinics and outlets for crafts made by women. To date, APWA is perhaps the largest service NGO in the country with regional headquarters in provincial capitals and offices in district headquarters. Its outreach varies from region to region. In Balochistan, it interacts with rural women, while in the Punjab and Karachi its primary focus is the urban poor.

FPAP is another NGO which operates in all four provinces of the country. The majority of its programmes and projects are in rural areas, but it also concentrates on slum areas in cities. It is the largest population and health NGO and is believed to be more active than government agencies in family planning promotion and services. FPAP has adopted a multi-sectoral approach for attaining its objectives, and its emphasis is on raising the status of women through training, skill development, and employment/self-employment opportunities.

FPAP has developed energy-saving stoves through user-participation, and has introduced kitchen-gardening and food conservation programmes as components of its community-based projects. It has also expressed interest in training its field personnel in forestry extension. FPAP's mixed-media information campaign has contributed to awareness regarding family planning methods.

Family Welfare Cooperative Organization (FWCO) in Lahore is a multi-sectoral organization with strong health and sewing-cutting-embroidery (traditional skills) development programmes. It has, over the years, added secretarial training and food processing to its wide-ranging programmes. Essentially a service-and-delivery organization, it runs a development workers' training course with the support of the Ministry for Women Development and Youth Affairs. FWCO reaches out to women in some of the villages on the periphery of Lahore.

Other known women's NGOs in this category are the Behbud Association, with branches in Lahore, Karachi, and Rawalpindi; Maternity and Child Welfare Association of Pakistan; and Voluntary Health and Nutrition Association (PVHNA). An association of a number of health-related NGOs, PVHNA runs a Women Development Workers' Academy in Karachi. Its network of women's organizations helps it access middle-level field workers for training.

A relatively new category of women's NGOs are resource centres involved in documentation, research, and publications besides advocacy, training, and networking. Their major contribution has been of generating a rich body of material on women and women's issues, which has provided sound documentation for the women's movement as well as for planners. These include AURAT, Shirkat Gah, Applied Socio-Economic Research, and Simorgh.

During the late 1980s and early 1990s, the rural areas have seen a spurt of women's CBO's in Sindh and to a lesser extent in NWFP and the Punjab. A major women's NGO is the women's wing of Sindh Rural Workers Co-operative Organization (SRWCO). SRWCO works among small and middle-level farm households and emphasizes the formation of local organizations to deal with problems like education, water supply, and health on a self-help basis. SRWCO has a women's wing which has established a network among women of several villages in Sindh. It has a cadre of trained women field workers who are responsible for imparting skills in poultry care, basic hygiene, and organization.

Informal women's networks exist within the framework of the social organization in rural areas. These operate in whole villages, or neighbourhoods in the case of larger villages, or on the basis of class and *biradri* (caste, clan) structures. Reflecting social norms regarding seniority, elderly women usually hold the position of authority in these informal networks. While no extensive examination of these networks is available, various case studies refer to their presence.

2.4. Environmental NGOs

Most developed NGOs now incorporate sustainable development in their mandate. Recently, a number of NGOs have emerged that focus exclusively on environmental issues. IUCN, an internation NGO that engages in research, policy advocacy, training, institutional building, public awareness, and environmental education, has been instrumental in catalysing the emergence of this category of NGOs, specially through the National Conservation Strategy (NCS) the formulation of which it facilitated. The Sustainable Development Policy Institute was established as a research NGO to help with the implementation of the NCS; it has various research programmes underway pertaining to sustainable development. Other NGOs focus exclusively on the environment, some from an advocacy perspective and others with a continuation of development and advocacy objectives, with varying degrees of effectiveness. They include Environment Protection Society of Pakistan; Environment Management Society; Pakistan Environment Protection Foundation; Society for the Protection and Conservation of the Environment; SHEHRI; Environment Conservation Forum; Friends of Earth and Trees; Society for Energy Environment and Development; PILER (Pakistan Institute of Labour Education and Research); Sungi; and Shirkat Gah (with a particular focus on women and environment).[2]

2.5. Donor Initiatives

There has also been much donor interest in participatory development spearheaded by development NGOs. ACTIONAID engages in direct implementation, while OXFAM is involved in capacity-building directly with NGOs, as well as with funding apex NGOs like Sungi, Pattan, and Baanhn Beli. The participatory approach to development has been incorporated into public sector organizations with donor support. The fundamental principles are those of organizing the community to ensure participation in order to identify and prioritize the community's needs and work out modalities of project implementation. While an exact count of such initiatives is not available, there are a number of noteworthy projects that have been initiated, reflecting the possibility of collaborative efforts between government, donor agencies, private institutions, and citizens.

Inspired by the AKRSP experience, several donor-assisted government projects have started in the NWFP. These include: the Pak-German Integrated Rural Development Project in Mardan and Swabi, the Pak-Swiss Kalam Integrated Development Project in Swat, the Pak-Holland Groundwater Irrigation Project in the Tribal Areas, and the Pak-Holland Social Forestry Project in Malakand. In addition, a number of rural support programmes have also been established on government donor initiatives, e.g. NRSP, SRSC.

In Balochistan, the Pak-German Self-Help Project has led to the formulation of the Balochistan Rural Support Programme. With German assistance, a dairy project was initiated by the Punjab government, which has been converted into an NGO, Idara-e-Kissan. This NGO, comprising of small farmers, is involved in milk production and collection for a milk processing plant. They have now expanded their product line to include yoghurt and fruit juices.

2.6. Major Issues

Pakistan has a fairly large number of NGOs varying in size, scope, and operations. They originated due to specific needs at a given time, but in most cases their impact and growth has remained limited. There is also evidence of NGOs becoming non-functional once the immediate reason for their creation is resolved. As mentioned earlier, 40 per cent of the NGOs in the TVO sample could not be located. The TVO Report did preface, in all fairness, that this is not likely to be different from the survival rate, say, in the business sector.

A study conducted in 1990 found the following issues facing the NGO sector in Pakistan (Husain 1990):

In the process of introducing latrines built on a low-cost, self-help basis, the project team (led by a woman) discovered the high levels of illiteracy and dropout rates in the area. The available schools were either too expensive, or the quality of education very poor. The problem was worse for girls who, due to social/cultural reasons, were not sent to school at all. The regular school hours meant that girls would not be available to help in the housework. It was also obvious that the girls themselves were keen to be educated.

The concept of home-schools evolved, keeping in view all the problems and constraints of the community. It involved intense mobilization, followed by the identification in each neighbourhood of the girl with the most education, who was chosen to start a primary level school in her home. All children between 4 and 12 years were eligible and school hours were fixed to suit the children. A minimum fee of Rs 5 was established and those who could not afford it were exempted from paying. Teaching materials were provided by the Soakpit Project. The teacher was also the mobilizer and in the initial period she went from door to door convincing parents to send their children to school.

The programme began in 1981 and within a year spread to 65 home schools, teaching about 1,800 students. Over the years, the number of home-schools grew to several hundred. The effort was vindicated when parents started to withdraw children from formal schools to admit them in home-schools because of the quality of education provided by them.

However, the home-school project was also confronted by problems. These included re-entry into the formal school system after completing the home-school phase, marriage of teachers and their change of locality, and low levels of income earned by the teachers. The Baldia Home School Teachers Welfare Association was formed to tackle these problems. The Association meets regularly and jointly deliberates over problems. It has organized vocational training for its members so as to enable them to increase their earnings.

The home-school teachers subsequently became mobilizers for UNICEF's health care programme for the community. Their schools doubled as Primary Health Care Centres (PHCCs), once their training in PHC, including immunization, was complete. In this manner, a network of health cover to the population of the entire area has been developed.

The project is an example of how community participation and initial success opens avenues for further expansion of activities that provide benefits to the whole community and, in this process, builds genuine development partnerships.

3.3. The Aga Khan Rural Support Programme (AKRSP)

AKRSP began its work in Gilgit District in 1982 and later expanded to Chitral and Baltistan districts. The area is marked by wide diversities, as the exposure of different villages to the outside world and forces of change varies greatly. AKRSP initiated work in the area to make agriculture more viable and improve to the living conditions of the people. The approach has been one of institutionalizaion of collective management with Village Organizations (VOs) integral to this concept.

VOs were created through active mobilization by AKRSP's social organizers. The process took time as did the acceptance of new ideas by VOs. By the end of 1993, there were about 2,809 VOs. All households of the village are represented in the VOs. Larger villages may have more than one VO, each representing a neighbourhood. Women participate through their own organization, i.e. Women's Organizations (WOs).

Initially formed to implement and maintain Productive Physical Infrastructure Projects (PPIs), such as irrigation channels, roads, and protective *bunds*, and to help create a trained cadre of village specialists (trained by AKRSP), the VOs have assumed an expanded role in planning for their villages. AKRSP's role is essentially that of a catalyst and provider of support services, e.g. technical training and managerial skills. The VOs receive cash grants from AKRSP for implementing their PPI projects. They are also encouraged to save, and this serves as collateral for loans for development projects. The recovery on loans, so far, has been good. The combined cumulative existing saving of VOs/WOs by December 1995 was Rs 257 million; the amount disbursed in various types of loans was Rs 483 million; the net amount outstanding was 34 per cent; and the net default was 1 per cent (*AKRSP* 1995, p.98-101)

Loan disbursement, payment to village specialists (vets, plant protection technicians), distribution of developed land, and options available to the village for further development are examined and discussed by the VOs and decisions are reached by consensus. A major impact of the AKRSP initiative (besides the formation of participatory social institutions) has been the two-fold increase in village cultivable area as well as in incomes.

Initially, efforts to involve women in Village Organizations did not succeed. However, the idea of separate women's organizations met with a positive response. Women hold separate meetings and maintain their own savings. By December 1995, there were 854 WOs with a total membership of 24,031, and a total saving of Rs 48 million (AKRSP 1995, p.98). WOs collaborate with the VOs on collective projects (e.g., land preparation for vegetable production and also marketing is in many instances, done by the VO). Women's projects have included home-based poultry and vegetable production packages. For the latter, women are provided improved seeds, training in new techniques, better tools, and fertilizers. For poultry production, a high-yield variety of poultry is supplied, and training is given in disease identification and vaccination. Both packages have been built on women's traditional activities, and have enhanced their incomes, and consequently the well-being of their families.

In upper Hunza, women have been trained to manage plant nurseries, a departure from the traditional activities of the people of the region, who are pastoral nomads. The decision to manage a forest nursery is a reflection of women's enhanced self-confidence in their ability to take on new projects.

AKRSP, as a catalyst, has facilitated the building of community organizations, introduced new ideas, provided essential information, and offered technological and material support. The programme is generously funded by all the leading donor agencies operating in Pakistan, and it is believed to have markedly improved the quality of life of the inhabitants of the region it operates in.

3.4. Orangi Pilot Project's Sanitation Programme

Orangi is the largest *katchi abadi* in Karachi, spread over 7,000 acres and inhabited by about a million people. The majority of the population belong to low-income groups—labourers, artisans, vendors, shopkeepers, and white collar workers. The Orangi Pilot Project (OPP) was founded in 1980 to promote infrastructural and other solutions through community participation and management. It works through a process of research, experimentation, and extensive education (Khan 1989). On the basis of this process, it has helped develop models of community participation and self-management in sanitation and housing, basic health education and family planning, female employment, education, and entrepreneurship development.

The Sanitation Programme of OPP was the entry point for what is now a prolonged involvement. Orangi, like other *katchi abadis*, had very poor sanitation, and no system of sewerage or drainage. The residents wanted an improved system but expected the official agencies to provide it. Recognizing that official interventions were unlikely, OPP first concentrated on devising a sanitation system that was low-cost, and could be self-built and self-maintained. Once it had done so with the help of engineers and technicians, bringing down the cost to a quarter of the market cost, OPP went about mobilizing residents lane by lane to build latrines. The next step was to form lane organizations so the installation of the underground sewerage system could be collectively undertaken and maintained. OPP's technicians provided the support services of surveying the lanes and preparing maps, plans, and estimates. It also loans tools and shuttering for the construction of latrines.

Once the residents were convinced of its efficacy the programme, expanded rapidly. By February 1995, 6,347 lanes (3,389 OPP and 2,958 non-OPP) consisting of 94,122 houses (49,941 OPP and 44,181 non-OPP) had been covered by the sanitation programme (OPP 1995, p.22). The most significant impact of improved sanitation has been on the health of the residents. In addition, the environment is cleaner and healthier, and the value of property has soared. Moreover, people's confidence in their ability to collectively decide and improve their lot has been established. The success of the programme opened the way for more interventions in the fields of health, education, and income-generation.

Based on OPP's success, the Sindh Government has recently established the Sindh Katchi Abadi Authority to promote sewerage facilities among *katchi abadis* in Karachi.

3.5. Aga Khan University's Preventive Health Care System

The Department of Community Health Sciences (CHS), Aga Khan University, established six functioning community-based primary health care (PHC) systems, five in *katchi abadis* and one in a coastal island off Karachi. These systems follow the principles of 'health for all, or equity in health, and care according to need' (AKU 1988 p.2).

The five *katchi abadi* sites served by PHC teams consist of 6,325 families and a total population of 43,321 (1988 figures). The programme is conceptualized with active community participation as an integral part of it, but the level of participation varies. In some communities, committees are fully in charge of some of the programme components and take a leading role in planning. In others, community involvement is more in the nature of co-operation rather than participation. However, with the visible impact of lowered malnutrition and better health among children, communities have started taking a greater interest in the programme.

Each field site has a community advisory committee to manage the PHC centre established in the area. Community organizers have been recruited to work with PHC teams to strengthen existing community organizations or to create new ones. In Baba Island, where the Baba Island Fisherman's Welfare Association, already existed, the NGO took the lead in the effort to bring PHC to the inhabitants of the island.

The PHC programme undertakes monthly household visits by the Community Health Worker (CHW) who reports risk factors for immediate action. Anyone requiring clinical assistance is referred to the field health centre. Immunization clinics are held once a week on the field sites. The CHWs makes special visits to motivate all families with children under five and pregnant women to come for vaccination. In Canister Goth, where CHS operates, only 2 percent of the children were not immunized.

Other components of the Programme are growth monitoring of children under five; grading the malnourishment levels of children (in cases of moderately or severely malnourished children, CHWs make special visits to monitor feeding patterns); encouraging mothers to bring children to the clinic; holding special health classes for diarrhoea management; family planning services; and basic curative care. Special clinics are conducted regularly for antenatal care; child care, and psychiatric care. Patients who have visited clinics are followed up by the CHWs.

There are very nominal consultation fees for both registered and non-registered patients who come to the health centre, and there are fixed medication charges, also nominal, for three days' dosage of medicines. At the end of 1988, the overall cost of providing health care was Rs 53 per person per year.

The CHS philosophy is that the task of building community relationships is one requiring perseverance and patience, but that such relationships are essential for developing PHC modules; further, that community needs are multidimensional, and that in order to promote 'health awareness' and 'health action' a multi-faceted, multi-sectoral approach is required. Thus, the CHS has involved other NGOs in education, women and development, and water and sanitation on the field sites. As part of its partnership-seeking efforts, the CHS is collaborating with the Sindh Government in developing rural health services in Thatta district, based on the principles of community participation.

3.6. Khuda ki Basti Project

The Khuda ki Basti project developed as a response to the urban housing crisis in Hyderabad. Initiated by the Hyderabad Development Authority, the official urban development agency, its objective was to provide land to the most needy at affordable prices without any down payment. Given the incidence of land speculation and land grabbing in urban Pakistan, this was indeed a challenge. The project has been patterned on the dynamics of the informal sector's land development systems. The difference is that it is a public sector service and hence legal. However, like informal sector activity, it is low cost.

The scheme involved the provision of an unserviced plot of land of 80 square yards at a low initial price. The major obstacle was to ensure that the land went to the targeted group. A system of careful scrutinizing of applications was set up to eliminate speculators. A very short period was fixed for starting construction to discourage speculative investment. Multiple checks were built in. Ownership documents were issued only after completion of the housing unit and clearance of development charges and continuous possession was considered proof to title of the plot. Allotment of plot of land left vacant could be cancelled by HDA, who could then allot it to some other applicant. Thus, very close monitoring and follow-up procedures were devised and are followed.

Khuda ki Basti faced initial difficulties but has tried to overcome them with creative solutions. In the first three years, 2,500 houses were built. Those who do not have the means to build *pucca* (solid) structures live in huts and *jhuggis*, improving these whenever they have the capacity to do so. As land was allotted and construction began, the formation of lane organizations encouraged. The OPP was inspired sanitation system was introduced, and the low-cost solutions offered reduced cost by 30 per cent.

The solutions to various issues evolved over a period of time through trial and error. For instance, it was discovered that the entire community could be organized only for certain objectives such as soliciting electricity. For sewerage and sanitation, lane organizations are more feasible. A system of block-level organizations and regular meetings emerged to deal with specific service-related problems. Under the initial scheme, there were 3,000 plots of land which were divided into 11 blocks of 250-300 plots. Each block has an account number where development charges are deposited. Open meetings of representatives of blocks are held with HDA staff, where service works are identified and prioritized and estimates prepared by the HDA staff are discussed. If funds in the block account are sufficient, a contractor is identified and the work commissioned. If the funds are inadequate, the residents of the block raise the necessary funds to pay for the work.

The Khuda ki Basti scheme has demonstrated that, without any fundamental change in social structures, people's needs can be met via grassroots mobilization and collective action.

4. THE LESSONS

The above case studies are successful models of development that demonstrate the possibility of achieving the goal of improving the quality of people's lives through innovative and sensitive approaches. The programmes/projects are peculiar to the circumstances and needs of a particular groups. This indicates that predetermined blueprints are not the answer to people's needs. Some fundamental principles are, however, established which can be adapted and applied to the specificities of varying groups and situations.

The central principle is that of community organization, which ensures participation of all in identifying needs, prioritizing activities, and arriving at implementation modalities. Corrupt and inefficient administrative systems, and weak and discredited traditional institutions require the creation of new institutional mechanisms that are democratic and capable of responding to people's immediate problems. New kinds of organizations are required where all members are active participants and take collective responsibility.

The process of mobilizing and motivating people requires a support system consisting of catalysts, trained social organizers/mobilizers, projects or programmes around which people organize, funds to initiate the project/programme, skills training, and technical support.

Since people react to a vast range of external pressures according to their material and psychological needs, the process of participatory organization can have long gestation periods. Interaction, dialogue, rapport, and confidence-building measures require time, perseverance, patience, and flexibility. Thus, interventions based on participatory approaches cannot be conceived of in rigid time-frames.

Monitoring and evaluation are critical to the participatory approach. Comprehension of obstacles is essential for dealing with them. Regular follow-up and assessments enable alternate solutions. Cost-analysis of projects is very critical. However, while initial expenditures are high, the long-term benefits and impact of participatory interventions are likely to outweigh the costs.

Once created, community organizations need to be equipped with managerial skills, professionalism, and sustainability. The process of growth and development is an ongoing one, with expansion into other areas of activity: from sanitation programmes to income generation for the OPP; from home-schools to PHC for Baldia; from VOs to Women's Organizations, and from PPIs to multi-sectoral initiatives for AKRSP.

Such approaches to development need to be seen in a long-term perspective, involved as they are in empowering communities and reducing their dependency. Building linkages and collaborating with other development agencies is another important aspect underscored by the above experiences. Since people's needs are multi-faceted, multi-sectoral responses are required which can be made possible through the development of networks and links with other NGOs, and official and private sector agencies. In Baldia, for instance, the Women's Division, a local philanthropist, CIDA, and UNICEF collaborated in nurturing and supporting the Home Teachers' Association. The CHS of AKU calls upon NGOs like the Teachers Resource Centre to provide guidance for non-formal schooling in its field sites. The BPWC uses its network to find outlets for new women entrepreneurs.

5. NGO–GOVERNMENT RELATIONS

In the various examples we have cited, NGOs like Khuda ki Basti and Idara-e-Kissan have the government's blessings. Some RSPs (like NRSP) have been established by the government, and others, like BRSP, rely partly on government funding. Government documents like *The Eighth Five Year Plan*, (1994, p.51, 69, p.97) acknowledge the special role of NGOs, particularly in service delivery. Prominent NGO leaders like Akhtar Hameed Khan and Shoaib Sultan Khan are on record explaining that the NGOs cannot and should not see themselves as competitors, but as complementing the government, partly by drawing on the vast network of government resources potentially available via the line departments. Thus, the philosophy is one of trying to make the government more effective and, in the process, giving government more credibility. Given all this, one would expect a harmonious working relationship between NGOs and the government.

As always, reality is often more complicated. It appears that, for various reasons, the government has felt threatened by NGO activity. By using the activity of various foreign NGOs operating in the NWFP as a hangover of the Afghan war as an excuse, it has sought to introduce an NGO Act which could, in principle, give complete control to the government over which organizations are registered as NGOs. Fortunately, the government did take the NGOs into confidence, and a prolonged debate spanning several sessions, ensued. NGO reservations regarding the proposed Voluntary Social Welfare Agencies Registration and Regulation (Amendment) Act, 1995, included the following:

1. The Government did not establish why this Act was needed.
2. The Government expressed two legitimate concerns.
    a. That NGOs should be accountable in terms of:
        i. documenting their activities and making this available to the general public;
        ii. having their accounts audited.
    b. That the government be informed of funds received by NGOs from foreign donors.

    With regard to 2a; the Acts that NGOs are currently registered under, and already require adequate accountability. With regard to 2b, the Acts that NGOs are currently registered under can be amended to include this clause (which essentially is Part II, clause 7 (d) of this 1995 Act). Many NGOs felt this was the only change needed.

The third concern expressed by the government about NGOs engaging in criminal acts is a red herring. Laws exist to deal with criminal activities.

3. The Act ignores the heterogeneity of NGOs. As portrayed in this Appendix, there are all manner of NGOs. For example, there are welfare organizations, charities, community-based organizations, advocacy organizations, denominational schools, various co-operatives, research organizations, implementing development organizations, support organizations, and various combinations of the above. The Acts these NGOs have currently registered under acknowledge the differences and the nuances (i.e. Societies Registrations Act, 1860, Co-operative Societies Act, 1925, the Companies Ordinance, 1984). This proposed Welfare Act is blind to these differences. Also, many NGOs are run by professional staff, and are not really voluntary. Thus, this Act does not apply to most NGOs in any case.
4. The Act opens up the possibility of the use of arbitrary authority. Part III, clause 9, 1-5, and clause 27 are very good examples of this.
5. Finally, why subject NGOs to re-registration (which itself could entail the exercise of arbitrary authority) when there is no prior case for the Act in the first place?

For these and other reasons, various NGOs opposed the new legislation. The revised version was deemed to be better by some NGO leaders, but many still felt that only a minimum change in existing legislation is all that is called for. The Act has not yet been approved by parliament but hangs over the NGOs like the proverbial sword of Damocles.[4] The government needs to speak with one voice. Does it support NGO activity and want to create an enabling environment for them as stated in *The Eighth Five Year Plan 1993-1998*, or does it feel threatened by NGO activity, and hence want to restrict the success and growth of this sector?[5]

6. SUMMARY AND CONCLUSIONS

The NGO sector in Pakistan is fairly large, but its impact is limited. NGOs operate largely as voluntary agencies providing relief and social service, and they vary vastly in their performance. Most follow the social welfare/charity approach, and are unprofessional and ad hoc. The government's interest in the NGO sector in the past has been minimal. Of late, the interest has been one of attempting to attain control.

Over a decade or so, new kinds of NGOs have been created and nurtured to shoulder the responsibility of meeting community needs. With the active participation of all those who are its members, such

NGOs are envisaged as institutions which will in the future have the capacity to tackle conflict and survival and engender development. While only a few NGOs have been in existence long enough to have reached sufficient maturity, efforts are needed to evolve development practices that ensure the growth of such NGOs for alleviating the impact of economic crises on the vulnerable.

Strategies for facing the challenge of the fall-out of economic crises and structural reforms can be both short-term and long-term. While short-term strategies can provide immediate relief, their sustenance over a period of time becomes difficult. It is, therefore, imperative to design long-term strategies that establish mechanisms that are sustainable and effective. Therefore, possible strategies for the future ought to:

i. adopt community-based initiatives which engender collective-action to overcome socio-economic problems;
ii. provide facilities for training professional cadres of social organizers/catalysts; address the problem of the acute shortage of mid-level field staff conversant in the techniques of participatory methods and comfortable with community interaction;
iii. identify the most basic needs of vulnerable groups and develop interventions around these;
iv. encourage collaboration among agencies and develop support networks/linkages between various NGOs to enable transformation of their approaches and activities.

The NGO sector has much promise for delivering just development. The above represents a plan of action for NGOs, the government, and the donors to realize this promise.

NOTES

1. ADHR Newsletter, July-Sep./95/No.1. The original sixteen members of the RSPN include the National Rural Support Programme, Sarhad Rural Support Programme, Balochistan Rural Support Programme, Orangi Pilot Project, AKRSP, Chitral Area Development Project, Dir District Development Project, Integrated Rural Development Programme, Idara-e-Kissan, Kalam Integrated Development Project, PATA Project, Sindh Katchi Abadi Project, Swiss NGO Programme Office, Swabi Irrigated Agriculture Project, and Trust for Voluntary Organizations. RSPN is debating opening membership to other organizations.

2. For details on environmental NGOs, see Aftab (1994).

3. The numbers are for the year 1991.

4. With the endorsement of the Pakistan NGO forum and the invitation of the Senate (November 1996) the NGOs had submitted, with legal assistance, an alternative NGO Act to the Senate Standing Committee constituted to consider the Act. Government reports continue to be hostile and so the final outcome of the proceedings in the Senate is uncertain.

5. Relying on NGOs to meet Plan objectives is a recurring theme of *The Eighth Five Year Plan 1993-98*. On p. 97, the authors state: 'Social Legislation will also be reviewed to promote maximum use of different welfare agencies and NGOs.' Few NGOs would view the proposed Voluntary Social Welfare Agencies Registration and Regulation (Amendment) Act, 1995, as meeting such an objective.

References

Aftab, S. (1994). 'NGOs and the Environment in Pakistan'. *SDPI Working Paper Series*, No. 21, Islamabad.

Agarwal, A., and S. Narain (1989). *Towards Green Villages*. Centre for Science and Environment, New Delhi.

Aga Khan University (1988). *Annual Report 1987-88*. Department of Community Health Science, Aga Khan University, Karachi.

Ahmad, E., and C. Allison, (1990). 'Poverty Growth and Public Policy in Pakistan'. Draft paper.

_____ and S. Ludlow (1989). 'Poverty, Inequality and Growth in Pakistan'. Background paper for the 1990 *World Development Report*, World Bank, Washington, D.C.

Ahmad M., C. K. Ming, A. K. Jalaluddin, and K. Ramachandra, (1991). *Basic Education and National Development: Lessons From China and India*. UNICEF, New York.

Ahmad N., and S. Zia, (1989). Women in Development. (mimeographed).

Akhtar S., (1988). *Poverty in Pakistan*. World Bank, Islamabad.

AKRSP (1995). *Thirteenth Annual Review*. Gilgit.

Alailima, P. (1984). Fiscal Incidence in Sri Lanka, 1973 and 1980, *World Employment Research Programme*. Working Paper WEP 2-32/WP.56, ILO, Geneva.

Alauddin T., (1975). 'Mass Poverty in Pakistan—A Further Study'. *The Pakistan Development Review*, Vol.14 (4).

_____ and Naqvi B., (1981). *Tax Progressivity in Pakistan*. Pakistan Institute of Development Economics Research Report No. 133, Islamabad.

Alderman H., J. R. Behrman, D. Ross, and R. Sabot, (1995). 'Decomposing the Gender Gap in Cognitive Skills in a Poor Rural Economy'. *Journal of Human Resources*, Forthcoming.

Altaf M. A., D. Whittington, H. Jamal, and V. K. Smith, (1991). 'New Perspectives on Rural Water Supply Policy in the Punjab, Pakistan'. AERC, Karachi. (mimeographed).

Amjad R., (1981). *Private Investment and Industrial Concentration in Pakistan*, Cambridge University Press, Cambridge.

_____ (1982). *Private Industrial Investment in Pakistan 1960-70*. Cambridge University Press, Cambridge.

Amadeo E. J., and T. Banuri, (1991). 'Policy, Governance and the Management of Conflict,' in T. Banuri (ed.). *Economic Liberalization: No Panacea*. Clarendon Press, Oxford.

Amin S., (1990). *Delinking: Towards a Polycentric World*. Zed Books, London.

Anderson W. T., (1987). *To Govern Evolution*. Harcourt Brace Janovich, Boston.

Apffel M. F., and S. A. Marglin, (1990). *Dominating Knowledge*. Clarendon Press, Oxford.

Azfar A., (1994). 'Designing New Models of Social Intervention: The Story of SAP in the Northern Areas'. Monitoring and Evaluation Section, AKRSP.

Azhar R. A., (1991). 'Education and Technical Efficiency During the Green Revolution in Pakistan'. *Economic Development and Cultural Change*, Vol. 39, No. 3.

Aziz M. A., (1986). *Review of Education Policies and Corresponding Five Year Plans, 1947-86*. Ministry of Education, Planning Wing, Government of Pakistan.

Banuri T., (1990). 'Modernization and its Discontents'. In *Dominating Knowledge*, F. Apffel Marglin and S. A. Marglin (eds.).

____ (1990). 'Development and the Politics of Knowledge'. In *Dominating Knowledge*, F. Apffel Marglin and S. A. Marglin (eds.).

____ (ed.) (1991). *Economic Liberalisation: No Panacea*. Clarendon Press, Oxford.

____ (1991a). 'Democratic Decentralisation'. Paper submitted for Conference on Strategic Issues for the Eighth Five Year Plan. Planning Commission, Islamabad.(mimeographed).

____ , and Schor J. B., (eds.) (1993). *Financial Openness and National Autonomy*. Clarendon Press, Oxford.

Behrman J. R., and A. B. Deolalikar, (1991). 'The Poor and the Social Sector During a Period of Macroeconomics Adjustment: Empirical Evidence from Jamaica'. *World Bank Economic Review*, Vol. 5, No. 2.

____ , and R. Schneider, (1994). 'An International Perspective on Pakistani Human Capital Investment in the Last Quarter Century'. *The Pakistan Development Review*, Vol. 32, No. 1.'

Bilqees F., and M. Mahmood, (1990). 'Women in the Labour Market in Pakistan'. ILO-ARTEP Working Papers, Delhi.

Bourguinon F., (1991). 'Optimal Poverty Reduction, Adjustment and Growth'. *World Bank Economic Review*, Vol. 5, No. 2.

Burney N. A., (1991). 'Trends in Income and Welfare Inequalities in Pakistan'. PIDE, Islamabad, (mimeographed).

____ , Z. Mahmood, T. Shabbir, and M. Akmal, (1991). *Human Development Report for Pakistan*. PIDE, Islamabad.

Cassen R. H., A. Duncan, , S. Guisinger, E. Hooper, and O. Noman, (1990). 'The Effectiveness of Aid to Pakistan'. A report to UNDP/ Government of Pakistan.

Chenery H. B., and M. Syrquin, (1975). *Patterns of Development*. Oxford University Press, London.

Cornia G. A., (1987a). 'Adjustment Policies 1980-85: Effects on Child Welfare'. In *Adjustment With a Human Face*, G.A. Cornia, *et al.* (eds.).Clarendon Press, Oxford.

____ (1987b). 'Economic Decline and Human Welfare in the First Half of the 1980s'. In *Adjustment With a Human Face*, G. A. Cornia, *et al.* (eds.).

____ (1987c). 'Social Policy Making: Restructuring, Targeting, and Efficiency'. In G. A. Cornia, *et al.* (eds.), *Adjustment With a Human Face*. Clarendon Press, Oxford.

____ (1989). 'Investing in Human Resources: Health, Nutrition and Development for the 1990s'. *Journal of Development Planning*, 19: 159-87.

_____ and Stewart F., (1990). 'The Fiscal System, Adjustment and the Poor'. *Innocenti Occasional Papers No. 11*, UNICEF, Florence.

_____ , Jolly R., and F. Stewart, (1987). *Adjustment with a Human Face: Protecting the Vulnerable and Promoting Growth*. Clarendon Press, Oxford.

_____ , Jolly R.and F. Stewart, (1987). 'An Overview of the Alternative Approach'. In *Adjustment With a Human Face*, G. A. Cornia, *et al.* (eds.).

Cornilesse P. A., and S. N. H. Naqvi, (1987). *The Wheat Marketing Activity in Pakistan*. Pakistan Institute of Development Economics, Islamabad.

Cotlear D., (1989). 'The Effects of Education on Farm Productivity'. *Journal of Development Planning,* Vol. 19: 73-99.

Davies R., and D. Sanders, (1988). 'Adjustment Policies and the Welfare of Children: Zimbabwe 1980-85'. In *Adjustment with a Human Face*, G. A. Cornia, *et al.* (eds.), Vol. II.

_____ , Sanders D., and T. Shaw, (1991). 'Liberalization for Development: Zimbabwe's Adjustment without the Fund'. *Innocenti Occasional Papers, Economic Policy Series*, 16, UNICEF, Florence.

de Krujik H., and M. V. Leeuwen, (1985). 'Changes in Poverty and Income Inequality in Pakistan During the 1970s'. *The Pakistan Development Review*, Vol. 24, No. 3-4.

Dreze J. H., and A. Sen, (1989). *Hunger and Public Action*. Oxford University Press, New York.

Duncan A., (1991). 'The Socio-Economic Role and Status of Women in Pakistan'. Paper submitted for a Conference on Strategic Issues for the Eighth Five Year Plan, Planning Commission, Islamabad. (mimeographed).

Durdag M., and A. R. Kemal, (1990). 'Budgetary Deficit and Performance of Pakistan's Economy'. World Bank, Islamabad. (mimeographed).

Ercelawn A. A., (1989). 'Poverty in Pakistan: Choice of Poverty Criteria'. Working Paper. Applied Economics Research Centre, University of Karachi.

_____ , Mahmood M., and K. Nadvi, (1991). 'The Relationship between Structural Adjustment, Structural Change and Poverty in Pakistan'. ESCAP Working Paper, Bangkok.

_____ , (1990). 'Absolute Poverty in Pakistan: Poverty Lines, Incidence, Intensity', AERC. Karachi, (mimeographed).

_____ , *et al.* (1991). 'The Social Costs of Economic Restructuring'. ESCAP, Bangkok.

Esrey S. A., R. G. Feachem, and J. M. Hughes, (1985). 'Interventions for the Control of Diarrhoeal Diseases Among Young Children: Improving Water Supplies and Excreta Disposal Facilities'. *Bulletin of the World Health Organization*, Vol. 63, No. 4.

Feroze, F. B. (1986). 'The Origins of Inflation in Pakistan 1959-82'. Ph.D. dissertation, University of Manchester.

Fishlow A., (1987). 'Some Reflections on Comparative Latin American Economic Performance and Policy'. WIDER Working Paper No. 22.

Galbraith J. K., (1990). 'Inefficiencies in the Soviet Economic System'. Lecture to the Quaid-i-Azam University, Islamabad.

Government of Azad Jammu and Kashmir. (1995). *Community Management of Rural Water Supply and Sanitation System*, Government of AJK and MSU, Mirpur.

Government of India. (1909). *Report of the Royal Commission on Decentralisation in India*. Vol. I, London.

Government of Pakistan. (nd.) *Report of the Pakistan Commission on the Status of Women*. Women's Division, Islamabad.

____ *Labour Force Surveys*. Federal Bureau of Statistics and Statistics Division, Various issues.

____ *Economic Surveys*. Finance Division, Various issues.

____ *Economic Survey, Statistical Supplement*. Finance Division, Various issues.

____ (1972). *25 Years of Pakistan in Statistics 1947-72*. CSO, Economic Affairs Division, Ministry of Finance and Planning and Development, Karachi.

____ (1981). *Census Report of Pakistan*. Statistics Division, Islamabad.

____ (1986). *Primary Education Improvement: Desired Measures*. Educational Development Series I, National Education Council, Islamabad.

____ (1987). *Secondary Education in Pakistan*. Education Development Series No. 2., National Education Council, Islamabad.

____ (1988). *Seventh Five Year Plan*. Planning Commission, Islamabad.

____ (1988a) *Pakistan Demographic Survey*. Federal Bureau of Statistics.

____ (1989). *Report of the National Manpower Commission*. National Manpower Commission, Islamabad.

____ (1990a). *Final Evaluation of the Sixth Five Year Plan*. Planning Commission, Islamabad.

____ (1991a). *Mid-Plan Review of the Seventh Five Year Plan*. Planning Commission, Islamabad.

____ (1991b). *Towards a Social Action Program: A Special Report for Consortium Meeting*. Planning Commission, Islamabad.

____ (1991c). *National Programme of Action for the Goals of Children and Development in the 1990s*. Planning Commission, Islamabad.

____ (1992). *Social Action Programme 1992-95*. Planning Commission, Islamabad.

____ (1993a). *Pakistan Integrated Household Survey: Final Results 1991,1992*. Federal Bureau of Statistics and Statistics Division, Islamabad.

____ (1993b). *Household Integrated Economic Survey*. Federal Bureau of Statistics, Economic Affairs Division, and Statistics Division. Karachi.

____ (1994a). *Eighth Five Year Plan (1993-98)*. Planning Commission, Islamabad.

____ (1994b). *Agricultural Census of Pakistan*. Ministry of Agriculture, Islamabad.

____ (1994c). *Agricultural Statistics of Pakistan 1992-93*. Ministry of Food, Agriculture and Livestock, Islamabad.

Guhan, S. (1992). 'Social Security Initiatives in Tamil Nadu' in Subramanian, S. (ed.). *Themes in Development Economics : Essays in Honour of Malcolm Adiseshiah*. Oxford University Press, New Delhi.

Haleem A., (1995). Desire for No More Children and Contraception Use in Pakistan. *The Pakistan Development Review, Forthcoming.*

Hamid N., I. Nabi, and A. Naseem, (1991). 'Pakistan'. *In The Political Economy of Agricultural Pricing Policy,* A. O. Krueger, *et al*. (eds.), Johns Hopkins University Press.

Hammond, R. (1989). *An NGO Guide to Trade and Finance In the Multilateral System*. United Nations, New York.

Herring R., (1983). *Land to the Tiller*. Yale University Press, New Haven.

Husain T., (1989). 'Managing the Environment: Social Organisation, The Informal Sector, and Participatory Approaches'. NCS Secretariat, Islamabad.

Husain T., (1990). 'Pakistan National Strategy: Perspective Paper on Grassroots Initiatives'. Development and Management Services, Islamabad.

International Union for the Conservation of Nature. (nd.) *The Pakistan National Conservation Strategy*. IUCN, Karachi.

International Monetary Fund. (1988). *Pakistan-Recent Economic Developments*. International Monetary Fund, Washington, D. C.

____ *International Financial Statistics*, Washington, D. C.

Irfan M., (1974). 'Shifting and Incidence of Indirect Taxes on Tobacco and Petroleum Products in Pakistan.' a *Pakistan Development Review*, Vol. 13, No. 1.

Irfan M., and R. Amjad, (1984). 'Poverty in Rural Pakistan'. In *Poverty in Rural Asia*, A. R. Khan, and Eddy Lee, (ed.), ARTEP-ILO, Bangkok.

____ , and R. Amjad, (1984). 'Poverty in Rural Pakistan'. In *Poverty in Rural Asia*, A.R. Khan, and E. Lee (ed.), ILO-ARTEP, New Delhi.

Israel, A. (1990). 'The Changing Role of the State: Institutional Dimensions'. Working Paper No. WPS495, The World Bank, Washington, D.C.

Jahangir A., (1991). 'Provisions for Speedy Justice'. Paper for Seminar on Eighth Five Year Plan, Planning Commission, Islamabad. (mimeographed).

Azad Jeetun, (1978). 'Incidence of Taxes in Pakistan'. Applied Economic Research Centre, University of Karachi, Discussion paper No.2.

Jimenez E., and J. Tan, (1985). 'Educational Development in Pakistan: The Role of User Charges and Private Education'. World Bank Discussion Paper No. EDT16, Washington.

Kemal A. R., (1982). 'Income Distribution in Pakistan: A Review'. Research Report No. 123, PIDE, Islamabad.

____ (1982). 'Incentive Structure for Manufacturing Industries of Pakistan'. Pakistan Institute of Development Economics, Islamabad. (mimeographed).

____ (1991). 'Industrial Sector Review'. A Study prepared for Asian Development Bank, Manila.

____ (1986). 'Elasticity and Buoyancy of Tax System in Pakistan'. Paper prepared for National Taxation Reforms Commission.

____ (1989). 'Fiscal Imbalances as an Obstacle to Privatization'. *The Pakistan Development Review*, Vol. 28, No. 4.

_____ (1990). 'Options for Financing the Budgetary Deficit, Money Supply, and Growth of Banking Sector'. *The Pakistan Development Review,* Vol. 30, No. 4.

_____ , F. Bilquees, and Z. Mahmood, (1990). 'Sustainable Development in Pakistan with a Focus on Environmental Issues.' PIDE, Islamabad. (mimeographed).

Khan A. F., (1991). 'International Migration and the Moral Economy of the Barani Peasantry'. *The Pakistan Development Review*, Vol. 30, No. 4.

Khan A., (1992). 'Direct Taxes, Policy Reform Proposal for Eighth Plan'. A paper presented to the Committee on Economic and Social Well Being, Pakistan Institute of Development Economics, Islamabad.

Khan A. H., (1989). 'A Case Study of Orangi Pilot Project's Low Cost Sanitation Programme'. Orangi Pilot Project, Karachi.

Khan M. H., 'Agricultural Development and Changes in the Land Tenure and Land Revenue Systems in Pakistan': In S. R. Khan, (ed.) *Fifty Years of Pakistan's Economy*. Oxford University Press, Karachi (Forthcoming).

Khan S. R., (1991). 'The Income Redistributional Impact of Financing Higher Education in Pakistan'. *World Development*, Vol. 19, No. 9.

_____ (1993). 'South Asia'. In E. M. King and M. A. Hall (eds.), *Women's Education in Developing Countries: Barriers, Benefits and Policies*. Johns Hopkins University, Baltimore.

Khan S. R., (1994) 'Equity in Public Sector Education'. SDPI Policy Paper Series No. 22, Islamabad.

_____ and S. Aftab, (1996). 'Devaluation and the Balance of Trade in Pakistan: A Policy Analysis for Pakistan'. *Economia Internationale*. Vol. XLIX, No. 2.

_____ *et al.* (1995). 'Education'. *Nature, Power, People: Citizen's Report on Sustainable Development*. SDPI, Islamabad.

_____ 1995, 'Structural Adjustment Labour and the Poor'. SDPI, Research Report No. 8, Islamabad.

Khan S. S., (1989). 'The Dynamics of Rural Development'. Paper for India-Pakistan Environment Conference, Lahore.

Kiranandana T., and K. Tontisirin, (1992). 'Eradicating Child Malnutrition: Thailand's Health, Nutrition and Poverty Alleviation Policy in the 1990s'. *Innocenti Occasional Papers*. Economic Policy Series, 23, UNICEF, Florence.

Kizilbash H., (1991) 'Education'. Paper submitted for Conference on Strategic Issues for the Eighth Five Year Plan, Planning Commission, Islamabad.

Kuznet S., (1955). 'Economic Growth and Income Inequality'. *American Economic Review*. Vol. 45, No. 2.

Levin, *et al.* (1984). *The Role of Family in Health: Appropriate Research Methods*. World Health Organization, Geneva.

Lewis S. R., (1970). *Pakistan: Industrialisation and Trade Policies*. Oxford University Press, Oxford.

Lockhead M. E., D. T. Jamison, and L. J. Lau, (1980). 'Farmer Education and Farm Efficiency: A Survey'. In King T., (ed.) *Education and Income*, World Bank Staff Working Paper No. 402, Washington, D.C.

Mahmood M., (1989). 'A Macro Appraisal of Poverty Alleviation Programs in Pakistan'. Report Prepared for the World Bank.

____ (1990). 'Change in Land Distribution in the Punjab: Empirical Application of an Exogenous-Endogenous Model for Agrarian Sector Analysis'. *The Pakistan Development Review, Vol. 29*, No. 3-4.

____ (1994). 'Why Children Do Not Go To School. Some Estimates and a Theoretical Framework'. *The Pakistan Development Review*, Vol. 33, No. 4.

____ (1995). 'Poverty in Pakistan', Asian Development Bank, Manila.

Malik M. H., (1988). 'Some New Evidence of Poverty in Pakistan'. *The Pakistan Development Review*, Vol. 27, No. 4.

Malik, *et al.* (1995). 'Poverty in Pakistan'. Asian Development Bank, Manila

Malik S. J., (1991). 'Poverty in Pakistan: 1984-85 to 1987-88'. International Food Policy Research Institute, Washington, D.C. (mimeographed).

____ (1991). 'Inter-temporal and Regional Aspects of Poverty in Pakistan: 1984/85 to 1987/88'. IFPRI, Washington, D.C.

Malik M. H., and N. Saqib, (1989). 'Tax Incidence by Income Classes in Pakistan'. *The Pakistan Development Review*, Vol. 28, No. 1.

Mata L., and Rosero. (1988). 'National Health and Social Development in Costa Rica: A Case Study of Intersectoral Action'. Technical Paper No. 13, Pan American Health Organization, Washington, D. C.

Matthais J., (1915). *Village Government in British India*. Unwin Limited, London.

Meerman J., (1979). *Public Expenditure in Malaysia: Who Benefits and Why?* Oxford University Press, New York.

Milanovic B., (1991). 'Poverty in Eastern Europe in the Years of the Crisis 1978-87: Poland, Hungary and Yugoslavia'. *World Bank Economic Review*, Vol. 5, No. 2.

Mujahid G. B. S., (1978). 'A Note on the Measurement of Poverty and Income Inequalities in Pakistan: Some Observations on Methodology'. *The Pakistan Development Review*. Vol. 17, No. 3.

Mujahid-Mukhtar E., (1991). 'Women in Development: Present Profile and Policy Prescription', Paper submitted for Conference on Strategic Issues for the Eighth Five Year Plan. Planning Commission, Islamabad. (mimeographed).

Mumtaz K., (1989). 'Towards Sustainable Development: Women and Resource Management in the Northern Areas of Pakistan'. Paper presented at IPEC, Lahore.

____ (1991). 'Initiatives to Help the Vulnerable Groups'. Study conducted for UNICEF, Pakistan. (mimeographed).

Nandy A., (ed.). (1988). *Science, Hegemony and Violence: A Requiem for Modernity*. Oxford University Press, Bombay.

Naseem S. M., (1977). 'The Economic Structure of Pakistan'. In *ILO Report on Poverty and Landlessness in Asia*. International Labour Organization, Geneva.

Nations, R. (1975). 'The Economic Structure of Pakistan and Bangladesh'. In R. Blackburn (ed.), *Explosion in the Subcontinent*. Penguin Books, London.

National Institute of Population Studies (1992). *Pakistan Demographic and Health Survey 1990-91*. Islamabad.

Naqvi S. N. H., and A. R. Kemal, (1991). 'Structures of Protection and Allocation Efficiency in Manufacturing in Pakistan'. International Growth Centre, New York.

Naqvi W. G., (1991). *The Health Sector and Social Policy Reform in the Philippines Since 1985*. Italy.

OPP (1995). *61st Quarterly Report- January-March 1995*, Karachi.

Osmani S. R., (1987). 'Controversies in Nutrition and Their Implications for the Economics of Food'. Working Paper No. 16, WIDER, Helsinki .

Perveen A., (1994). 'Proximate Determinants of Fertility in Pakistan'. *The Pakistan Development Review*, Vol. 33, No. 4.

Qureshi M. L., (1988). 'Incidence of Federal and Provincial Taxes and Appraisal of Economic and Distributive Effects of Direct Taxes'. Study prepared for National Taxation Reforms Commission, Development Studies Institute, Lahore.

Raven J., (1989). 'Democracy, Bureaucracy, and the Psychologist'. *The Psychologist*. Vol. 2, No. 11.

Robertson R. L., (1985). 'Review of Literature on Costs of Health Services in Developing Countries'. Report Prepared for the World Bank, Population, Health, and Nutrition Department, Washington, D.C.

Rehnema M., (1991). 'Global Poverty: A Pauperizing Myth'. *Interculture*. Vol. XXIV, No. 2.

Rivero C. C., R. L. Ascencio, and J. Q. Vinagre, (1991). *The Impact of Economic Crisis and Adjustment on Health care in Mexico*. Italy.

Rukanuddin A. R., and M.N.I. Farooqui, (eds.) (1988). *The State of Population in Pakistan 1987*. NIPS, Islamabad.

Sathar Z. A., (1979). 'Rural Urban Fertility Differentials: 1975'. *The Pakistan Development Review*, Vol. 18, No. 3.

_____ and S. Kazi, (1988). *Productive & Reproductive Choices of Metropolitan Women: Report of a Survey in Karachi*. PIDE, Islamabad.

Selowsky M., and L. Taylor, (1973). 'The Economics of Malnourished Children: An Example of Disinvestment in Human Capital'. *Economic Development and Cultural Change*, Vol. 22, No. 1.

Sen, A. (1991). 'Towards a Food Security System in South Asia'. Paper contributed at Independent Group for South Asian Cooperation, Dhaka, WIDER, Helsinki (mimeographed).

Siddiqui T. A., (1991). Innovation and Success in Sheltering the Urban Poor. (Mimeographed).

Society for Advancement of Higher Education (SAHE) (1989). *Report on Education*. Lahore.

Squire L., (1991). 'Poverty and Adjustment in the 1980s'. *The World Bank Economic Review*. Vol. 5, No. 2.

Stewart F., (1990a). 'Alternative Macro and Meso Policies', in G. A. Cornia, *et al.*, (eds.), *Adjustment with a Human Face*. Clarendon Press, Oxford.

Stewart F., (1990b). 'Supporting Productive Employment Among Vulnerable Groups', in G. A. Cornia, *et al.* (eds.), *Adjustment with a Human Face*. Clarendon Press, Oxford.

TVO (1994). *Database and Directory of NGOs. January 1990 to December 1993*. Islamabad.

Ul Haque N., (1993). 'Agricultural Pricing policy in Pakistan'. IFPRI, Islamabad. (mimeographed).

____ and S. Kardar, (1994). 'Financial Sector Reform,' ADB. (mimeographed).

UNDP (1990). 'The UN System In Pakistan and WID: An Inter-Agency Review', 5-3 November 1989, UNDP, Islamabad.

____ *Human Development Report*, Oxford University Press, New York, Various issues.

____ (1991a). *Balanced Development: A Prescription for Social Action in Pakistan*, Islamabad.

____ (1991b). *NGOs Working for Others: A Contribution to Human Development*, Vol. I. Islamabad.

UNICEF (1986). 'Review of EPI in Pakistan'. GOP/WHO/UNICEF, (1991, EPI Programme Review in Bangkok), Islamabad.

UN (1988). *World Population Prospects No. 106*. UNDP, New York.

____ (1991). 'Beyond the Debit Crisis Structural Transformations'. Final Report of the International Women's Seminar, New York.

Valerio F., (1991). *Fiscal Shock, Wage Compression & Structural Reform: Mexican Adjustment and Educational Policy in the 1980s*. Italy.

Warren B., (1974). *Imperialism the Highest Stage of Capitalism*. Routlege and Kegan Paul, London.

Vickers J., and G. Yarrow, (1989). *Privatization and Economic Analysis*. MIT University Press, Boston, Cambridge, Mass.

World Bank (1987). *The Trade Regime in Pakistan,* Industry, Trade, and Finance Division, Washington.

____ (1991). *Towards a Social Action Program for Pakistan: Impediments to Progress and Options for Reform*. World Bank, Washington, D.C. (Country Department I).

World Bank, 1993, *The East Asian Miracle: Economic Growth and Public Policy*. A World Bank Research Report, Oxford University Press, Oxford.

____ World *Development Report*. Oxford University Press, Washington, D.C. Various issues.

Zaman A., and R. M. Zaman, (1991). 'Psychology and Development: A Conceptual Itinerary, NIP, Islamabad.

Zamora M. D., (1990). *The Panchayat Tradition*. Reliance Publishing House, New Delhi.

Index